Limited Classical Reprint Library

THE BIRTH

OF

CHRIST

BY

H.P. LIDDON

&

JAMES ORR

Foreword by
Dr. Cyril J. Barber

Klock & Klock Christian Publishers, Inc.
2527 GIRARD AVE. N.
MINNEAPOLIS, MINNESOTA 55411

THE

𝔐𝔞𝔤𝔫𝔦𝔣𝔦𝔠𝔞𝔱

SERMONS IN ST. PAUL'S
AUGUST, 1889

By H. P. LIDDON, D.D., D.C.L., LL.D.

LATE CANON RESIDENTIARY AND CHANCELLOR OF ST. PAUL'S

Foreword by
Dr. Cyril J. Barber

Misericordias Domini in æternum cantabo.   *Alleluia*

Klock & Klock Christian Publishers, Inc.
2527 GIRARD AVE. N.
MINNEAPOLIS, MINNESOTA 55411

Originally published by
Longmans, Green, & Co.
London, 1891

ISBN: 0-86524-058-2

Printed by Klock & Klock in the U.S.A.
1980 Reprint

FOREWORD

When we take up a study of the incarnation, it is surprising to read in the writings of a man whose *Daily Bible Studies* have been so widely received that

the Virgin Birth is a doctrine which presents us with many difficulties; and it is a doctrine which our Church does not compel us to accept in the literal and the physical sense (I,10).

If the conception of Jesus was purely physical and strictly according to nature, then we may well question the validity of Old Testament prophecy, and ask, Who died on the cross? If the answer is a mere man, then we have no salvation. However, if it was the Son of God, then a miraculous conception is a logical necessity and everything pertaining to His life and ministry is of the utmost importance to us.

One Bible scholar who has expounded chapter 1 of Luke's Gospel with clarity and insight is Henry Parry Liddon (1829-1890), a graduate of Oxford University (B.D., and D.D., 1870), and for many years Ireland Professor of Exegesis in that institution. Well known for his outstanding *Explanatory Analysis of St. Paul's Epistle to the Romans* and famous Bampton Lectures on the *Divinity of Our Lord and Saviour Jesus Christ*, Professor Liddon's sermonic treatment of Dr. Luke's record of the events surrounding the birth of the Christ-child remains one of the most stimulating and satisfactory studies ever written.

With deftness and skill, Liddon describes the events leading up to "God being in Christ in order to reconcile the world to Himself." With equal dexterity he links Scripture with Scripture to show how momentous was the event that took place in a stable in Bethlehem. With eloquence and true reverence he leads the believing reader to worship Him "by Whom are all things, and we by Him."

These messages are delightful in their simplicity, yet profound in their handling of the praises and predictions recorded by Luke in his Gospel. It is a joy to see this work being made available to believers at this time.

Cyril J. Barber
Author, *The Minister's Library*

PREFACE TO THE SECOND EDITION

THIS edition has no advantage over its predecessor,
beyond the improvement of a few phrases of
doubtful meaning. But a friend, to whose criticisms
the writer attaches particular value, remarks that in
these sermons too much is made of the historical import
of the Magnificat to leave room for doing justice to
its practical aspects. To this, perhaps, it may be replied
that the historical occasion of the Magnificat is of greater
relative importance than is the case with any other
Psalm or Hymn that ever was uttered.[a] If so much be
granted,—and what Christian can hesitate to grant it?
—the question is reduced to one of time and space. It
might have been better to devote eight sermons to such
a subject than four; but, in days like ours, it would
have been more difficult to secure attention. For the
rest, the bearing of the Hymn of Mary on our daily

[a] A sentence to this effect might well have been introduced at p. 8.

lives lies more on the surface of the language than does its relation to the Incarnation. And its practical value for us is likely to be enriched and intensified if we bear in mind as much as may be, when the words that are so often on our lips were first uttered, and by whom.

3, AMEN COURT, ST. PAUL'S, E.C.,
Whitsuntide, 1890.

PREFACE TO THE FIRST EDITION

THESE sermons are published for the reason which has compelled the recent publication of some earlier volumes. If a man's words are in any case to remain behind him, he would rather give them to the world himself, and correctly. The author cannot be responsible for any version of these discourses which does not bear the name of his present publishers.

It has not been an object with him to discuss the grave controversies which at once present themselves when the name and office of our Lord's Blessed Mother come into question. If her true place in the hearts of Christians has been often exaggerated, it has been as often unrecognized or denied. If the language and practice of some Christians with respect to her may seem to encroach on what is due to the incommunicable and awful prerogatives of God, the terms in which she is referred to by others would appear to show that they have forgotten Whose Mother she is, and what He may be thinking of a lack of love and reverence for her on the part of those who own His Name. In these sermons it has seemed better to dwell on the inspired language which she herself has left us; and for the rest to bear in mind the wise words of Bishop Pearson:[a] "If Elisabeth cried out with so loud a voice, 'Blessed art thou among women,' when Christ was but newly conceived in Mary's womb, what expressions of honour and admiration can we think sufficient now that Christ is in heaven and that Mother with Him! Far be it from any Christian to derogate from that special privilege granted her which is incommunicable to any other. We cannot bear too reverent a regard unto the Mother of our Lord, so long as we give her not that worship which is due unto the Lord Himself. Let us keep the language of the Primitive Church: 'Let her be honoured and esteemed, let Him be worshipped and adored.'"

3, Amen Court, E.C.,
    Advent Sunday, 1889.

[a] Pearson, *On the Creed,* Art. III., p. 218.   Oxford: 1847.

I.

MARY OUR MODEL IN PRAISING GOD.

St. Luke i. 46–48.

And Mary said,
My soul doth magnify the Lord,
And my spirit hath rejoiced in God my Saviour.
For He hath regarded the low estate of His handmaiden.

No fact is more attested by wide experience, and few facts are more pregnant with significance and warning, than the tendency of the human mind to lose its hold of the sense and power of language, especially of religious language, after constantly repeating it. Words, although sacred, and designed for universal use by the Highest of all authorities, and richly endowed with spiritual power, do yet become to us, through the process of constant usage, barren and unfruitful, unless an effort be made from time to time to recover and reassert in the human mind their original sense and import. So it is even with that most sacred Prayer which our Lord Himself prescribed for the use of His disciples. Neither the associations of ages, nor

the varied experiences of our own souls, which
have gathered round the several petitions of the
Lord's Prayer, will avail to save us from saying
it in a thoughtless and formal way, unless we
constantly remind ourselves of what it means; of
what it has meant to millions, of what it might
mean to ourselves. And as this is true of words
which our Lord Himself bids us use, so it is no less
true of other inspired words, which His Church has
selected from the Sacred Records, as being especially
suited for constant employment in public worship.
It holds good of those psalms which, like the ninety-
fifth or the hundredth, or the seven psalms of Peni-
tence, have been chosen for frequent use on account
of their spiritual intensity ; and even of those three
hymns in which the earliest saints of the New
Testament heralded the Birth of the Divine Redeemer—the song of Zacharias,[a] or the Benedictus ;
the song of Simeon,[b] or the Nunc Dimittis ; and
the song of Mary,[c] or the Magnificat. In view of
this tendency to lose our hold on the sense of
language which on account of its excellence we
repeat most frequently, it may be well to devote the
Sunday afternoons of the present month, to such
consideration as time will permit, of the familiar, but

[a] St. Luke i. 68–79.   [b] *Ib.* ii. 29–32.   [c] *Ib.* i. 46–55.

not always well-understood words of the first in
order and the greatest of Christian hymns—the
Magnificat.

I.

There is no mistaking the prominence assigned
in the English Prayer-book, as in many older
Prayer-books of the Christian Church, to the Hymn
of Mary. It is the centre and heart of our Evening
Service. All else leads up to it, or expands it, or
radiates from it. We mount upwards to it by
successive steps; by confession of the sins which
disqualify the soul of man for true communion with
God; by the great prayer which makes all communion with God easy and natural; by psalms which
express the longings of the human heart for some
nearer contact with God, or which sadly deplore
whatever may hinder it, or which joyfully anticipate
its realization. We mount yet a step higher as we
listen to some Lesson from the Old Testament,
which, whether it be history or prophecy, narrative
or moral teaching, poetry or prose, everywhere and
always speaks of Jesus Christ, to those who have
ears to hear; suggesting Him as the contrast to the
human failures, or as the crown of the human ex-
cellences which it describes; or announcing Him as

the Heavenly Visitant Who, by-and-by, will still
man's fears and warrant his hopes. Now, as of old,
unless there be a vail over the heart[a] in the
reading of the Old Testament, the Great Teacher
accompanies us through its pages, and, beginning
at Moses and all the Prophets, expounds to
us in all the Scriptures the things concerning
Himself.[b] And thus we approach the Hymn
which proclaims that all for which Psalmists and
Prophets have yearned has in very truth and
deed come to be. Mary might seem evening
by evening to stand in the church of her Divine
Son, while in strains which we shall consider, she
celebrates an event compared with which all else in
human history is insignificant indeed. As from her
thankful heart the incense of praise ascends to
the Eternal Throne, first in one and then another
incense-wreath, each having its own beauty of
tint and form, we reflect that the hardest questions
of man's mind have been answered, and that the
deepest yearnings of his heart have been satisfied.
The Only Begotten Son has come down from
heaven to be born of a human Mother, to die at
the hands of His creatures, and to rise again.
After this all else might seem, in some sense must
seem, pale and poor ; but it is this great truth, set

---

[a] 2 Cor. iii. 14.   [b] St. Luke xxiv. 27.

forth or latent in every line of the Magnificat which carries us on to the end of the Evening Service; through the Second Lesson, in which the Incarnate God speaks to us Himself or by the lips of His Apostles; to the Nunc Dimittis, in which we take leave of His message with thankful joy; to the Creed, in which we brace ourselves for the toils and pains of life by a new profession of our faith in Him; to the concluding prayers, in which His omnipotent Intercession is at once the warrant of our praying at all, and of the confidence that we shall be heard, not for our merits, but for His.

It may seem strange that, from time to time, persons who have felt no difficulty about the use of the old Hebrew psalms in Christian worship, have been disposed to take offence at the public use of the Magnificat, or, indeed, of all the Christian hymns which are preserved for us in St. Luke's Gospel. Such a feeling, however, found expression shortly after the Book of Common Prayer had come into use.[a] It was maintained that unless we could all be in the exact circumstances of Zacharias at the birth

---

[a] The permission to sing the psalms Cantate Domino and Deus Misereatur, instead of the Magnificat and Nunc Dimittis, dates from 1552. But even this serious concession did not appease the Judaizing temper which was offended by any use of the Evangelical Canticles.

of the Baptist, or of Simeon after seeing our Lord
in the Temple, or of Mary at the Visitation, we had
no adequate reason for singing their hymns.[a] This
amounts to saying that no hymn or psalm is to be
used by any other person than its composer, unless
the circumstances of the composer can be exactly
reproduced in the case of the man or the Church
which sings his hymn. Not to enquire how this
rule would apply to modern and uninspired com-
positions which are largely in use among us, we
may observe that it would forbid any use whatever
of the Psalter itself in public or private devotion—
a use to which, however, oddly enough, those old
objectors who have been referred to, do not seem to
have objected. For every psalm was composed in
a special set of circumstances, some of which can,
while some cannot, be ascertained; and yet it does
not seem to have been argued that, because we
cannot make these circumstances our own, we
are precluded from using the psalms. We are
none of us in the position of David persecuted by
a jealous sovereign,[b] or insulted and rebelled against

---

[a] Cf. Hooker, *Eccl. Pol.*, v. 40. See 1 *Adm. apud Whitg.*
Def. 494, quoted by Keble. Some Puritans objected to the
frequent use of the *Venite;* cf. *A parte of a register, contayninge
sundrie memorable matters*, Edinburgh, 1593, p. 73.

[b] Ps. viii., lii., lvii., lviii., lix.

by a favourite son,[a] or bringing the ark to the
sanctuary of Zion,[b] or ordering a royal household
according to the Divine Law.[c]   The glories of
Solomon,[d] the conquest and humiliation of Reho-
boam,[e] the repulse of Sennacherib,[f] the ruin and
desolation of Jerusalem by the Babylonian con-
queror,[g] the sadness of the captives weeping by the
waters of Babylon,[h] the laying the corner-stone of
the new temple after the exile,[i]—these, and many
other like subjects or events, are the occasions of
psalms, which yet we use at this day to express the
fears, or hopes, or resolves, or aspirations of our own
souls.   Clearly, if such a difference of circumstances
does not forbid the recitation of Hebrew psalms, it
cannot preclude us from using New Testament hymns;
which, as Richard Hooker has said, " concern us so
much more than the songs of David, as the Gospel
toucheth us more than the Law, the New Testament
than the Old.[j] "   But in truth, whether it be Jewish
psalm or Christian hymn, we Christians use them
because their inspiration lifts them above the limits
of the time, the place, the events which witnessed
their composition.   As a work of natural genius,

[a] Ps. iii.–vii., lv., lxi.   [b] *Ib.* xxiv.   [c] *Ib.* ci.
[d] *Ib.* lxxii.   [e] *Ib.* lxxxviii.   [f] *Ib.* xlvi., lxxiii., lxxv., lxxvi.
[g] *Ib.* cii.   [h] *Ib.* cxxxvii.   [i] *Ib.* cxviii.   [j] *Eccl. Pol.*, v. 40, 42.

whether it be poem, or speech, or painting, or statue, has that in it which detaches it from the study of the poet, the audience of the speaker, the workroom of the artist, and makes it belong to all times and countries ; so much more do words that are supernaturally inspired carry with them the certificate of an universal applicability, which is independent of places, and events, and epochs, and authorship, and, indeed, of everything save His Mind from Whom they proceed, and that heart and understanding of His creatures which needs and welcomes them.

The Magnificat, then, is the Hymn of the Incarnation. It was uttered in circumstances the like of which had never before, and have never since, surrounded any human being whatever. Mary had been told at Nazareth by a heavenly messenger that she was to be the Mother of Him in Whom all God's best promises to Israel and to the human race were to be fulfilled.[a] And she was to be His Mother, not in the ordinary way of nature, but, as became His pre-existing glory, and as was needed in order to cut off the entail of evil which came down from the first father of our race, in a new and supernatural way. "The Holy Ghost"—so ran the prediction—"shall come upon thee, and

[a] St. Luke i. 30-33.

the power of the Highest shall overshadow thee:
therefore also that Holy Thing Which shall be born
of thee shall be called the Son of God."ᵃ   Mary
knew that she was to be the Mother of the Divine
Messiah, when she traversed the land from Nazareth
to a country house some few miles from Jerusalem,
on a visit to her cousin Elisabeth, the future
mother of the Baptist.   It was their meeting which
was the immediate occasion of the Magnificat.
Elisabeth had no sooner heard from the lips of
Mary the wonted salutation, of " Peace be to thee !"
with which religious Jews greeted each other after
a long absence, than, under the influence of the
holy spirit of prophecy which filled her soul, she
broke out into words which mark the high significance of Mary's destiny scarcely less clearly than
does Mary's own Magnificat.   " She spake with a
loud voice, and said, Blessed art thou among
women, and blessed is the fruit of thy womb.   And
whence is this to me, that the Mother of my Lord
should come to me ?"ᵇ   The Mother of my Lord !
Elisabeth was the elder woman, and, as the wife
of Zacharias, she was in a higher social position
than Mary; but few things in religious history are
more beautiful than her ready and unstinted recog-

ᵃ St. Luke i. 35.   ᵇ *Ib.* 42, 43.

nition of the loftier vocation of her younger relative. Her next sentence was at once a blessing and a prophecy; but they touched a secret spring in the illuminated soul of Mary, and she forthwith uttered her hymn of praise.

She uttered it, as might seem, in a single jet; but as it passed from her lips, as is usual with eastern poetry, it fell, not of set design, but by an instinct of intrinsic fitness, into divisions of unequal length, which we moderns should call strophes.

Mary begins by offering up to God, with the whole strength and resource of her spiritual being, that praise which she knows to be His due at all times, and especially in view of the signal privilege and honour that has been vouchsafed to her—

"My soul doth magnify the Lord,
And my spirit hath rejoiced in God my Saviour.
For He hath regarded the low estate of His handmaiden."

Then, in a second strophe, she dwells for a moment on the singular and gracious distinction whereby she has been chosen to be the Mother of the Incarnate Son—

"For behold, from henceforth all generations shall call me blessed.
For He That is mighty hath done to me great things;
And holy is His Name.
And His mercy is on them that fear Him throughout all generations."

But during these moments of thankful exultation her vision has widened to embrace new
horizons, and, in a third strophe, she sets forth
some relations of the Birth of her Son to the action
of God's Providence in the history of human nations
and human lives—

" He hath showed strength with His Arm;
  He hath scattered the proud in the imagination of their
  hearts.
  He hath put down princes from their thrones,
  And hath exalted men of low degree.
  He hath filled the hungry with good things;
  And the rich He hath sent empty away."

Once more, in a concluding strophe, she traces the
great gift which, through her, has been bestowed
on the race of man, up to its sources in the Compassion and the Faithfulness of God.

" He remembering His Mercy
  Hath holpen His servant Israel;
  As He promised to our forefathers,
  Abraham and his seed, for ever."

It has more than once been suggested that such
a Hymn as this is not the kind of response which it
would be natural for us to make in reply to such
a congratulation as Elisabeth's;[a] and it is hinted

---

[a] Strauss, *Leben Jesu*, i, 3, § 31, cannot understand how
two friends, visiting one another, should " even in the midst
of the most extraordinary occurrences, break out into long
hymns."

that the composition may be really due to some later writer, whether the Evangelist or another.

Upon this we may remark that "natural" is a term of varying import; and that what is natural to one person, or people, or age, is far from being natural to another. We have only to look around us in order to discover that persons of different temperaments meet similar occasions very differently. One man is reserved and sparing of his words, another is effusive; this man checks his feelings, that man indulges them; one is as literal and prosaic as may be, another almost inevitably expresses himself in the language of poetry. Then the Eastern and Western nations differ now in these respects as they have always differed. To many an Arab at this hour it is perfectly natural to discuss an everyday occurrence in words which have the form and rhythm of a poetical composition. That which an European would put into a sentence, the Arab will expand into what is virtually a poem, with rhythmic rise and fall, and refrains and repetitions, and appeals to all kinds of higher considerations, not perhaps foreign to the subject, but not necessary to its due discussion. No Englishman who had just lost his king and his friend would forthwith break out into an

effusion such as that in which David laments the
death of Saul and Jonathan on Mount Gilboa;[a]
but in David, as in many another Eastern, ancient
or modern—apart from any question of inspiration
—it was almost a matter of course to do so. And
Mary, instinct with the spirit of prophecy, answers
Elisabeth's congratulations in a burst of inspired
poetry, based on older words which she has known
from infancy, and which she so transfigures as
to make them express the fact which fills her
grateful soul with wonder and joy. To measure
her utterance by the prosaic rules of our Western
temperament, is to forget the most obvious laws
of equitable criticism.

Nor, we may confidently add, is there any real
ground for the assertion that Mary's Magnificat
was the work of any other than Mary. Like the
songs of Zacharias and Simeon, it is something
more than a psalm, and something less than
a complete Christian hymn. A Christian poet,
living after the Resurrection of Christ, would
surely have said more ; a Hebrew psalmist would
have said less than Mary. In this Hymn of hers
we observe a consciousness of nearness to the
fulfilment of the great promises, to which there is

2 Sam. i. 19–27 ; cf. Acts iv. 24–30.

no parallel even in the latest of the psalms; and
yet even Mary does not speak of the Promised One
as an Evangelist or an Apostle would have spoken
of Him, by His Human Name, and with distinct
reference to the mysteries of His Life and Death
and Resurrection.[a] Her Hymn was a native product
of one particular moment of transition in sacred religious history, and of no other; when the twilight
of the ancient dispensation was melting, but had
not yet melted, into the full daylight of the new.

Certainly the Magnificat is an inspired Psalm;
it belongs to the highest degree of inspiration, and
yet it does not claim an absolute originality. It
is, in truth, modelled very largely, although not
altogether, on an older Psalm,[b] which Hannah had
sung many a century before at the door of the
tabernacle in Shiloh, when she brought to it
her infant son Samuel, as she said, to "lend
him to the Lord as long as he liveth."[c] Hannah's
history had an especial place in the heart and
thoughts of every Jewish woman. Not only
because she was the mother of the great and
austere prophet, who may claim in some respects

---

[a] Cf. Mill, *Observations on the Attempted Application of Pan-
theistic Principles to the Theory and Historic Criticism of the
Gospels*, p. 119.

[b] 1 Sam. ii. 1–10.   [c] *Ib.* i. 28.

an unrivalled importance in the history of the
people of Revelation, but also and because her
deferred hopes, her bitter disappointments, the
rough misunderstanding to which she was exposed
even at the hands of the gentle and weak old man
who then held the office of high priest in Israel,
have a human pathos that is all their own. At last
her longings were fulfilled, and when, in accordance with the terms of her vow, she consecrated
her son as a Nazarite to the lifelong service of God,
her thankful heart found vent in a Hymn of Praise,
in repeating which many a Jewish mother and
maiden from that time forth associated herself with
the sorrows and the joys of Hannah. Listen to
Hannah first and then to Mary, and you will
perceive how closely their hymns are related to
each other. Each of these inspired women finds
her joy in God ;[a] each traces God's Hand in the
exaltation of the humble and in the humiliation
of the proud ;[b] each closes her song by dwelling
on God's fulfilment of His promises.[c] Mary, we
see plainly, has reproduced the very ideas, the
order of ideas, nay, sometimes the very phrases,
of the older hymn ; but she has made them sub-
servient to a truth which was seen, if at all, very

---

[a] i Sam. ii. i.   [b] *Ib.* 6–8.   [c] *Ib.* 10.

dimly, across the ages, by the older songstress, and which is close and clear to herself. When Strauss observes that if the Virgin's Hymn had been inspired from on high we might expect in it more of originality,[a] it is not out of place to reflect that God the Holy Ghost is not bound to adopt the exact standard of originality which may approve itself to a modern literary man of a sceptical turn of mind. Originality does not consist always and only in the production of new material, new thoughts, new phrases; the truest originality may display itself when old ideas and old phrases are enlisted in the service of some newly proclaimed truth. When, in her inspired Magnificat, Mary draws so largely upon the ancient Hymn of Hannah, she is only doing what inspired souls had done again and again before her. We cannot read the Bible carefully, without noting how Psalmist borrows from Psalmist, Prophet from Prophet, nay, it even might seem, one Evangelist from another; the first object with all the sacred writers being not the creation or the vindication of a poor repu-

---

[a] *Leben Jesu, u.s.* Strauss thinks it "surprising that a discourse emanating immediately from the Divine Source of inspiration should not be more striking for its originality, but should be interlarded with reminiscences from the Old Testament."

tation for one species of originality, but the clear exhibition of truth through the employment of those precise words and thoughts which are best able to do it justice.

II.

The first strophe of Mary's Hymn is a burst of praise. And we may note here three matters for consideration.

1. There is, to begin with, the fact that in the order of Mary's thoughts the praise of God comes first. To give God His due is not, with Mary, an afterthought ; it is not appended to something relating to her friends or to herself. In Mary's soul God takes precedence of all besides. And therefore, in her Hymn, the praise of God takes the lead of all other topics. This, be it observed, is the case, although her Hymn is also an answer to the congratulations of a near relative. She is replying to Elizabeth, but she instinctively, inevitably, turns the eye of her soul upwards. She addresses her first words to God.

Now let us consider what would, in all probability, have been our own course of procedure.

You have achieved, let us suppose, some consi-

c

derable success, or you have escaped some disaster,
or some position or distinction has been conferred
on you. Friends surround you with congratulations ; some of them conventional and perfunctory ;
many of them, let us be assured, sincere. Your
friends paraphrase, after an earthly fashion, the
words of Elisabeth to Mary. They tell you that
your success, your escape, your distinction, is a
gain and a joy to them. They associate themselves,
by the expression of a warm and intimate sympathy,
with your satisfaction and delight; they are
honoured, they are decorated, they have succeeded
and been distinguished, because you, their friend,
have won distinction and success.

How do you reply? You begin by thanking
them for their kindness. To succeed in a world
where no friends are left to express their joy,
would be success robbed of two-thirds of its
value. The old sometimes observe, pathetically,
that success and honours have come to them too
late. And so you tell your friends with perfect
sincerity that their congratulations are more precious to you than anything that has been done
by or done to yourself, and that your first thought
on this auspicious occasion is the satisfaction which
you have given them. The first verse of your

real Magnificat, if it were written out, might perhaps run thus : " My soul doth magnify the kindness and sympathy of my friends, and my spirit
hath rejoiced in the pleasure which they have
enjoyed on my account."

Or, it may be, you give your first thoughts to
yourself. You do not wish to say too much about
yourself, but at the same time you will not affect
a false modesty. You cannot deny—that is the
form which a sense of personal merit takes when
tempered with some misgivings as to the wisdom
of expressing it—you cannot deny that it is a great
satisfaction to you that efforts, long persevered
in without success, have at last succeeded ; that
merits, which it might have seemed were entirely
overlooked, have at last been recognized. You do
not wish to dwell too much on the subject ; but,
on the other hand, your conviction of what is the
fact, and what you call a " proper pride," compels
you to say thus much. With this view you would
make the first verse of your Magnificat something of
this sort : " My soul doth magnify myself, and my
spirit hath rejoiced in the efforts or merits which
have at length been rewarded as they deserve."

But you are a Christian, or at least a Theist.
You remember that, after all, there is such a Being

as God. If the truth is to be told, you do not feel
Him to be very near to you, but you do not wish
to forget Him altogether. If He exists,—and you
believe that He does exist,—He must have something to do with everything that goes on. It is
only right that you should recognize this. You
recognize it somewhat tardily, and as a matter to
be touched on lightly; because, in fact, God is less
real to you than you are to yourself, or than your
friends are. You would not ignore God; still less
would you deny His existence. But you think of
Him, in many of your moods of mind, as an idea
or conception rather than as a living Being; a
conception from which man's mind can really sub-
tract something, or to which it can add something,
as the ages pass. You do not think of Him as
of One Who is entirely independent of you, but
Who is also as near to you as are the influences
which you can measure and the creatures which
you can touch, about which you talk to other
men, or of which you read in the newspapers.
He is there; but on a somewhat distant and
dim horizon of your thought. He is there, and
something must be said about Him; but that
something must befit your very thin and precarious
idea of what He is. And so at last, you say your

Magnificat after a third fashion: "A sense of intellectual fitness leads me to magnify the Lord; and I experience a satisfaction in admitting that now, as at other times, something may be due to a higher Power than myself."

How pathetically is all this in contrast with Mary! No doubt, to Mary, the joy of Elizabeth was a real joy; and she cannot but have known that by lineage and training she herself had been prepared for her own high destiny. But her first thought is of Him from Whose goodness all else proceeds; both the warm hearts, and kindness of friends, and the gifts, whether of nature or of grace, which she had herself received. God must claim her first acknowledgments. Before Him she is as nothing; and yet He, in His condescending Mercy, had deigned to visit her, as none of His creatures had been visited before. She can only think of the contrast between her nothingness and His Magnificence. If she glances for a moment at herself, it is to wonder that she should have been noticed at all by her Creator. "He hath regarded"—not the humility, not the lowly temper; these graces were undoubtedly hers in a very eminent degree, but she is not thinking of them; the original word will not lend itself to such a sense.—"He hath regarded

the low condition [a] of His handmaiden." Because
the contrast between Him and herself is thus
present to her; because she is convinced that she
has exerted no claim on Him, and that whatever
she has received has come from Him; she must
begin with praise—

"My soul doth magnify the Lord,
And my spirit hath rejoiced in God my Saviour."

2. Then Mary praises God with all the faculties
and resources of her spiritual being. "My soul
doth magnify," "my spirit hath rejoiced." "Soul"
and "spirit" are not two different names for the
same thing. When St. Paul prays that the "whole
spirit and soul and body of the Thessalonian
Christians may be preserved blameless unto the
coming of our Lord Jesus Christ," [b] he does not use
two words where one would have sufficed. No
doubt, alike in Biblical and popular language, both
soul and spirit are sometimes used alone for the
whole immaterial part of man; as when our Lord
asks, "What shall it profit a man, if he shall gain

---

[a] ταπείνωσιν. The word may have been chosen to express
among other things the reduced circumstances of the House of
David.   Meyer, *in loc.*, takes it more generally: "Maria meint
die Niedrigkeit ihrer Person."   [b] 1 Thess. v. 23.

the whole world, and lose his own soul?"[a] or when the Preacher says "that the spirit shall return to God Who gave it."[b] But when, as here, the words occur together, in more or less obvious contrast with each other, they stand for the lower and higher parts of that invisible half of man which accompanies his body, yet is distinct from it.[c] Soul is nearer to the bodily nature; spirit nearer to the nature of God. Soul in man is analogous to the higher life of the animals; the animals |have in them nothing that corresponds to spirit. Soul receives impressions both from the external world and from spirit: and so, as here, it utters through the bodily organs that thought or emotion which has previously[d] been present to spirit. Soul is the seat of passion, of imagination, of impulse; spirit, while, as we see in this Hymn, it is, like pure thought, capable of sublime joys all its own, is specially the seat of the self-measuring and reflective reason, of memory, of deliberate and imperative will. Soul, it is plain, lives not far from the frontier of the things of time and sense; spirit

---

[a] St. Mark viii. 36.   [b] Eccles. xii. 7.

[c] Delitzsch, *Bibl. Psychol.*, p. 179.

[d] Observe the present μεγαλύνει to express the action of ψυχή, in contrast with the aorist, ἠγαλλίασεν, which describes that of πνεῦμα. Cf. Meyer, *in loc.*

belongs to a sphere on which the things of time
and sense need not, and often do not, intrude.
Between them soul and spirit include the whole
incorporeal nature of man, with all its powers ; and
Mary summons them all, the highest and the lowest,
the faculties which traverse the world of sense, and
the faculties which live among the highest and most
abstract truths, to the solemn work of praise.   Her
"soul" must magnify the Lord, because, as she
sings, her "spirit" has rejoiced in God her Saviour.

Is there not here also a lesson to be learnt from
Mary ?   Some men appear to think that a single
power of the soul may be told off, like a domestic
servant or a soldier, when sent on a particular
errand, to discharge the duty of praise.   One
man bids his fancy engage in the work ; and
another his affections ; and another his ·reasoned
sense of the fitness of things ; and another his
instinct of beauty, turned towards the higher
horizons.   Nay ! it might sometimes seem as
though no mental or spiritual faculty was bidden
to engage in praise at all ; and Christians who
make a serious effort to pray, and would be
shocked at the neglect to do so, leave the duty of
praising the great Creator to their neighbours, to
the choir, to the choristers, or, it might almost

seem, to the organ. And yet what a demand on all the faculties of our being is made by one simple and oft-repeated act of praise, such as, for instance, the Gloria Patri! We say it before we begin the Psalms; we repeat it at the end of each Psalm and each Canticle, excepting the Te Deum. It consists only of two verses, and yet what infinite spheres does it bid us traverse! Our souls rise first to the Three Almighty Incomprehensible Sub-sistences within the Being of the Godhead—" Glory be to the Father, and to the Son, and to the Holy Ghost." And then, remembering that the Eternal Three have ever been and ever will be what They are, our thought reaches backwards into an unbegun, and forwards into an unending eternity, while seeking for an instant to touch the present, which, as we touch it, has already mingled with the past— " As it was in the beginning, is now, and ever shall be, world without end." If any of us should have cause to think that we have paid but scant atten-tion and embarked little or no spiritual effort in this oft-repeated act of praise, let us bethink our-selves of the import of Mary's words. She would summon the whole mental and moral nature to the work of praise; a work in which, as in a vast orchestra, each mental faculty has its place, and

may bring its due and needed contribution to
swell the harmony of the mighty whole. No variety
of emotion is so poor and lowly that it cannot
utter something in honour of the Creator; no
power or resource of thought is so great that it is
humbled by joining in the tribute which is due
from all finite minds to the Infinite.   The old
exhortation to the Temple choir may be paraphrased
as addressed to the faculties of the Christian soul—

> " Praise Him with the sound of the trumpet,
> Praise Him upon the lute and harp.
> Praise Him in the cymbals and dances:
> Praise Him upon the strings and pipe.
> Praise Him upon the well-tuned cymbals:
> Praise Him upon the loud cymbals.
> Let everything that hath breath
> Praise the Lord." [a]

3. Lastly, observe the title under which Mary
praises God.   " My Saviour."   " My spirit hath rejoiced in God my Saviour."

This designation, as you would know, although
associated by Christian faith, in an especial manner,
with our Lord Jesus Christ, is much older than the
New Testament.   It grew naturally out of Israel's
faith in God's especial and protecting Providence.
" It is Thou that savest us from our enemies," [b] was
the voice of the chosen people from age to age.

[a] Ps. cl. 2–6.   [b] Ps. xliv. 8.

But the enemies were generally political foes, and
the salvation was victory in the field or deliverance
from bondage. This outward and temporal salvation was, indeed, also a religious salvation. Israel
was the people of God; the defeat of Israel was the
defeat of the cause of God; the victory or salvation
of Israel was the victory or the triumph of that
cause. But it is probable that a new impulse was
given to this more spiritual meaning by what would
have seemed to pious Jews the profane assumption
of the title of Saviour by the pagan kings, who,
after the death of Alexander the Great, founded
dynasties in Syria and in Egypt.[a] If henceforth
the God of Israel was to be addressed as Saviour, it
must be in a lofty and spiritual sense; and thus
Mary praises God as the Saviour, not of her country
from temporal ruin, but of her own soul from
eternal death. The expression cannot be explained
by the clause, " He hath regarded the low estate of
His handmaiden;" which, while it assigns the
motive for Mary's praise, does not explain the title
she gives to God. The honour put on her by the
Incarnation might be described by many other
names. But high office is one thing, personal

---

[a] Antiochus I., of Syria, the son of Seleucus Nicanor, took
the title of σωτήρ, after his victory over the Gauls. It was
also assumed in Egypt, by Ptolemy I., the son of Lagus.

salvation another; and if Mary calls God her
Saviour, it is for reasons independent of the rank
and duties which He has assigned to her.

Let us reflect on the meaning of this expression
on Mary's lips. Unique as was her office, magnificent as was the endowment of grace bestowed on
her, singular as were her humility, her purity, her
likeness to the Most Holy, she has and she needs a
Saviour. She does not stand outside that universal
law, that "all have sinned, and come short of the
glory of God."[a] Hers is not a soul which finds its
way to the courts of heaven without recourse to
that One "Name under heaven given among men,
whereby we must be saved."[b] There is, in fact, no
intermediate position in the kingdom of grace
between the Saviour and the saved; no neutral
post, in which nothing is received and from which
nothing is bestowed. There is one Saviour, and all
others are simply saved, be their place in the spheres
of glory what it may, and whatever the graces that
may have been here bestowed on them. Mary
owed, and owes what she was on earth, what she
is in heaven, no less entirely to the merits and the
Precious Blood of her Divine Son, than does the
humblest Christian among us at this hour; and she

[a] Rom. iii. 23.   [b] Acts iv. 12.

offers the best praises that her soul can offer to God, not as manifested first or only in the awful attributes of Knowledge or Power, but as her Saviour.

And in this, too, most assuredly she is a model for us. It is well indeed that we should think deeply and often on other aspects of the Divine Nature, each one of which is a fitting object of adoring praise. It is meet and right that we should give thanks to God for the great glory of His Power, His Intelligence, His Love. But the sense of natural gratitude which He has put in our hearts bids us remember that " God commendeth His love to us, in that, while we were yet sinners, Christ died for us."[a] There is much else for which we may praise God ; we must bless Him " for our creation, preservation, and all the blessings of this life." But if we know what indeed we are, and what has been done and may yet be done for us, we shall do more than thank Him for these fruits of His bounty. We shall bless Him, above all, for His " inestimable love in the Redemption of the world through our Lord Jesus Christ ; for the means of grace, and for the hope of glory," which, through that Redemption, He has bestowed on us.

[a] Rom. v. 8.

II.

PRIVILEGES OF THE VIRGIN MOTHER.

St. Luke i. 48–50.

For behold, from henceforth
All generations shall call me blessed.
For He That is mighty
Hath done to me great things.
And holy is His Name :
And His mercy is on them that fear Him
Unto all generations.

Last Sunday we left Mary, at the end of the first strophe of her Hymn, beginning to disclose the motive that had inspired the burst of praise with which she had replied to the salutation of Elisabeth. All the powers of her spiritual nature, ranging from the heights of pure thought to the depths of passionate emotion, were engaged, like the variously accomplished members of a great choir, in chanting the glory of the Eternal Being; especially in His character of the Saviour of herself and of the whole race of mankind. But the fact which immediately prompts her song is that He, in Whose sight every

creature is manifest,[a] and Whose eyes are in every
place, beholding the evil and the good,[b] has deigned
to cast on her a look of profound significance.
" He hath regarded the low estate of His handmaiden." The blood of David flows in her veins.
But for some generations the royal race has lived
in seclusion, among the poor; cherishing the
secret of its high descent, but resigning itself
to the destiny which God, in His Justice and
His Love, had for the time assigned to it. The
low social estate of Mary was, in her eyes, associated
with a low spiritual estate ; a condition which
could pretend to no excellence or merit in the
eyes of God. Nevertheless, He had " looked upon
her," after such a fashion, that she must needs
break out into thankfulness and praise. It may be
that her memory was haunted by some words of a
later Psalmist, describing an event which, like the
Annunciation, though in an immeasurably lower
sense, was the reversal of a great humiliation.

> " He taketh the simple out of the dust,
> And lifteth the poor out of the mire ;
> That He may set him with the princes,
> Even with the princes of His people." [c]

She thinks of herself as of the handmaiden, or,

[a] Heb. iv. 13.   [b] Prov. xv. 3.   [c] Ps. cxiii. 6, 7.

more exactly, the bondwoman[a] of God; a slave
who was simply His property, who could plead
no personal rights in arrest of His Will. And yet
what had He not done for her ? Before she goes
further she must, out of sheer gratitude, own His
bounty; and this she does in the second strophe
of her Hymn, in which one remarkable result of
the high honour conferred on her, the Source to
which it is due, and the sense in which a kindred
distinction may be shared by all the true servants
of God, are successively touched on.

> "For behold, from henceforth
> All generations shall call me blessed.
> For He That is mighty
> Hath done to me great things ;
> And holy is His Name.
> And His mercy is on them that fear Him
> Throughout all generations."

I.

Mary places her finger first of all on one very
startling consequence of the honour assigned to
her as Mother of the Divine Redeemer.[b] She would

---

[a] δούλης.

[b] It is not easy with Meyer to paraphrase ἀπὸ τοῦ νῦν by
"nach den begeisterten Worten der Elisabeth." The fact
which Elisabeth recognized by the words ἡ μήτηρ τοῦ Κυρίου
μου gave her address its real importance.

live for ever in the memory of mankind. Elisabeth had said, "Blessed art thou among women;"
and Mary, so far from deprecating this high estimate of her privilege, goes considerably beyond it.
"Behold," she exclaims, "from henceforth all generations shall call me blessed."

Undoubtedly there are in the Hebrew Scriptures
sentences which Mary, when thus speaking, may
have had in her mind. Thus, at the birth of Asher,
his mother Leah exclaimed, "Happy am I, for the
daughters will call me blessed;"[a] and the child's
name Asher, "the happy," expresses the feeling of
his mother. And in the Book of Proverbs the
children of the virtuous woman arise up and call
her blessed;[b] and Malachi predicts a day when all
nations would recognize the blessedness of Israel as
having been the people of God.[c] But there is
nothing in these sayings which is really comparable
to Mary's unique prophecy about herself; in which
she anticipates the judgment, not of some, but of
all the generations of living men. "All generations
shall call me blessed."

That which, at first sight, must strike us in
this language is its boldness. Mary is sure of that

---

[a] Gen. xxx. 13.   [b] Prov. xxxi. 28.
[c] Mal. iii. 12. See Dr. Pusey, *in loc.: Minor Prophets.*

D

which, in ordinary experience, seems to lie beyond
the range of probable conjecture. She is sure of
the future. Average human common sense, looking
out upon the future, declares that nothing is probable except the unforeseen. But Mary, too,
surveys the future, and she has no hesitation in
foretelling the terms in which distant ages will
speak of herself. " Behold," she cries, " from
henceforth all generations shall call me blessed."

She is sure, first of all, that she will be remembered. Let us reflect what this means. In every
generation of men, only a small minority of the
dead is remembered at all. A name commonly
lives in a family for two or three generations at
most. If a man is known to a wider circle, it
may cherish his memory for a few years. But
the circle dies, and the man is forgotten. There
are, of course, some few memories that survive :
rulers of peoples, leaders of political parties, dis-
coverers in art or science, masters in literature.
But you can almost count them on your fingers;
and their names, too, when a century has gone by,
are often enough on their way to pass into general
oblivion, even though they should linger in the
notebooks of students and on the shelves of
libraries. As a rule, all quickly disappear. A

human life drops like a pebble into the ocean of
Eternity; for a few moments there are ripples on
the surface, growing fainter as the circles widen,
and then, so far as this world is concerned, the life
which has passed from sight is as forgotten as
though it had never been lived.

> " ' Men fade like leaves, they drop away
>   Beneath the forest shade :
> Others again succeed ; but they
>   Are in oblivion laid.'
> So spake the sire of Grecian song ;
>   Through each succeeding age,
> The words are caught and borne along
>   By poet, saint, and sage." [a]

This, I say, is the rule ; but Mary is confident
that she will be an exception to it. She is, to all
seeming, but a poor Syrian peasant-girl. And yet
she dares to predict that this ordinary law of forget-
fulness of the dead will be suspended in her favour.
Remember that, as yet, nothing has happened out-
wardly to warrant her confidence. No Apostle has
yet been called to the service of her Son; no miracle
has been worked by Him; no one has yet heard of
His Resurrection or of His Sermon on the Mount ;
nay, He is still invisible ; He has scarcely laid aside
the glory which He had [b] with the Father before the

[a] Williams, *Christian Scholar*, p. 23.   St. John xvii. 5.

world was; He has not yet entered by birth into the world of sense. Mary has only the angel's promise to fall back upon. Yet she sees in it a warrant that she will live in the memories of men to the furthest limits of time.

But Mary not only knows that she will be always remembered; she declares that she will be congratulated on her blessedness as long as her memory shall endure among men.

Let us reflect here, that when a memory does survive, it often survives only to be associated with a very different judgment from that which was once accorded to it. A time comes when all who knew a living man or woman have passed away; when the dead can only be studied in documents, in such documents as may be still procurable. And then a reputation is forthwith cast into the crucible of criticism, which constantly, under the guise of historical impartiality, ministers to the passions or to the prejudices of the age. Criticism, indeed, is sometimes just; it destroys unworthy idols, and it redresses the injustice of contemporaries. But it is a very uncertain guide to absolute truth; and it often illustrates by its capricious activity the point on which I am insisting; it shows how transient may be an earthly reputation. Scarcely any two writers

who have discussed him, during the seventy years
that have passed since his death, have agreed as to
the merits or demerits of the first Napoleon. And if,
to come nearer to our present subject, we recall the
names of women who have figured on the scene of
human history—Hatapsu, Semiramis, Zenobia, the
Countess Matilda, Catharine of Medici, Elizabeth of
England, Mary Stuart, Maria Theresa, Catharine
II.—how various have been the world's judgments
about them! But of such a vacillation respecting
herself Mary has no apprehension whatever. Filled
with the spirit of prophecy, she looks down the long
procession of the coming ages, with their incessant
vicissitudes of races and opinions, and she knows
that her name will ever carry with it associations
which must secure for it a universal welcome. "From
henceforth all generations shall call me blessed."

And is she not right?   Nearly nineteen centuries have passed since she spoke; and what
man of average information, interested only in the
concerns which affect our race, has not heard of
the Virgin Mary? A man cannot help hearing
of her; so conspicuously does she loom in the
pages of human history. True enough it is that
around the solid records in the Gospels respecting
her religious imagination has been especially busy.

Early in the history of Christendom there were documents,[a] which the early Church rejected as apocryphal,[b] and in which Mary's birth and infancy, and the exceptional distinctions supposed to have been accorded to her after her death, are described with a freedom which might have passed as poetry if only it had not been treated as sacred prose. Into this subject it is not consistent with our present purpose to enter. Suffice it to say, that whatever the exaggerations and fables which have thus gathered around the name of Mary, they cannot obscure the greatness which is assigned to her in the pages of the Gospel, while in their wildest forms they should remind us of the place which she herself claimed to occupy, and has occupied ever since her death, in the minds of men.

Compare Mary, from this point of view, with some of the great ladies who were nearly or exactly her contemporaries. While Mary was fetching water day by day from the well of Nazareth, or gathering

[a] For the *Psuedo-Matthæi Evangelium*, and the *Evangelium de Nativitate Mariæ*, cf. Tischendorf, *Evangelia Apocrypha*, pp. 50–114. For the Κοίμησις τῆς ἁγίας θεοτόκου, and the two versions of the *Transitus Mariæ*, cf. Tischendorf, *Apocalypses Apocryphæ*, pp. 95–136.

[b] Cf. S. Hieron., *Contr. Helvid.* cxii., ad Matt. xxv. 35-sqq.; Credner, *Gesch. d. Canons*, 215–217; Tisch., *Ev. Ap.*, Prol. xxv.–xxvii.; and *Apocalyps. Apocryph.*, Prol. xxxiv.–xlvi.

wood and wild fruits on the hill above the village, these stately dames, surrounded by a crowd of slaves, swept proudly through the halls of the Cæsars. But, if we except a professed student of history here or there, what do men know about them now? What do you know of Livia, who parted from an honourable husband that she might be the wife of Augustus; or of Julia, the ill-used daughter of Augustus and wife of Tiberius; or of Octavia, the sister of Augustus, whom Antony divorced that he might wed Cleopatra; or of Antonia, the high-minded daughter of Octavia, who lived, they say, to be poisoned by her grandson Caligula; or —somewhat later—of such empresses as Messalina, Agrippina, Poppœa,—better perhaps unmentioned in a Christian church—who are associated with the courts of Claudius and Nero? The names of these ladies were once as familiar to the vast population of the Empire as are those of the members of our own royal family to ourselves. For a few years they filled the thoughts, and—by their crimes or their misfortunes—they supplied materials for the gossip, of the world. Now they are, for all practical purposes, forgotten; while the lowly maiden who was living unknown in a remote province of the vast Empire that was ruled by their nearest relatives, is at this hour more borne in mind by civilized men than any other member of her sex who ever lived.

II.

But what is the justification of this astonishing confidence on the part of Mary that she will be remembered as blessed to the utmost limits of time? It is not anything that she has personally achieved. It is not any grace or excellence peculiar to her mind or character. That she was personally endowed with graces of the highest excellence and beauty we may be well assured: in coming among us, the Eternal Son would, by His Spirit, make ready a fitting temple prepared for Himself. But Mary dwells on nothing of this kind; on nothing personal to herself. She only knows that she has been the recipient of an astonishing privilege, conferred on her by the free bounty of her Creator.

> "He That is mighty hath done to me great things;
> And holy is His Name."

She refers, of course, to what was implied in the message of the Angel Gabriel at the Annunciation: "Hail, thou that art highly favoured, the Lord is with thee: blessed art thou among women. . . .

Fear not, Mary : for thou hast found favour with God. . . . Thou shalt bring forth a Son, and shalt call His Name Jesus. He shall be great, and shall be called the Son of the Highest : and the Lord God shall give unto Him the throne of His father David : and He shall reign over the house of Jacob for ever ; and of His kingdom there shall be no end." [a] And in answer to Mary's expression of wonder the Angel added, " The Holy Ghost shall come upon thee, and the power of the Highest shall overshadow thee : therefore also that Holy Thing Which shall be born of thee shall be called the Son of God." [b] Mary had received these assurances in submissive faith. "Behold the handmaid of the Lord ; be it unto me according to thy word." [c] And they were the warrant of the confidence which she expresses, that " all generations shall call me blessed." How, indeed, could it be otherwise, if she was to be the Mother of the superhuman Heir of David's throne and promises ? if He Who was to be born of her was, in virtue of the supernatural conditions of His Birth, to be recognized as the Son of God ? Nothing that she had done or could have done, nothing that she was or could have been, could have merited this extraordinary distinction ; and Mary is bent upon

---

[a] St. Luke i. 28–33.   [b] *Ib.* i. 35.   [c] *Ib.* i. 38.

ascribing it unreservedly to God. "He That is
Mighty hath done great things to me."

Be careful to observe that Mary dwells here,
not on her person, but on her office in the economy
of the Incarnation. Not once in the Magnificat
does she let fall a single word which points to a
sense of personal desert or excellence ; her joy is
that "He That is Mighty hath done great things to
me." And she adds, "Holy is His Name." She does
not understand why she should have been singled
out for such high honour ; but she is sure that,
since He wills it, all is well. For His Name, which
is to her apprehension inseparable from, since it
unveils His Nature, is Holy. Holiness is the rule
and measure of that which He ordains. Elisabeth
had wondered, " Whence is this to me, that the
Mother of my Lord should come to me ? " Mary
does not repudiate the honour ; to have done so
would have been to make little of God's bounty. But
she insists that she is whatever she is by the grace
and favour of God, and in this respect is on a level
with all His creatures.

In all this is she not an example to an age like
ours, which has no very robust faith in the Presence
and the gifts of God, but does pay exceptional
homage to the merits or accomplishments of indi-

vidual men? Even the modern Church of Christ
has not wholly escaped the disposition to think less
of a sacred office than of the man who holds it; to
dwell lightly on the gift or the commission which
is common to the holder with all his brethren, and
to devote exceptional attention to anything that
is strictly peculiar to the man, and that may be
supposed to be the product of his own industry or
character. It may well be that we of the clergy have
not always been sufficiently on our guard against
a tendency to disparage the ministerial character
which Christ has given us in comparison with some
fancied or real endowments which we dream of as
our own. Any such mistake is tacitly rebuked by
Mary in her Magnificat. She never leads us to
think of what she personally is; but we do not for
a moment forget that she is by office the Mother of
the Divine Redeemer.

Indeed, when we review the terms in which she
refers to her surpassing privilege, it is impossible
not to be struck with their guarded and reserved
tone. "He hath regarded the low estate of His
handmaiden;" "He That is mighty hath done
to me great things." We wonder, perhaps, that
she is not more explicit; that, knowing what she
knows of her extraordinary place in the order of

Divine Providence, she does not say more about it; does not, at least in outline, describe what it is. " He That is mighty hath done to me great things." An ordinary Christian might say as much, we think, after recovering from a dangerous illness, or after a spiritual change, which had altered profoundly all his views and purposes in life. Mary is designated as Mother of the Eternal Son; she is, as the poet says with literal truth, "favoured beyond archangel's dream;"[a] and yet she might seem to desire to draw a veil over her prerogatives, by phrases which, while implying, in her mouth, something extra-ordinary, convey no definite idea of what it is. Can we venture in any way to account for this?

It would seem, then, that here Mary is teaching us a lesson which has never been unneeded since religion—the commerce between the human soul and God—has had a place in the life of man. She is teaching us the duty of speaking very sparingly, if we speak at all, of any blessings which we may have reason to believe that God has conferred on us and on no others. It cannot be wrong to insist on the common facts of Christian experience. We cannot be mistaken, when a good opportunity

[a] *Christian Year*, Hymn for the Annunciation of the Blessed Virgin Mary.

offers, in pointing out the power of prayer, the
value of Christian example, the instruction and
encouragement to be gained from Holy Scripture,
the grace and efficacy of the Christian Sacraments.
We cannot err in bearing our witness to truths
which are the common inheritance of Christians;
the reality of His love for us, Who died for us on
the Cross, and intercedes for us on His throne in
heaven; the incalculable issues of life; the certainty
and nearness of the eternal world. To say what
we may with sincerity and reverence on these
high subjects is indeed to

> "Praise God in His holiness,
> Praise Him in the firmament of His power,
> Praise Him in His noble acts,
> Praise Him according to His excellent greatness." [a]

But when we come to matters which touch us, and
us alone; to blessings which we only have received;
to experiences which, so far as we know, have been
shared by no others;—the case is different. As to
these, the best rule is to say nothing at all about
them, if we can help it; or, if we must say something, to say as little as possible.

That God does at times visit one particular soul
as He visits no other, can hardly be doubted. The

[a] Ps. cl. 1, 2.

Bible teaches us that He does so in a variety of
ways ; and here Christian experience has ever been
in accord with the mind of Holy Scripture. Such
favours or gifts to individuals are suited to the
needs or the temperament of those who receive
them ; they cannot be catalogued or reduced to a
system. Sometimes God gives to a soul a peculiar
satisfaction and joy in prayer ; sometimes a vivid
sense of His Presence in times of anxiety or trouble ;
sometimes a clear presentiment of the blessedness
of the world to come. There is no question here
of communications made, whether in prayer or
otherwise, to a single soul for the sake of others ;
as when, during that stormy night in the Mediter-
ranean, the angel of the Lord stood by Paul, and
assured him of the safety of himself and his fellow-
voyagers.[a] But much may pass between God and
a soul which has no reference to others; as when our
Lord encouraged and guided the Apostle in the vision
at Corinth,[b] or strengthened him during the second
imprisonment at Rome.[c] Such things may take place
in any Christian life. There is no reason for doubt-
ing the reality of these special favours, but there is
great reason why those who have received, or
who think that they have received them should

[a] Acts xxvii. 24.   [b] *Ib.* xviii. 9, 10.   [c] 2 Tim. iv. 17.

say as little about them as they may. For,
first, there is always the possibility that what
looks like a spiritual visit, endowment, or grace,
especially if it be of an unusual character, may
be in truth an illusion of natural emotion. That
such illusions exist is no less certain than the existence of the spiritual graces or gifts which they
counterfeit. And, next, supposing there to be no
element of illusion at all, a soul cannot but suffer
loss if, like Hezekiah, when entertaining the mes-
sengers of Merodach-Baladan, it displays its treasures in an ostentatious temper; [a] and the danger
of such ostentation is very subtle, and may
exist where it is least suspected. Then, thirdly,
there is the ever-present risk of exaggeration; not
in the coarse form of representing something to have
occurred which never did occur at all, but in the more
common forms of giving distinctness and outline
to that which was indefinite, or colour when everything was colourless, or vividness and point where
such elements of interest were really wanting.

Probably we have all heard of meetings of
earnest people, in which first one and then another
member of the company has retailed his experiences.
If these experiences were strictly confined to sins,

[a] 2 Kings xx. 12-18; Isa. xxxix. 1-7.

such meetings might be very improving. In the
early Church of Christ, Christians confessed their
sins in public; and such confession, it need hardly
be said, was a very good lesson in the difficult
work of learning to be really sincere and humble.
But to talk in public about any tokens of God's
especial favour towards us, or still more about our
good points, even if our estimate of them is an
accurate one, is surely very dangerous; dangerous
to those graces of truthfulness and self-forgetfulness
which are, in the Christian life, of almost more
account than anything else. I do not say that no
occasion can ever arise to justify departure from
this rule; one such occasion, we know, did present
itself in the lifetime of St. Paul. He had been
traduced by his opponents at Corinth, as an
ambitious, scheming, and, above all, unspiritual
man; who was really working against Christ's older
Apostles, Peter and James, and who acted as he did
because, unlike Peter, he had never witnessed such
a sight as the Transfiguration—the vision of Christ
in glory. Had his own reputation or comfort only
been at stake, the Apostle would have been
silent. But, if his opponents were unanswered, his
whole work for Jesus Christ at Corinth would have
been imperilled. And therefore very reluctantly he

partially, only partially, withdraws the veil from an occurrence of which, but for the ill-natured gossip of the Corinthian sectaries, we should never have heard. In doing this he only half admits that he is the subject of his own narrative; he refers to the receiver of the singular distinction which he records as if he were or might be some one other than himself.

"I knew a man in Christ fourteen years ago, (whether in the body, I cannot tell; or whether out of the body, I cannot tell: God knoweth;) such an one caught up to the third heaven. And I knew such a man, (whether in the body, or out of the body, I cannot tell: God knoweth;) how that he was caught up into Paradise, and heard unspeakable words, which it is not lawful for a man to utter. Of such an one will I glory: yet of myself I will not glory, but in mine infirmities." [a]

We see how a reference to this striking passage in his life was wrung out the soul of the unwilling Apostle by the sheer pressure of spiritual necessity; and something of the same kind must have been the case with the Blessed Virgin, when for the honour of her Son, and to promote the true and full knowledge of the Gospel, she communicated

[a] 2 Cor. xii. 2–5.

E

to the Evangelist St. Luke the details of all that
passed at the Annunciation between herself and the
angel. When she is acknowledging Elisabeth's
congratulations, she is under no such necessity;
and therefore she veils what has happened beneath
the more general phrases of the Magnificat. It is a
point of spiritual prudence to know how to say
enough to give God His due, and yet not enough
to feed that subtle self-approbation which is one of
the worst foes of our true well-being.

III.

Mary concludes the second strophe of her Hymn
by lines which lead our thoughts away from God's
dealings with herself, to a general law of His
Providence—

> " His mercy is on them that fear Him
> Unto all generations."

And yet in these words she may well be classing
herself among those who fear God, and whom God,
in consequence, visits with His mercy, whatever
form the visitation may take. By "fear" she means
that sincere and awe-struck apprehension of the
Presence and Majesty of God which is the beginning of all spiritual wisdom, since without it

the soul can take no true measure either of itself, or of what is due to the Author and End of its existence. Such fear may coexist with love; although love in such degree as it becomes "perfect"[a] expels from fear the element of terror, while preserving that of reverent and watchful apprehension. It is in this sense that "perfect love casteth out fear." Fear and love are the twin guardians of the higher life of the soul; and God never fails to help and govern those whom He brings up in His steadfast fear and love.[b]

Mary, then, shows, by what took place at the Annunciation, that she had this fear, or reverent apprehension of God, in her heart; that she was looking out for intimations of His Will. And, accordingly, His mercy lighted upon her; He made her the Mother of His Son. But the same law of His action would hold good for all coming time. Not by natural works of righteousness which man had done, but according to His mercy,[c] would Jesus Christ save men from their sins; and this mercy would be accorded to those who had in their hearts that sensitiveness to what was amiss in them which some apprehension of what God is alone can give.

[a] 1 St. John iv. 18.
[b] Collect for Second Sunday after Trinity.   [c] Tit. iii. 5.

So it was with those earliest believers who waited
for the Consolation of Israel;[a] so it has been with
every soul which has come, in adult life, out of the
darkness of heathenism or unbelief to the knowledge
and love of Jesus Christ.   To the end of time Jesus
is the channel and dispenser to the human race of
the infinite Mercy of God, and He dispenses it to
those seekers who begin with fear.

But Mary's words have another and a deeper
meaning.   It is that for the endless well-being of
the soul those earliest stirrings of life which are
due to a Divine influence, and which we call fear
and love, are more important even than religious
privileges.   They are more important, not in themselves, but to us.   Without fear and love the greatest
religious privileges are but as seed dropped into the
sand of the desert,—they cannot bear fruit, or indeed
do anything for us.   We may dare to say that even
to Mary it was more necessary that she should have
the fear of God in her heart than that she should
be the Mother of the Incarnate Son; since our
Lord Himself has told us so.   You remember that
striking scene in after-years, when one in a crowd
of eager listeners around Him, in a transport of
enthusiasm, essayed to win His heart by reference

[a] St. Luke ii. 25.

to the blessedness of His Mother : " Blessed is the womb that bare Thee, and the paps that Thou hast sucked." [a] What was His answer ? He does not disparage, much less deny, the high standing and privilege of His Mother Mary ; but He insists that both for her and for all others the more important thing is that temper of obedient fear, which alone makes great religious privileges other than dangerous. " Yea, rather, blessed are they that hear the Word of God and keep it." He does not here imply that His Mother did not satisfy this condition of true blessedness ; we are told, indeed, that she kept in view all God's providential dealings towards her, and pondered them in her heart. [b] But He would draw attention away from religious privilege, however eminent, to those vital conditions without which no spiritual advantages can be turned to good account.

We can never afford to lose sight of this truth. The human mind is constantly tempted to think that the possession of high religious office, or of special religious opportunities, is of itself a warrant of religious security in time and for eternity. Nothing is less true. A man may be an Apostle, and yet a Judas. He may be a companion of

[a] St. Luke xi. 28.　　　　[b] *Ib.* ii. 19.

apostles, and yet a Demas. He may be a receiver of that greatest of all the gifts of God—that gift by receiving which we are most nearly likened to Mary—the Sacrament of Christ's Body and Blood —and yet he may eat and drink his own condemnation, not discerning the Lord's Body.[a] Warm or excited feelings are often full of illusion, but the important matter is that sensitiveness of conscience to the Will and the Presence of God which the Bible calls "fear." "Blessed is the man that feareth the Lord; he hath great delight in His commandments;"[b] "Blessed are all they that fear the Lord, and walk in His ways. For thou shalt eat the labours of thine hands: O well is thee, and happy shalt thou be."[c]

And thus we are led to reflect—even in presence of the highest religious distinction that ever was conferred on a human being—that, after all, religion places all men on a level more truly than any other force or agency in this world. The great inequalities between human lives are due to causes which are rooted in the nature of things and always operative; if these inequalities could be suppressed by legal enactment to-morrow, they would reappear in a week's time. The rich and poor, the powerful and

---

[a] 1 Cor. xi. 29.   [b] Ps. cxii. 1.   [c] *Ib.* cxxviii. 1, 2.

the defenceless, the honoured and the neglected, will ever be found in human society, for the simple reason that men enter life with different equipments of natural power, and this difference will certainly express itself in consequences beyond. Some men, who have dwelt constantly and even bitterly on the social and other inequalities of life, have endeavoured to console themselves by reflecting that nature and books redress the balance. Whatever be our position in life, they say, we are all equally free to enjoy a writer like Shakespeare; monarchs and working men are, for the moment, on a level before the genius and insight which instructs and delights us all. Again, whatever be our position in life, we are all equally free to enjoy nature. The outline of the great mountain, the first burst of spring, the glories of the autumnal sunset, the mystery of the heavens on a clear night, the sea with its ever-changing moods of storm and calm; —these are common property. Undoubtedly to a certain extent this is true. But in order to relish the masterpieces of literature, at least some education is needed; and men who would enjoy nature most thoroughly are not always free enough or wealthy enough to visit her where she may be seen to the best advantage. It is otherwise with those elemen-

tary movements of the soul, upon which God sheds
His mercy, and which are the first steps, as they are
the crowning accomplishments, of a religious life.
Every human heart may fear and love the Being
Who made it. Religious instruction and religious
opportunities are indeed precious; and when they
are within reach, fear and love will conspire to
make the most of them, since assuredly they cannot
be neglected without peril. But when they are not
to be had, if there be the fear of God in the heart,
there, most surely, is His mercy too. And where
there is the love of the Perfect Moral Being, there
also is within reach a Presence in the soul which
may even compare with that vouchsafed to Mary.
" If any man love Me, he will keep My words : and
My Father will love him, and We will come unto
him, and make Our abode with him." [a] Only one
woman could be the Mother of the Most Holy
when He vouchsafed to enter our human world ;
but there is no reason why each and all of us
should not know by experience what the Apostle
means by that astonishing yet most blessed saying,
" Christ in you, the Hope of glory." [b]

[a] St. John xiv. 23.   [b] Col. i. 27.

III.

VICISSITUDES OF MEN AND NATIONS.

St. Luke i. 51–53.

He hath showed strength with His Arm;
He hath scattered the proud in the imagination of their hearts.
He hath put down princes from their thrones,
And hath exalted them of low degree.
He hath filled the hungry with good things;
And the rich He hath sent empty away.

BETWEEN the second strophe of the Magnificat and the third, there is a contrast which makes the transition from one to the other appear somewhat abrupt. In the second strophe, so far as her humility would permit, Mary was speaking of herself; she foretold her place throughout all time in the memories and hearts of men; she touched upon the great things which God had done to her; she was not excluding a personal reference when she sang of that Mercy of God which unto all generations is on them that fear Him. But in the strophe which is before us to-day, she is surveying the wide field of human history; she sees God's

Arm of power displayed in it conspicuously; she
notes the changes which God makes in the fortunes
of dynasties and nations; and His rule of action
in the kingdom of grace.

"He hath showed strength with His Arm;
  He hath scattered the proud in the imagination of their
    hearts.
  He hath put down princes from their thrones,
  And hath exalted them of low degree.
  He hath filled the hungry with good things;
  And the rich He hath sent empty away."

What is the connection between that more
personal history and this larger survey of the
action of God in the civil and religious affairs of
man? How does Mary come to have passed so
rapidly from one to the other?

Here let us take note of a common experience
of the human mind in all ages, whether within the
sphere of inspiration or outside it. At times of
deeply moved feeling, whether of joy or sorrow, the
soul of man is raised above the level of its average
existence, and enjoys the command of a larger
outlook. The petty cares of life are lost sight
of in these moments of unwonted elevation; and
wide and extended horizons, which are ordinarily
beyond the range of sight, come into view. From
the crest of the wave that is bearing him towards

an unknown shore, the mariner looks out for an
instant on a distant prospect, it may be of pre-
cipitous cliffs, it may be of hills and valleys and
peaceful homesteads, and all that recalls the security of a landsman's life ;—but he has no sooner
descried it than he sinks forthwith into the trough
of the sea. And the human soul is able, when
borne upwards by a wave of feeling, to perceive
larger fields of truth than usual, even though the
vision fades almost at the moment of its being
enjoyed. Something of this kind has often been
observed at the approach of death. Men who are
not generally given to hazard predictions, or even
to enunciate general principles, will sometimes
speak on their death-beds as though they were
invested with a kind of prophetic character ; so
large would seem to be their range of view, so clear
and confident their opinion as to what will or will
not happen after they are gone. A great joy will
sometimes have a like result; and we may have
observed how recovery from the extremity of ill
ness, or the birth of a son, or unlooked-for deliverance from impending ruin, will lead even taciturn
people to speculate aloud on the influences which
govern human life, and with which they feel themselves for the moment to be in vivid contact.

Mary's inspiration would not have withdrawn her
from the operation of this law of the special
illumination which is attendant on certain states
of elevated feeling.   Her own experience would
lead her to reflect on God's general principles
of government.   For the principles on which He
deals with single souls are the same principles as
those which control His dealings with nations and
races and Churches; the difference lies in the scale
of their application.   When Newton saw an apple
fall from the tree, and had asked himself why
it did not go upwards instead of downwards, he
had discovered the law which governs the movements of the heavenly bodies; and when Mary
surveyed her own history closely, she recognized
the principles of God's general government of the
world.   She was a descendant of David's line; and
she knew how in the past her ancestors had been
put down from their thrones, while she, in her low
estate, had been exalted to a far higher honour than
is conferred by any earthly crown.   Like every
true Israelite, she had longed to see God's promised
salvation; and lo! she was to be the Mother of
the Promised One.   Such experiences could not
but lead her to consider the general truths which
they so strikingly illustrated; but, before she

announces them, she pauses to do homage to a fact
which takes precedence of them, and which throws
them out into full relief.

I.

That fact is the active and never-failing Provi
dence of Him Who ordereth all things both in
heaven and earth.   No fact, perhaps, is so widely
confessed and so practically forgotten as God's
action in the affairs of the world and of men's
separate lives.   Yet those who believe in God may
always verify it, since it explains, and it alone
explains, much which takes place ; while if much
also takes place which it does not explain to our
apprehensions, we may reflect that, alike in what
He does and in what He permits, God, as the Infinite Being, naturally does and allows much which
we could not understand.   But Mary sings that
"He hath showed strength with His Arm."   The
human arm represents man's working power.   The
arm executes the orders of the will ; and it is in
the vigorous, quickly moving arm that we recognize
a will of energy and decision.   Thus, in the language
of the Hebrews, the word "arm" was generally used
in the sense of power ; as when the man of God

prophesied to Eli the downfall of his family:
"Behold, the days come, that I will cut off thine
arm, and the arm of thy father's house;"[a] or when
Jeremiah exclaims that the "arm of Moab is
broken;"[b] or Ezekiel, speaking in the Name of
God, "I have broken the arm of Pharaoh King of
Egypt."[c] A word thus employed to denote human
power was naturally used of the Power of God,
without, of course, implying that the Divine Being,
in ages before the Incarnation, had taken on Him
any likeness to the human form. Thus God is
often said to deliver His people from Egypt, and
from later oppressions, "with an outstretched
Arm,"[d] that is, by a special exertion of His power.
And a Psalmist sings how God "with His own
right Hand and His holy Arm hath gotten Himself the victory;"[e] and another, that "He had
scattered His enemies abroad with His mighty
Arm."[f] And Isaiah speaks of God's showing
"the lighting down of His Arm;"[g] and he predicts that the Arm of the Lord shall be on the
Chaldeans;[h] and he invokes the Divine attribute of
power in favour of captive Israel: "Awake, awake,

[a] 1 Sam. ii. 31.   [b] Jer. xlviii. 25.   [c] Ezek. xxx. 21.
[d] Deut. v. 15; vii. 19; xi. 2; xxvi. 8; Ps. cxxxvi. 12.
[e] *Ib.* xcviii. 1.   [f] *Ib.* lxxxix. 10.
[g] Isa. xxx. 30.   [h] *Ib.* xlviii. 14.

put on thy strength, O Arm of the Lord ; " ª and he asks, with reference to the future Redeemer, considered as embodying and exhibiting to men the Power of God, "To whom is the Arm of the Lord revealed ?" ᵇ These, as all readers of their Bibles would know, are only a few of the passages which might be quoted; so that Mary was using old and consecrated language when she described God's power by the metaphor of an "arm." But what does she mean by saying that God had "showed strength with His Arm" ? Clearly that His incessant energy had brought about particular results which were calculated to impress human minds with the sense of His power, as vividly as though they had seen the heavens open, and an arm of irresistible might stretched out to shape the course of men and events according to the good pleasure of their Invisible Ruler. One of the principal uses of the historical books of the Old Testament is to accustom us to look at all history in this way; to see God's Hand and Arm in it; to trace in circumstances which might seem trivial or a matter of course, the strong action of His Holy Will. God is not less present in English than in Jewish affairs ; nor has He less concern with our separate

---

ª Isa. li. 9.   ᵇ *Ib.* liii. 1.

lives than with those of the forefathers and heroes
and saints of Israel ; the great difference is that, as
a rule, we do not see Him, whereas they did. Mary,
at any rate, before she goes further, will not leave
the matter in doubt; God, she says, "hath showed
strength with His Arm."

II.

She passes on to note one particular series of
events, running through long periods of history in
which this action of the Arm of God is especially
manifested—

"He hath scattered the proud in the imagination of their
  hearts.
He hath put down princes from their thrones,
And hath exalted them of low degree."

Mary here, it seems, looks backward and forward ;
she is at once historian and prophetess ; she is
proclaiming principles of the Divine Government
which will be as true in the remote future as they
have been true in the distant past. She looks
backward over the ages of history, and she beholds
kingdoms which have fallen from great prosperity
into utter ruin ; and princes whose names were once
the terror of the world, while their thrones have
long since been vacant, or humbled with the dust.

" He hath scattered the proud," or literally, " the
insolently proud." [a] The word which she uses ac-
curately describes the prevailing temper of the
average occupant of an Eastern throne. It is the
temper which is naturally produced by long-con-
tinued success, by the accumulation of much wealth
and power. It is to be found on a small scale in men
among ourselves in private life, who have had everything their own way, made money rapidly, achieved
social and perhaps some political importance, and
above all have had many years of unbroken health.
To prosper after this fashion, and to remain humble,
self-distrustful, unselfish, mindful of the real conditions of life, of the nearness of death, of the
weakness of the strongest man, and of the awful
Presence and Power Which is around and above
us,—this is the exception rather than the rule.
The rule is, that when very prosperous men are
not under the influences of religion, they become
haughty and self-asserting, even although they
should have sufficient good taste, as distinct from
religious principle, to check the exuberant exhibition
of these tendencies in what they do and say. But if
such a temper exists in Christendom and in private
life, think what may happen when a man is in

[a] ὑπερηφάνους.

F

the position of one of the ancient kings of Egypt
or Assyria; with unchecked power over the lives
and fortunes of his subjects; with vast wealth, large
armies, and a great company of accomplished slaves
altogether at his disposal. Wonderful indeed it
would be if, without the control of the true religion,
the heart of a man in such a position did not swell
with an intolerable pride; wonderful if he did not
altogether lose sight of the real measure of things,
of the place of every dying man in the universe
of God, of his true relations with God and with
his brother-men. Mary knows this, and thus she
sings of God's scattering the insolently proud *in*, or
rather *by*, the imaginations of their hearts.[a] The
false estimate of self, of men and things, which is
engendered by the temper in question, is constantly
fatal to the position which has appeared to warrant
it. It overrates its own resources; it underrates
the resources of others; it overrates material wealth
or power; it underrates the strength of those moral
convictions which lie deep in the hearts of millions
of men; it is so inflated by the successes of the

[a] Meyer's theory that διανοίᾳ is here a dative of more precise definition, would make the phrase too nearly tautolo-
gous. Pride cannot exist outside the διάνοια τῆς καρδιάς of
the proud.

past, that it cannot coolly take account of the con-
tingencies of the future ; it is so full of its Auster-
litz and its Jena, that it cannot anticipate what
may happen amid the snows of Russia, or during
a retreat from Moscow.   It is not a peculiarity of
the ancient, as also it is not of the modern, world ;
it is not less true in private than in public life, that
God in His own time and way scatters to the
winds highhanded insolence as being too full of self
to recognize the conditions on which any position
is held in this world, by any man or any people
whatever.

Mary, no doubt, would often have heard her
parents discuss the fall of those ancestors of hers
and theirs who had last sat in Jerusalem on the
throne of David ; and consider how far their temper
and conduct or that of some of their predecessors
had helped to bring it all about ; and repeat the
solemn truths contained in those warnings of Jeremiah, which to the last kings of Judah and their
courtiers appeared to be so unpatriotic and dis-
loyal.   But if these monarchs of what was only an
inconsiderable state had to learn that they would
not therefore reign because they closed themselves in
cedars,[a] their fall was, in the outward scale of events,

[a] Jer. xxii. 15.

of trifling importance when compared with that of
the occupants of the mighty thrones around them.
The Egyptian hieroglyphics and the cuneiform
characters have yielded up their secrets to the
industry of modern scholars; and we have before
our eyes the proud inscriptions in which the
old kings of Egypt and Assyria announced their
will or proclaimed their triumphs to their subjects
and to the world. Nothing is more remarkable in
these inscriptions than the astonishing self-assertion
which from first to last inspires them : they are the
language of men who sincerely believe that no
bounds to their power exist, and that to traverse
their will is an unpardonable crime. The Egyptian
kings believed that they were deities in human form,[a]
and they spoke and acted accordingly. More than
one Syrian monarch after Alexander described himself as " God." [b] And the Bible bears a like witness
to the temper of the ancient monarchies. Ezekiel
records a saying of the contemporary Pharaoh about
the Nile : " My river is mine own, and I have
made it for myself." [c] Daniel tells us that Nebu-

[a] Cf. quotations from the inscriptions in Renouf's Hibbert
Lecture for 1879, p. 162 sq.

[b] Antiochus II., Antiochus IV., the great oppressor of the
Jews, and Antiochus VI., describe themselves on their coins
as ΘΕΟΣ.   [c] Ezek. xxix. 3.

chadnezzar " walked in the palace of the kingdom of
Babylon ; and the king spake, and said, Is not this
great Babylon, that I have built for the house of
the kingdom by the might of my power, and for the
honour of my majesty?"[a] And how does Ezekiel
address a much less considerable potentate, the
Prince of Tyre? "Thine heart is lifted up; thou
hast said, I am a god, I sit in the seat of God, in
the midst of the seas."[b] In a later age there was
a scene at Cæsarea which illustrates the point
before us, when "Herod, arrayed in royal apparel,
sat upon his throne, and made an oration" to the
embassies from Tyre and Sidon ; "and the people
gave a shout, saying, It is the voice of a god, and
not of a man."[c]

Mary knew what had happened to Egypt; she
knew what had been the fate of Tyre and of
Babylon. Before her eyes there passed a long
procession of vacant and ruined thrones. Assyria
had gone down before Babylon; Babylon and
Egypt before the Persians; the Persians before the
great Alexander. Alexander's generals in Egypt
and in Syria had set up monarchies which by
turns oppressed Israel in the later stages of its
history ; never did a nation sustain a more

[a] Dan. iv. 29, 30. [b] Ezek. xxviii. 2. [c] Acts xii. 21, 22.

exhausting struggle for its very life than did the
Jews under the Maccabees. But these oppressors
too had recently gone their way; in Egypt and Syria
they had alike been humbled before the Roman
power. It might be said that when Mary sang, the
East was still echoing to the crash of falling thrones;
and one power remained supreme on earth—at least
to the apprehension of populations that had never
heard of what was even then going on in India and
China—the Imperial power of Rome.

But Mary is a prophetess no less than an historian; and as she could foretell her own place in
the memory of the grateful Church, so she could
divine what would happen to the great world-
Empire. She speaks of what God *has* done. "He
hath scattered;" "He hath put down;" "He hath
exalted;" "He hath filled;" "He hath sent away."
But this is sometimes the style of a prophet, who is
by no means obliged to use a future tense when
foretelling a future time. The vision of the future
passes before the prophet's soul; and he describes
what he sees as actually occurring, or as already
accomplished. Thus it is that Isaiah, in the latter
part of his book, foretells the captivity in Babylon
as though it had already produced a state of things
in the midst of which he was actually living; and

the prophets sometimes use a past tense advisedly,
as expressing as vividly as possible their conviction
that the predicted future is as certain as the past.
If, then, Mary speaks of God as having put down
princes from their thrones, she may mean Roman
emperors to come no less than the dynasties which
had long since ruled on the Nile or on the Euphrates.

When Mary sang, Rome was at the height of
her power; the greatest part of the known world
obeyed her laws. Her legions had planted their
eagles on the Rhine, on the Danube, on the Euphrates, on the Nile, in the deserts of Africa. Her
civilization, with its blessings and its vices; her
institutions, her manners and motives, even her
language, had followed. The world was already
Roman, not only in name, but to a large extent in
sympathy and purpose ; and no social and political
fabric that had ever bound civilized men together
seemed so strong or so durable as that which stood
around the throne of the Cæsars. And yet the
causes which had brought about the downfall of
earlier powers were at work within the great Empire. Material splendour had blinded men's eyes to
the secret symptoms of decay, and to the truths and
virtues which could alone avert it ; and at last the
rash came. It nearly came in the third century,

after Christ, two hundred years before its time. It did come with overwhelming terrors in the fifth, when everything that had been venerated for centuries, save only the Church of God, was involved in one vast catastrophe, and when Goths and Huns, and Vandals and Lombards, swept like waves of angry men over the wreck of the old civilization. Thus at last the words were fulfilled which St. John had heard in ecstasy, "Babylon the great is fallen, is fallen!"[a]

But the work of the Arm of God, as Mary watches it from afar, is not merely or chiefly destructive; it scatters and destroys only that it may gather and rebuild. As the Church says with such truth and beauty, "God declareth His Almighty Power most chiefly in showing mercy and pity."[b] When Mary sings that God hath exalted the humble and meek, or rather, them of "low estate," she may well be thinking of the position of Israel among the nations of the world; surrounded by mighty monarchies, while itself occupying a territory not much larger than an English county, yet chosen to be the people of Revelation, and to exercise an altogether unrivalled influence on the future of the human race. Or she may have in her mind such careers as those of

[a] Rev. xiv. 8.   [b] Collect for Eleventh Sunday after Trinity.

Joseph at the court of Egypt in one age, and of Daniel and Esther at the courts of Babylon and Persia in another.   Nor can she but have borne in her grateful soul an ever-present and overwhelming sense of the exceptional honour put upon herself. What royal distinctions were in reality ever comparable to hers who was the chosen Mother of Emmanuel; to hers, of whom—as St. Paul said of her race—as concerning the flesh, Christ came, Who is over all, God blessed for ever ?[a]

And may we not here also observe that Mary's words have a reference to the future as well as to the past ?   Does she not already descry a far-off time, when the disciples of the Crucified would succeed to the empire of the world; when "the meek would inherit the earth, and be refreshed in the multitude of peace"?[b]   The triumph of Christianity, notwithstanding the faults of individual Christians, was on the whole a victory of purity and patience, of humility and conscientiousness, over the corruption, violence, pride, lack of serious moral principle, which so largely characterized the social fabric of the old empire.   And Mary beheld the coming victory; she saw that it was involved in the angel's promise respecting her Son.   "He shall reign over

[a] Rom. ix. 5.   [b] Ps. xxxvii. 11.

the house of Jacob for ever; and of His kingdom
there shall be no end." [a]

How far happier would men be, if they could
only be sure that their future place in another
world, if not here, will be the reverse—I do not
say of their place, but—of their temper, whether of
self-effacement or of self-assertion, in this! Doubtless there have been paupers who have cherished in
their rags the pride of discontent in a measure not
unworthy to be compared with Sennacherib's pride
of success;[b] and there have been kings whom crown
and sceptre, and the fascinations of power, and the
adulations of a court, have not rendered incapable
of cultivating the humble and patient temper of a
Christian saint.   The position counts for little;
the important point is the temper.   As it is the
self-asserting temper which God deposes from its
throne of pride, so it is the self-renouncing temper
which He exalts to His realm of glory.   How could
it be otherwise, when the Most Holy, being in the
form of God, did not deem His equality with God a
prize to be eagerly grasped, but emptied Himself of
His glory, and took on Him the form of a servant,
and was made in the likeness of man, in order that
this same mind might be in us which was also in

[a] St. Luke i. 33.   [b] 2 Kings xviii. 33–35.

Himself, Christ Jesus?[a]   And what more natural
and fitting than that the Mother of the Incarnate
God should proclaim a moral truth which is the
first lesson of the Incarnation of her Son?

III.

Corresponding with this law of the depression
of the insolent and the exaltation of the unpre-
tending, is God's rule of administration in the
purely spiritual world. They who are sensible of
their needs and deficiencies, who are seeking truth
and longing for grace, are, sooner or later, satisfied.
They who deem themselves to have need of nothing
from on high, who are sure that they see at once to
the bottom of every question, who hold that they
can do right without any aid from the Author of
all goodness—the self-reliant and the self-compla-
cent,—these men are excluded from a share in the
Divine bounty.

> " He hath filled the hungry with good things;
> But the rich He hath sent empty away."

This principle, that a sense and confession of
want must precede in intelligent men any communication of God's best blessings, is in keeping, as

[a] Phil. ii. 6, 7.

Mary's metaphor suggests, with the law of nature.
If food is to invigorate the body, if it is not to be
an incumbrance, and a cause of discomfort and
disease, it must be welcomed by appetite. Appetite
is nature's certificate that food will not be injurious.
And if a soul is to be benefited by truth or grace,
that soul must desire the blessing. No fact is
more constantly insisted on in Holy Scripture than
this; unless it be another fact which follows as a
consequence, namely, that God withholds His best
blessings when men do not seek them.

This is the constant teaching of the Old Testament. "Open thy mouth wide, and I will fill it." [a]
"Call upon Me," says God, by the mouth of Jeremiah, to Israel—"call upon Me, and I will answer
thee, and show thee great and mighty things, which
thou knowest not." [b] "If," says Solomon, "thou
criest after knowledge, and liftest up thy voice for
understanding; if thou seekest her as silver, and
searchest for her as for hid treasures; then shalt
thou understand the fear of the Lord, and find the
knowledge of God." [c] And so a Psalmist during the
exile sings: "Blessed are they that keep God's testimonies, and seek Him with their whole heart. . . .
I have had as great delight in the way of Thy testi-

[a] Ps. lxxxi. 10. [b] Jer. xxxiii. 3. [c] Prov. ii. 3-5.

monies as in all manner of riches. . . . Open Thou
mine eyes, that I may see the wondrous things out
of Thy Law. . . . My soul hath longed for Thy
salvation, and I have a good hope because of Thy
Word.   Mine eyes long sore for Thy Word, saying,
O when wilt Thou comfort me ? . . . I have longed
for Thy saving health, O Lord ; and in Thy Law is
my delight.   O let my soul live, and it shall praise
Thee." [a]

This teaching and these prayers would have been
familiar to Mary ; and her Son and Lord confirmed
their import in after-years.   " Ask, and ye shall
have ; seek, and ye shall find ; knock, and it shall
be opened unto you.   For every one that asketh
receiveth ; and he that seeketh findeth ; and to him
that knocketh it shall be opened." [b]

On the other hand, Mary proclaims that " the rich
He hath sent empty away."   God does not force
Himself on those who think that they can do without Him.   He offers them His good things ; and if
He meets with the indifference of an imaginary
sufficiency, He passes on.   They who deem themselves too well off to need Him, are taken at their
word ; and they cannot complain if it be so.   So it
was in the days of our Lord and His Apostles.

[a] Ps. cxix. 2, 14, 18, 81, 82, 174, 175.   [b] St. Matt. vii. 7, 8.

Herod, Pilate, Felix, all came close to truth, and were sent empty away ; while Simeon and Anna, and first one, and then another Apostle—the fishermen, the tax-gatherer, the tent-maker—and later on, Cornelius the centurion, were filled with the good things of faith in the Unseen, and hope in an endless inheritance, and love towards God and man. And as with individuals, so with classes of men. The average Greek, satisfied with his shallow pride of culture, had no eye for the realities of the moral world, or for his own deep need of pardon and grace. He toyed with some one of the current philosophies ; and if it told him nothing certainly about those things which it most concerns a thinking man to know, it at least produced in him a sense of tranquil satisfaction with life and with his own powers. And the average Jew was either a hard-headed sceptic like the Sadducees, or a man of phrases and proprieties like that Pharisee who is apostrophized by St. Paul : "Behold, thou art called a Jew, and restest in the Law, and makest thy boast of God, and knowest His Will, and approvest the things that are more excellent, being instructed out of the Law; and art confident that thou thyself art a guide of the blind, a light of them which are in darkness, an instructor of the foolish, a teacher of babes, which hast the form of knowledge and of the truth in the Law."[a] This is a picture of the temper of a great number of Jews in the Apostolic age ; and we can understand how, in such a state of mind, " they being ignorant of God's righteousness, went about to establish their own righteousness, not submitting themselves to the righteousness of God."[b] The earlier chapters of the Epistle to the Romans are devoted to breaking down, in Gentile[c] and Jew[d] alike, this fatal temper of satisfaction with self, and to proving that, since all the world is guilty before God, all need that gift of pardon and peace which is offered by His Blessed Son, Incarnate and Crucified for men.

This consideration may enable us to answer two questions which are often asked nowadays, and which are sufficiently practical in their bearings.

And first, Why do so many people, who have opportunities of knowing Christian truth, and have good natural abilities, often know so little about its real character ?

The answer, at least in a great many cases, is, that they do not make a serious effort to find out what it is. They take it for granted that while

[a] Rom. ii. 17–20. [b] Rom. x. 3.
  Ib. i. 18–32. [d] *Ib.* ii. 17–iii. 31.

you cannot master a science or learn a new language
without some serious trouble, religious knowledge
will somehow come to them as a matter of course.
They have learnt something about it many years
ago, and that, they think, will do.   They give the
real energy and vigour of their minds to the things
of this world ; they reserve a few spare moments
for religion.   Religion, they say to themselves, being
meant for all, can be thoroughly understood, with
a very little effort, by any person of average
ability ; and to spend too much labour on it would
be a waste of time.

Now, natural ability has nothing necessarily to
do with the real apprehension of religious truth.
It can master the surroundings of religion ; the evidences on which the Creed depends ; the historical
circumstances which accompanied the appearance
of our Lord among men ; the outline of Church
history ; the controversies which have arisen on
religious matters from century to century.   But the
essential point, the appeal which our Lord makes
to the moral and spiritual faculty in a man, has no
more to do with his intellectual capacity than it has
with his accomplishments as an athlete or as an
artist.   And unless the spiritual faculty be on the
alert, hungering to be satisfied with the good things

of God, religious truth falls dead upon the soul, whatever a man's natural ability may be. It is one thing to read about religion, and to use religious language; and a very good thing too, as far as it goes. But it is another to perceive the reality of religion from its perfect adaptation to the wants and aspirations of a man's own soul. And this perception is impossible if we allow ourselves to think that, as we already know all about religion, there is no need for further trouble. However much he may have learnt about God, a true Christian is always learning; and he ever bears in mind, that, since he, a finite being, is face to face with the Infinite, there must always be something, or rather much, to learn. He is always forgetting those things that are behind, and pressing forward to those things that are before.[a] The moment he ceases to do this; ceases to desire to know more of God and of our Lord Jesus Christ; the pores of his soul close up, and a process of spiritual atrophy begins to develop itself. To him, not less than to souls that are choked with the cares and riches and pleasures of this life, is addressed the solemn warning: " Because thou sayest, I am rich, and increased with goods, and have need of nothing; and knowest

[a] Phil. iii. 13.

G

not that thou art wretched, and miserable, and poor, and blind, and naked : I counsel thee to buy of Me gold tried in the fire, that thou mayest be rich; and white raiment, that thou mayest be clothed, and that the shame of thy nakedness do not appear; and anoint thine eyes with eyesalve, that thou mayest see." [a]

And the other question is, Why do many of us apparently get so little moral and spiritual strength from the Holy Communion ? Considering what that Sacrament really is, and Who it is That we meet in it, and the purpose with which He comes, we may wonder that it is, in so many cases, to all appearance, so unfruitful in spiritual results.

Well, my brethren, there may be some other answers to that very important question; but one answer, doubtless, is that we do not sufficiently long for it. Our Lord Himself said of the last Passover at which He met His disciples, " With desire have I desired to eat this Passover with you before I suffer;" [b] and every communicant ought to be able to say to our Lord, before each Communion, " With desire have I desired once more to receive this Thy Sacrament before I die." Such desire must grow out of and be prompted by an unaffected sense of our weakness, nay, of our impotence, without the

* Rev. iii. 17, 18.   [b] St. Luke xxii. 15.

strengthening Presence and aid of our Lord Jesus Christ; but to a soul that has any relish for spiritual things, this desire is not less spontaneous than is the craving for food in a hungry man.   Such a desire prompts and guides preparation for Communion; review of conscience, confession of sins, prayers for the dispositions of repentance, faith, hope and love, which befit the approach to this great means of grace. The spirit of this desire is that of the Psalmist in exile on the hills of Bashan, who, as his thoughts wandered to the services in the distant temple, beheld at his feet the wild gazelles tracking the water-courses that furrowed the mountain-sides in search of some spring which might slake their thirst: " Like as the hart desireth the water-brooks, so longeth my soul after Thee, O God.   My soul is athirst for God, yea, even for the living God: when shall I come to appear before the Presence of God?"[a]

May our Lord Jesus Christ, of His great Mercy, empty us of all which so satisfies the soul as to make it insensible to His supreme attractions; and then may He fill us with such true love of Himself, that we, loving Him above all things, may obtain His promises, which exceed all that we can desire !

Ps. xlii. 1, 2.

IV.

GOD'S MERCY AND FAITHFULNESS IN THE DIVINE INCARNATION.

ST. LUKE I. 54, 55.

He hath holpen His servant Israel,
In remembrance of His mercy
(As He promised to our forefathers)
Towards Abraham and his seed for ever.

TO-DAY we reach the closing strophe of Mary's Hymn; and it is obvious to remark how naturally, as the utterance of a religious mind, this strophe follows on all that have gone before it. Mary has told us how all the powers of her soul and spirit were engaged in praising God for the great and distinguishing honour which had been vouchsafed to her; she has described this distinction, so far as she might, in itself and in some of its consequences; she has dwelt upon the connection between it and the great rules by which God governs the world at large, and the kingdom of souls. And now she would follow the gracious mystery confided to her up to its source in the Life of God; and she finds it in His attributes of Mercy and Faithfulness.

> " He hath holpen His servant Israel,
> In remembrance of His mercy
> (As He promised to our forefathers)
> Towards Abraham and his seed for ever."

" He hath holpen His servant Israel." Mary, of course, is referring, under cover of this general statement, to the Incarnation of the Son of God, Whose Mother, as the Angel had announced, she was to be. The terms she uses are vague and distant, as in earlier verses of her Hymn: " He hath regarded the low estate of His handmaiden. . . . He That is mighty hath done great things unto me." When we consider what the coming of the Eternal Son of God, clothed in our human nature, into this our world, really meant, for all races and for all times, it might be deemed little enough to say that by such an event God had brought help to Israel. But, in fact, Mary's vagueness and reserve is not without a reason. In the earlier lines of her Hymn, as we have seen, it may be explained by the instincts of a sanctified character, when touching upon subjects that intimately affect personal standing before God.[a] In

---

[a] See pp. 44-50.

the last strophe it is dictated by her immediate purpose, which is to find the source of the Incarnation
in God's attributes of Lovingkindness and Truth.
This could but be done by pointing to His past
relations with Israel ; since the Birth of His Only
begotten Son of a Jewish Mother was the fitting
complement and crown of those relations. " He
remembering His mercy towards Abraham and his
seed for ever, hath holpen His servant Israel."

I.

The Incarnation of our Lord, then, is ascribed
by Mary, first of all, to God's remembrance of His
mercy towards Abraham and his descendants. The
words, " Towards Abraham and his seed for ever,"
are certainly connected in the original with the
words, " For a remembrance of His mercy," although
the line, " As He spake to our forefathers," is
parenthetically inserted between the two halves of
the clause. It was not, as in other places, God's
mercy over all His works, or over all the race of
mankind, but His mercy towards Abraham and
certain of His descendants, that God is here said to
have remembered. Why He should have selected
this particular family to be the object of His

especial favour ; to be constantly visited by His
envoys ; to be the guardian of His Revelation and
His Will ; to be thus chosen out of all nations for
a post of spiritual and exceptional distinction;—is a
subject on which we may speculate, but can arrive
at no certain knowledge. We can only say with
the Apostle that He has mercy on whom He will
have mercy.[a] The unequal distribution of gifts and
privileges among His creatures by the Creator is
unintelligible to that passion for equality which is
a conspicuous ingredient of the social or political
temper of our day. But, whatever we may think
about it, there it is ; it is written on the face of God's
works. If, without detriment to His attributes
of Justice and Love, God could create the various
orders of living beings which we see around us, and
which differ so surprisingly in the qualities which
enable them to maintain and protect life ; if, as
human beings come into the world, they find themselves equipped by the Creator, some with the
highest gifts of genius, and others with so low an
order of intelligence as scarcely to deserve the
name ; if even the moral as well as the mental
and physical advantages of men are so various ;
then God's choice of Israel is at least in harmony

[a] Rom. ix. 15.

with the general rule of His administration, and is governed by considerations and motives which, as lying behind creation itself, are out of the reach of human criticism. He hath mercy on whom He will have mercy ; and, if we are satisfied that His decisions are those of a perfectly holy Will, we bow our heads and are silent.

The family of Abraham was God's choice; and in this choice there lay the earnest of blessings yet to come. For the calling as well as the gifts of God are without repentance.[a] They are, as befits the majesty and generosity of the Giver, irrevocable. They may take different forms from age to age, as the temper and dispositions of men may require ; but God's "mercy towards Abraham and his seed for ever" was as much a part of His Will as the existence of any separate order of rational or irrational life ; and Mary sees a signal proof of it in the fact that the Son of God was to be born of a Jewish Mother. "He remembering His mercy towards Abraham and his seed for ever, hath holpen His servant Israel."

But, further, it is plain from the terms of the promises to the patriarchs, that, in the Divine Mind, Israel included others than the race of men

[a] Rom. xi. 29.

who were lineally descended from the patriarchs,
and whom the Apostle calls Israel "after the flesh."
Mary had already sung of God's mercy as being on
them that fear Him throughout all generations;[a]
and this earlier phrase of hers, probably, does not
mean anything very different from God's Mercy
towards Abraham and his seed in its wider sense.
For who are the real "seed" or descendants of
Abraham? Not only they, St. Paul has told us,
who could claim descent from Abraham by blood,[b]
although such were so far from being excluded from
a higher relationship with Abraham than the
merely physical one, that they had a first claim to
it.[c] But the Apostle insists that Abraham's seed
includes millions who had no blood-relationship
with the patriarch whatever; that the promise that
in Abraham's seed all nations of the earth should
be blessed, imposed upon the idea of descent, in
Abraham's case, a much wider and more spiritual
meaning; that the children of this promise, those
who by faith in and union with Jesus Christ made
it their own, were counted for a seed,—were
reckoned among Abraham s descendants,—though
they belonged to races utterly distinct from the
stock of Abraham.

[a] St. Luke i. 50.   [b] Rom. ix. 8, cf. iv. 16.   [c] *Ib.* xi. 17.

This is not so strange an idea as it may appear
at first sight, if we will reflect that there are two
ways in which a man may be said to live on in this
world after he has left it.   He may live on by the
transmission of his blood, and by the transmission of
his convictions, ideas, type of character.   They are
by no means incompatible forms of survival—God
forbid ; but they are at least very distinct from each
other.   Jonadab the son of Rechab, who was associated with King Jehu at a critical period in his
career,[a] is an instance of a man who combines the
two fatherhoods in a remarkable degree ; he was
the spiritual as well as the natural ancestor of his
descendants, the Rechabites.   He lived on from
age to age, not only in their strong Bedouin
frames, but in their method of life.   They were
wandering   men,   dwelling   in   tents,   and   were
bound by him to certain ascetic observances ; and
long after he was gone, as we know from Jeremiah,
when they were forced by the Chaldean invasion
to take refuge within the walls of Jerusalem, they
could not be induced to transgress the rule of their
progenitor.[b]   A man may be the parent of an enormous family without transmitting to them anything
whatever except the gift of physical life.   Or he

[a] 2 Kings x. 15, *seq.*   [b] Jer. xxxv. 19.

may be childless, and yet may live after his death in the convictions of thousands whom he has formed by his precepts and his example. And, if the question be raised which is the nobler sort of ancestry —the purely zoological, or the spiritual, the parentage of mere animal life, or the communication of principles and ideas which govern life—surely there can be no doubt about the answer. There can be no doubt which of these kinds of ancestry is common to man with the animals below him; and which is his prerogative distinction as a being in whom an immortal and spiritual nature is linked to a bodily form, but without waiving its claim to superiority and leadership. St. Paul resists the Jewish boast that descent from Abraham is limited to those in whose veins the blood of Abraham still flows; he claims for Abraham the immeasurably larger family of those who have inherited Abraham's firm hold of and trust in the Unseen, as shown in his practical obedience.[a] And this loftier and vaster spiritual ancestry underlies Mary's language, too: the objects of God's mercy are not only or chiefly the natural descendants of the patriarch, but the millions whose faith in the Unseen is counted to them for righteousness.

[a] Rom. iv. 12, 18–22.

Why, let it once more be asked, should either Israel—the Israel by blood or the Israel through faith—be objects of the Divine Mercy? Why, but because Mercy radiates from God as do light and heat from the natural sun? When we Christians name God, we do not mean only a resistless force, which has brought about and maintains all that is; we do not mean only a boundless intelligence, which has left marks of design and contrivance in all that is; we mean also and especially that moral quality which is revealed in the gift of self; we mean love. Only by His desire to surround Himself with creatures who might be the objects of His love, can we account for the mystery of creation;—that first and greatest innovation on the Eternal Life of God. And when love looks out upon a world, or a race, or a single being, in whom sin, need, pain, dissatisfaction with life as it is, are manifest, love takes the form of mercy. Mercy is love in its attitude towards the suffering, the sinful, and the fallen; and God's Mercy was ever presiding over the destinies of Israel. You remember that later Psalm, which so often attracts the attention of young children by the peculiarity of its structure, and in which this truth is brought out more vividly than anywhere else in the Psalter.[a] Act after act

[a] Ps. cxxxvi.

of God, from the making of the heavens, and
laying out the earth above the waters, down to
the deliverance from the prison in Babylon, is
followed by the line, " For His mercy endureth
for ever." It was this enduring Mercy which
accounted for the wonders in Egypt; for the overthrow of Pharaoh; for the passage through the
wilderness; for the conquest of Sihon and Og; for
the inheritance of Canaan; for the escape from the
exile. " His mercy endureth for ever." And Mary
would place the Divine Incarnation, too, in the
light of this luminous and gracious Attribute, of
which it was indeed in human history the crowning
and supreme expression. " He remembering His
mercy hath holpen His servant Israel," by the
Incarnation of His Son.

II.

But a second account of the help thus vouchsafed to Israel follows. God was pledged. " He
hath holpen His servant Israel, as He promised," or
spake, " to our forefathers."

The question has been asked how God could
ever have pledged His word to man ; and a sort of
antecedent impossibility of His doing so has in

some quarters been taken for granted, to the discredit of the Bible narrative. This is only a
variety of the general presumption supposed to
lie against Revelation which has been made to do
duty for serious argument. Why should not God,
if He so wills, do that which any of His reasonable
creatures can do at their pleasure ? Why should
He not, if He so wills, unveil His Mind ? Why
should He not, if so He wills, pledge His word of
promise ? The assumption that, for some undefined
reason, He cannot do these things, breaks down as
soon as we look it steadily in the face. The Author
of all intercourse between one of His creatures and
another, can Himself, surely, hold intercourse with
any as seems best to Him. Doubtless, His methods of
revealing His Will vary in different ages of human
history. An angel, an inspired soul, even a dream,
may be the channel of a promise or a revelation.

Among the promises to the patriarchs which
Mary glances at, those may be presumed to be
especially in her view which stated, whether distinctly or by implication, that the Promised One
would be born of their descendants. Thus the promise ran to Abraham, in Haran: " In thee shall all
families of the earth be blessed ; " [a] at Hebron : " I

[a] Gen. xii. 3.

will establish My covenant with Isaac for an everlasting covenant, and with his seed after him;" [a]
in the plain of Mamre: "Abraham shall surely
become a great and mighty nation, and all the
nations of the earth shall be blessed in him;" [b]
after the offering of Isaac: "In thy seed shall
all the nations of the earth be blessed; because
thou hast obeyed My voice." [c] To Isaac, in
Gerar: "I will perform the oath which I sware
unto Abraham thy father; and I will make thy
seed to multiply as the stars of heaven, . . . and
in thy seed shall all the nations of the earth be
blessed." [d] To Jacob, in Bethel: "Thy seed shall
be as the dust of the earth, and thou shalt
spread abroad to the west, and to the east, and
to the north, and to the south; and in thee and
in thy seed shall all the families of the earth be
blessed." [e]

These promises, besides connecting the anticipated blessing with the descendants of Abraham,
make two other assertions about it. It was to
extend to the whole human race: so each of the
three patriarchs was in turn assured, as if to rebuke
by anticipation the narrow national prejudice of

---

[a] Gen. xvii. 19.   [b] *Ib.* xviii. 18.   [c] *Ib.* xxii. 18.
[d] *Ib.* xxvi. 3, 4.   [e] *Ib.* xxviii. 14.

the later Jews. And it was to last. Unlike other
promises to nations or dynasties, it was not conditioned ; it would not be transitory in its effects ;
it would not depend upon the fortunes of a people
or a form of government ; it would outlive the
vicissitudes of human affairs ; it was embodied in
" an everlasting covenant ; " it would hold good for
ever. The promise to the patriarchs was made
more definite to their descendants. Its realization
was limited first to the tribe of Judah, then to the
family of David. Then the Person of the Promised
One comes more clearly into view. Isaiah foretells
His miraculous Birth,[a] His atoning Sufferings,[b] His
eventual triumph ;[c] and, with a nearly contemporary Prophet, Micah,[d] though in different terms, proclaims His Divinity.[e] Lastly, Daniel fixes the date
of His appearance ;[f] and Malachi announces His
coming to His Temple,[g] and the triumph of His
Name and His worship in the heathen world.[h]

Reflect how such a promise as this would have
been talked over again and again from generation
to generation, from century to century, in every
Jewish household ; how the old people would pass

---

[a] Isa. vii. 14.   [b] *Ib.* liii. 4–10.   [c] *Ib.* 12.
[d] Micah v. 2.   [e] Isa, ix. 6.   [f] Dan. ix. 24–26.
[g] Mal. iii. 1.   [h] *Ib.* i. 11.

it on to the younger ; and how these, at first, perhaps, thinking little of it, as young people do, as of a tradition mainly interesting to a past generation, came in time, as they grew older, to perceive its importance. Great indeed was its importance. For two reigns only, and for a period far short of a century, did Israel attain to anything like political splendour or even consideration. When Solomon had been laid with his fathers, and the division of the ten tribes and the two had taken place, the nation's place in the world was, to all outward appearance, insignificant indeed as compared with that of the great surrounding monarchies. There was little, or nothing, of this world's splendour to stir the imagination or feed the national pride of the descendants of the patriarchs; there were no walls or palaces like those of Babylon; there was no navigable stream teeming with industry and life, like the Nile; nay, the Temple of Jerusalem itself was of diminutive proportions when contrasted with the mighty structures that had existed in Egypt from a date long before the days of Moses. Not only had the divided people little to show in the way of distant conquests ; they gradually lost the territories that had been won by David and Solomon: and as years went on, there was less and less reason for thinking

that Israel could ever again be a great power
in the East. Thus, in the absence of grounds
for satisfaction with their present public circumstances, religious men were led to think more of
the promise which had been handed down to them.
If they had no great share in the present, they had
good hope for the future; if man was not likely to
do much for them, they had a confidence that one
day God would do much, both for them, and through
them, for others. But years passed; first came one
disaster, then another; the captivity of Israel by the
Assyrians; the destruction of Jerusalem by Nebu-
chadnezzar; the bondage of Judah in Babylon;
with its profound distress and humiliation; the
many vicissitudes which followed the return; and
notably, the hard struggle against Antiochus Epi-
phanes, who desired to substitute Greek paganism in
thought and life for the religion revealed to Moses
and the Prophets. Often, in days when all seemed
going to ruin, and men's hearts were faint, the
question must have been asked in many a humble
home up and down the land, whether God had
forgotten to be gracious, and whether He would shut
up His lovingkindness in displeasure.[a] So Isaiah
anticipates the complaints of Israel in exile:—

[a] Ps. lxxvii. 9.

" But Zion saith, The Lord hath forsaken me,
  And my Lord hath forgotten me.
  Can a woman forget her sucking child,
  That she should not have compassion on the son of he
      womb?
  Yea, they may forget, yet will I not forget thee.
  Behold, I have graven thee on the palms of My hands;
  Thy walls are continually before Me." [a]

And when the prospect of impending ruin was
darker than ever before, Jeremiah reminds his
despairing countrymen—

" Behold, the days come, saith the Lord,
  That I will perform that good thing which I have
      promised
  Unto the house of Israel and to the house of Judah.
  In those days, and at that time,
  Will I cause the Branch of Righteousness
  To grow up unto David. . . . Thus saith the Lord;
  If ye can break My covenant of the day, and My covenant
      of the night,
  That there should not be day and night in their season;
  Then may also My covenant be broken with David My
      servant,
  That he should not have a son to reign upon his throne." [b]

And so the years passed on. It was a long night
of expectation, and generation after generation died,
as it had lived, in hope ; but at last the first streaks
of dawn were seen in the East : it was understood

[a] Isa. xlix. 14-16.   [b] Jer. xxxiii. 14, 15, 20, 21.

that the Sun of Righteousness [a] was rising on the world. Says Zacharias—

"He hath raised up a mighty salvation for us,
  In the house of His servant David;
  As He spake by the mouth of His holy Prophets,
  Which have been since the world began;
  That we should be saved from our enemies,
  And from the hands of all that hate us;
  To perform the mercy promised to our forefathers,
  And to remember His holy covenant;
  To perform the oath which he sware to our forefather Abra-
    ham
  That He would give us." [b]

Or, as Mary sings—

"He hath holpen His servant Israel,
  For a remembrance of His mercy,
  As He spake unto our forefathers."

III.

Now, the Gospel which was preached by Mary's Divine Son, and which has Him for its central Subject as well as its Author, contains, as St. Peter reminds us, "great and precious promises; that by these we might be partakers of the Divine Nature, having escaped the corruption that is in the world through lust." [c] But the fulfilment of these

---

[a] Mal. iv. 2. [b] St. Luke i. 69–74. [c] 2 St. Pet. i. 4.

promises is, in large measure, yet to come.   Many men find it easy to believe in God's past faithfulness, simply because the past witnesses to His faithfulness.   But they hesitate about the future.   They assume, without saying it, that He is less present to us than He was to our forefathers, and that, in accordance with modern ways of talking and thinking, His "Hand is shortened that it cannot save." [a]

At any rate, we cannot doubt that God may be trusted to keep His word in the world of nature. We lay out our lives upon that presumption.   We go to bed night after night without any misgivings as to whether the sun will rise the next morning. We make plans for the autumn, feeling sure that it will be followed by winter; and for the winter, knowing that it will be succeeded by spring, and, in due time, again by summer and autumn.   All the proceedings of our farmers and our sailors, nay, of our chemists and physicians, are based on the calculation that God will be true to His general rules of working; that He has given to the world of nature a law which shall not be broken. [b]   So too our men of science cross the Atlantic to take observations of an eclipse, which they are sure will begin to be visible in a certain

[a] Isa. lix. 1.   [b] Ps. cxlviii. 6.

place at a given hour and minute, because long observation has taught them that the Almighty Worker never fails to keep His appointments exactly.   Indeed, so exact is He, that they themselves will often fail to remember that He works or lives at all; the mechanism of nature by its faultless regularity shuts out from their view the Great Engineer.   Sometimes too His constant observance of His rules is pleaded as a reason for foregoing the duties of prayer and thanksgiving, since all, it is presumed, will go on without failure, whether we address our prayers to Him or not.   And this, indeed, is why now and then He stays His beneficent Hand, and shows us, in what we call, through our ignorance, the caprices of nature,—in the drought, the storm, the deluge of waters, the destroying plague,—that He is ever at work behind the veil, and that we cannot with impunity trifle with Him; as though He were only an unintelligent force strangely engaged in the complex and subtle manipulation of matter.

But if God keeps His appointments in the world of nature, much more does He keep them in the moral sphere.   For while nature might have been, in countless ways, otherwise ordered than as it is, the moral law could not have been other than it

is, since it expresses in human speech the Nature of
God, in relation to the circumstances of human life.
God might have made us men with differently
shaped bodies, with differently furnished minds.
But, without being untrue to Himself, He never
could have said to us, "Thou mayest do murder;
thou mayest commit adultery; thou mayest steal."
If the laws of nature, as we call them, fail not,
much more impossible is it that the laws of the
moral world should fail. If seedtime is followed by
harvest, and day by night, much more certain is it
that "God is not mocked;" and that "whatsoever a
man soweth, that shall he also reap;"[a] that "he that
soweth to the flesh shall of the flesh reap corruption, but he that soweth to the Spirit shall of the
Spirit reap life everlasting."[b] God's own essential
Nature is concerned in maintaining the unfailing
regularity of His rules for governing the moral
world. "Wherefore should the wicked blaspheme
God, while he doth say in his heart, Tush, Thou
God carest not for it? Surely Thou hast seen it;
for Thou beholdest ungodliness and wrong."[c] And
on the other hand, "God is not unrighteous, that
He will forget your works and labour that pro-
ceedeth of love."[d] Even a heathen like Sophocles,

[a] Gal. vi. 7. [b] *Ib.* 8. [c] Ps. x. 14, 15. [d] Heb. vi. 10.

contemplating the moral order of human life, could recognize

> " The steadfast laws that walk the sky—
> Laws born and reared in the ethereal heaven,
> Of which Olympus is alone the sire ;
> To which no race of mortal man gave birth,
> Nor ever shall oblivion lay to sleep." [a]

And we Christians know that God's righteousness standeth like the strong mountains; that His judgments are as the great deep.[b]

The Gospel contains Divine promises to the Christian Society or Church, and to the Christian soul. Why should we think that they are less likely to be observed than God's rules for the movements of the stars, or for the enforcement of virtue and the repression of vice ?

To the Church, for instance, there has been made the great promise that " the gates of hell shall not prevail against it." [c] This promise enables a believing Christian to survey, not, indeed, without distress, but certainly without misgiving, much that he sees around him in the Realm of Christ. Our Lord prayed[d] for unity, and everywhere we behold division. Our Lord made holiness a note of

---

[a] *Œd. Tyr.*, 863, *sqq.*   [b] Ps. xxxvi. 6.
[c] St. Matt. xvi. 18.   [d] St. John xvii. 20, 21.

His kingdom,[a] and holiness among Christians is the
exception rather than the rule.   Our Lord promised
His Spirit to guide into all truth,[b] and we see men
adding to or taking away from that truth into which
the Apostles were guided.   Nor is the difficulty to
be removed by saying that one fragment of the
Church is the whole of it, or that the true
Church of Christ is an invisible society.   These
are the rude expedients of a supposed controversial
necessity ; they will not bear the wear and tear of
reflection.   No ! we must admit that an enemy has
sown tares among the wheat.   Of the Gospel Vine,
too, it must be said that whereas

> " The hills were covered with the shadow of it,
>   And the boughs thereof were like the goodly cedars,"

it has come to pass that she lies, with " her hedge
broken down," so that " all they that go by pluck
off her grapes "—

> " The wild boar out of the wood doth root it up,
>   And the wild beasts of the field devour it." [c]

Certainly the Church's weakness is the opportunity if not the triumph of unbelief, which, since the
earliest age of the Christian Faith, never was so

---

[a] Isa. lx. 21 ; Jer. xxxi. 33, 34; St. John xiii. 35.
[b] St. John xvi. 13.   [c] Ps. lxxx. 10–13.

threatening, never had enlisted so many fine intellects in its service, as to-day.   But there lies our charter—"the gates of hell shall not prevail." There may be temporary discouragement and defeat; a falling away of prominent men, of large classes; the withering of entire branches of the Sacred Vine.   We do not know, but all this and more is possible.   What is not possible is that the Divine kingdom should perish from off the face of the earth before the day of our Lord's coming.

So also will the Christian soul recall many and precious promises, on which it may lean during the days of its earthly pilgrimage, and of the eventual fulfilment of which there can be no room for doubt. Promises of deliverance from spiritual foes; promises of victory over insurgent passions; promises of an inward Presence Which can make man a true temple of God; promises of joy and peace in believing; promises which transcend this world and pierce the veil of the next, and embrace in their mighty scope not only time but eternity. "Come unto Me, . . . and I will give you rest. Take My yoke upon you, and learn of Me; . . . and ye shall find rest for your souls."[a]   "If any man love Me, he will keep My words: and My Father will

---

[a] St. Matt. xi. 28, 29.

love him, and We will come unto Him, and make
Our abode with him."[a] "In My Father's house are
many mansions : if it were not so, I would have told
you. I go to prepare a place for you. . . . I will
come again, and receive you unto Myself; that
where I am, there ye may be also."[b] "To him that
overcometh will I give to eat of the tree of life,
which is in the midst of the Paradise of God."[c] "He
that overcometh, the same shall be clothed in white
raiment; and . . . I will confess his name before
My Father, and before His angels."[d] "To him that
overcometh will I grant to sit with Me in My throne,
even as I also overcame, and am set down with My
Father in His throne."[e]

There are times when even good Christians
are tempted to ask whether such bright and
gracious words will be realized. Let them remember how long Israel waited before the promises
spoken to the patriarchs were fulfilled in the Son of
Mary. Be sure that no word of God returns to
Him empty, or without accomplishing that purpose
for which He sent it.[f] It is so with God's laws in
nature ; it is so with His moral law ; it cannot be
otherwise with His promises to His servants. If

[a] St. John xiv. 23. [b] *Ib.* 2, 3. [c] Rev. ii. 7.
[d] *Ib.* iii. 5. [e] *Ib.* 21. [f] Isa. lv. 11.

He was true to His word in dealing with the old Israel, He will not fail those who belong to the Israel of God.

The conviction that God will keep His pledges to help us carries us, as nothing else can, through the trying changes of our outward circumstances. These changes will sometimes go far to break down the faith of men who have believed for years. Narrow means, weak health, the death of those for whom we care most on earth,—why, men ask, if He is alive, and if He loves us, should God permit it?

Christians sometimes forget that they are to be tried as other men are not; that they are not to count such trials strange;[a] that "whom the Lord loveth He chasteneth;"[b] that "our light affliction, which is but for a moment, worketh for us an exceeding and eternal weight of glory."[c]   That which seems so accidental or purposeless, is designed to train us gradually for a higher life; those great sorrows which are sometimes pointed to as showing that we are the sport of some heartless chance, are in truth but so many blows of the chisel of the Eternal Artist, Who is fashioning each character for its high destiny out of the rude material which passes under His Hand and Eye.

[a] 1 St. Pet. iv. 12.   [b] Heb. xii. 6.   [c] 2 Cor. iv. 17.

No one trial, be sure of it, is aimless or unneeded; poverty, sickness, loss of friends, each has its appointed work to do. And, beyond all, is the certainty that He will be true to His promises; true to those who overcome the temptation to doubt His word. The bright Morning may not be far distant from thee when thou shalt praise Him

"Who saveth thy life from destruction,
   And crowneth thee with mercy and lovingkindness;
   Who satisfieth thy mouth with good things,
   Making thee young and lusty as an eagle." [a]

And this same conviction braces us to encounter those trials of the mind and heart which sometimes bear more hardly on a man than anything outward. You have done your best, you say, and you have met with nothing but disappointment; you have done your best for a noble cause, and you are credited with devotion to purely selfish ends; your love and energy has met with ingratitude or contempt. You have spent prayer, time, money, upon the bringing up your children in the nurture and admonition of the Lord, and they only attain to manhood to wound you by their neglect, or to shame you by their frivolity or their misconduct. What, you are tempted to ask, is the good of efforts which lead to nothing, at least, so far as

[a] Ps. ciii. 4, 5.

you see, in those for whose sake they are made?
And then you are out of heart about yourself. You
have meant sincerely to consecrate your life to God,
and lo! you find that which should be a temple of
His perpetual Presence degraded by a hundred
little sins which are utterly alien to Him; by some
vulgar social pride, by some ill-natured and spiteful
grudge, by unchristian acts, by words that breathe
only covetousness or envy. You had hoped that you
had gone far enough on the road to the heavenly
Jerusalem to be out of the reach of these igno-
minious sins; but there are days when they seem
to have been so numerous, and to represent so much
of unsubdued passion and of decomposing faith,
that your spirit fairly sinks within you, and you
doubt whether you will ever reach the heavenly
goal. Certainly you cannot fall back for comfort
on your own heart, which is not in the same mood
for two days running. You know it to be per-
petually changing, or, as the Bible says, " deceitful
above all things." [a]   In the morning you are happy
and hopeful, and before night you are in misery
and despair. To-day you are in ecstasies as if with
Paradise in full view; to-morrow you are a victim
of the most gloomy depression. One week the
heaven of your inner life is as the clear blue sky,

[a] Jer. xvii. 9.

with the brilliant rays of the Eternal Sun playing
upon you ; the next, all is overclouded, and you
are apparently in the darkest shadow.   Certainly
this poor, changeful, vacillating heart of ours yields
but a sorry resource in the troubles of life.   Our
only real deliverance lies in rising out of ourselves,
and taking firm hold of the promises and the
Person of Him Who sitteth above the waterflood [a]
of human feeling, and Who does not change.[b]   In
His own time He will be as good as His word ; the
disappointments will be seen to have been steps in
our probation ; the temptations to humiliating
faults, after teaching us self-distrust, will have
vanished ; the varying moods of joy and depression
will have been exchanged for a tranquil and assured
happiness.

This is the closing lesson of the Magnificat.
Mary leaves us with the conviction that God's
promises may for long remain unfulfilled, but that
they will be fulfilled at last.   " He hath holpen His
servant Israel, as He promised to our forefathers."
For us too of to-day " the vision is yet for an
appointed time, but at the end it shall speak, and
not lie : though it tarry, wait for it ; because it will
surely come, it will not tarry." [c]

[a] Ps. xxix. 9.   [b] Mal. iii. 6.   [c] Hab. ii. 3.

THE

VIRGIN BIRTH OF CHRIST

BY

JAMES ORR

Foreword by
Dr. Cyril J. Barber

"Thou didst not abhor the Virgin's womb."

Klock & Klock Christian Publishers, Inc.
2527 GIRARD AVE. N.
MINNEAPOLIS, MINNESOTA 55411

Originally published by
Charles Scribner's Sons
New York, 1907

ISBN: 0-86524-058-2

Printed by Klock & Klock in the U.S.A.
1980 Reprint

FOREWORD

It is a comparatively easy matter to look back over the years and select the major works produced in any given discipline. For example, where it concerns the life of Christ, several important studies immediately spring to mind: Andrews' *The Life of Our Lord Upon Earth,* Edersheim's *Life and Times of Jesus the Messiah,* and Farrar's *Life of Christ,* and many others.

Likewise, when we consider the virgin conception of the Lord Jesus, the the same mental process takes place. We immediately think of Machen's *Virgin Birth of Christ,* Robertson's *The Mother of Jesus: Her Problems and Her Glory,* and James Orr's famous work.

Reflecting on the major contributors of the past is not hard, but if the spotlight were suddenly turned on us and we were asked to produce a book which would stand the test of time, we would suddenly be faced with the difficulty of the task imposed upon us. To produce a work of significant quality would require many years of diligent study. Some of the ideas we entertain would be retained, while others would be discarded. The process would become one of "unconscious incubation." Finally, however, we would find ourselves in the position of being able to make a unique contribution to a particular discipline or area of investigation. Such was the experience of the late James Orr (1844-1913), Professor of Apologetics and Church History, United Free Church College, Glasgow, and editor of the well-received *International Standard Bible Encyclopedia.*

The Minister's Library (1974) carries the following comment about Dr. Orr's *Virgin Birth of Christ:*

These chapters contain lectures delivered at the chapel of the Fifth Avenue Presbyterian Church, New York, in 1907. They evaluate the criticisms levelled against the virgin conception of Christ and provide a scholarly rebuttal to these antisupernaturalistic theories.

But there is more that should be said about this fine book. The lectures were delivered under the auspices of the Bible Teacher's Training School. They were designed for and delivered to laypeople. There is one addition: The book contains an appendix which will delight every preacher's and Christian worker's heart! Eighteen evangelical scholars of international repute, from different countries and different denominations, provide a "digest" of quotable material in which they express their own convictions relating to Christ's incarnation.

"But," someone will ask, "what intrinsic value does Orr's book have that might not be found in the writings of contemporary men of the Faith?" and "What is there in this book that merits my time and the investment of my money?"

These are good questions!

In preparing this material, Dr. Orr's aim was avowedly apoligetic. He wrote in the Preface:

The aim of these lectures is to establish faith in the miracle of the Lord's incarnation by Birth from the Virgin, to meet objections, and to show the intimate connection of fact and doctrine in this transcendent mystery. The organism of truth is one, and there is much need, in these days of loose ends in thinking, to fortify what may be called the doctrinal conscience by showing how the parts of divine truth cohere together. For the rest, this book speaks for itself.

In executing his task, Professor Orr marshalls evidence, both biblical and historical, to prove the credibility of Christ's remarkable conception and birth. He also discusses the supposed silence about the incarnation in the remaining books of the New Testament. His comments are preceptive and enlightening. Furthermore, an entire chapter is devoted to relating the prophecies of the Old Testament to the birth narratives of Matthew and Luke. All of this is of the utmost significance to us today, for modern trends in theology have tended to ignore the evangelical contributions of the past and repeat the errors of their predecessors (albeit with certain refinements).

In three concluding chapters, Dr. Orr discusses the mythical theories advances by some rationalists to account for the virgin birth of Christ; the imperative necessity of the virginal conception of Christ if the Lord Jesus was to be both sinless in His person and unique in His mission; and finally, a treatment of the doctrines of the Christian faith built upon and supported by the scriptural teaching of Christ's divine conception.

When this book is viewed from the perspective of its contents, its intrinsic worth becomes evident. When it is evaluated in terms of its cost and its lasting value, it becomes one which Christians of all persuasions should read and have as a constant source of reference in their homes.

Cyril J. Barber
Author, *The Minister's Library*

PREFACE

THESE lectures were delivered during the month of April, 1907, in the Chapel of the Fifth Avenue Presbyterian Church, New York, under the auspices of the Bible Teachers' Training School of that city, and they are now published, practically as prepared for delivery, under the same auspices. The author regrets that their revision for the press had to be undertaken at a distance from facilities for checking quotations and references in his pages; but he trusts that these, if not so copious as he could wish, will be found generally correct. The papers summarised in the Appendix came into the author's hands in New York after his own work was completed, and he has made no use of them in the text.

The aim of the lectures is to establish faith in the miracle of the Lord's Incarnation by Birth from the Virgin, to meet objections, and to show the intimate connection of fact and doctrine in this transcendent mystery. The organism of truth is one, and there is much need, in these days of loose ends in thinking, to fortify what may be called the doctrinal conscience by showing how the parts of divine truth cohere together. For the rest, the book must speak for itself. The writers to whom the author has been chiefly indebted, and to whom he makes grateful acknowledgment, will be found mentioned in the footnotes.

September, 1907.

CONTENTS

SYNOPSIS OF LECTURES

I

STATEMENT OF THE CASE—ISSUES AND PRELIMINARY OBJECTIONS

II

THE GOSPEL WITNESSES—GENUINENESS AND INTEGRITY OF THE RECORDS

III

SOURCES OF THE NARRATIVES—HISTORICAL AND INTERNAL CREDIBILITY

IV

THE BIRTH NARRATIVES AND THE REMAINING LITERA-
TURE OF THE NEW TESTAMENT—ALLEGED SILENCE
OF THE NEW TESTAMENT

V

RELATION TO OLD TESTAMENT PROPHECY—WITNESS OF EARLY CHURCH HISTORY

VI

MYTHICAL THEORIES OF ORIGIN OF NARRATIVES OF THE VIRGIN BIRTH—ALLEGED HEATHEN ANALOGIES

VII

DOCTRINAL BEARINGS OF THE VIRGIN BIRTH—PERSON OF
CHRIST AS INVOLVING MIRACLE: SINLESSNESS AND
UNIQUENESS

VIII

DOCTRINAL BEARINGS OF THE VIRGIN BIRTH: THE INCAR-
NATION—SUMMARY AND CONCLUSION

APPENDIX

THE VIRGIN BIRTH OF CHRIST

LECTURE I

LET me first of all say—I hardly need to say it—
that I am not here to attack any individual, to inter-
fere with any church or its discipline, to presume to
judge of the Christian standing of any man, whether
he agrees with me or not, even on the very vital point
which brings us together. I am here to discuss with
you calmly and temperately an important part of divine
truth which has been of late years most vehemently,
and, in my judgment, most unjustly assailed. The
question which is to occupy us is a very grave one. It
is not a question simply of liberty to the individual
conscience, of tenderness and forbearance towards Christian brethren whose minds may be in doubt and perplexity on this subject: that is a totally different matter. It is a question, actually, of the right of the
Church to retain in its public creed this fundamental
article of the oldest of all creeds—an article based on
express declarations of two of our Gospels, and found

1

in the creeds of every important branch of the Christian Church in the world at the present hour—the article, namely, that Jesus Christ, our Saviour, was " conceived by the Holy Ghost, born of the Virgin Mary." The right to retain this article, you must be aware, is, in the name of modern thought and criticism, boldly, even peremptorily, denied us. With whatever graceful acknowledgment of the poetry that may lie in the heart of the old Christmas story, the time has come, we are told, when that story must be parted with, and the belief it enshrines once and for ever left behind as serious affirmation.

We are growing accustomed to stronger language even than denial. I take two examples. The first is from a recent, often-quoted writer, Soltau, in his book on *The Birth of Jesus Christ*. " Whoever makes the further demand," he says, " that an evangelical Christian shall believe in the words ' conceived by the Holy Ghost, born of the Virgin Mary,' wittingly constitutes himself a sharer in a sin against the Holy Spirit of the true Gospel as transmitted to us by the Apostles and their school in the Apostolic Age." [1] It is sin against the Holy Ghost to ask belief in the Virgin Birth!

The other example is from Mr. R. J. Campbell's newly published book on *The New Theology*. " The

---

[1] *Die Geburtsgeschichte Jesu Christi*, p. 32 (E. T., p. 65). The passage is put in bold type. Soltau's own theory is discussed in Lect. VI, pp. 173–5.

credibility and significance of Christianity," Mr. Campbell says, " are in no way affected by the doctrine of the Virgin Birth, otherwise than that the belief tends to put a barrier between Jesus and the race, and to make Him something that cannot properly be called human. . . . Like many others, I used to take the position that acceptance or non-acceptance of the doctrine of the Virgin Birth was immaterial because Christianity was quite independent of it; but later reflection has convinced me that in point of fact it operates as a hindrance to spiritual religion and a real living faith in Jesus. The simple and natural conclusion is that Jesus was the child of Joseph and Mary, and had an uneventful childhood." [1] Truly the Evangelists who introduced this story into their Gospels have much to answer for!

There is abundant need and call, therefore, for discussion of this question. I bear in mind that I am here to deal with the subject, not in scholastic fashion, but on the lines of a broad, popular presentation. I am not to enter into minute discussions of philological, exegetical, historical, or even theological points, such as might be appropriate to the class-room; but am to try to lift the question out of the cloud of learned subtleties in which it is becoming continually the more enveloped, into a strong, clear light, where all may be able to see the real character of the problem, and the true

[1] *The New Theology*, p. 104.

nature of the issues that are involved in it. I shall
probably be able to say little that is really new; nothing, I am afraid, that has not already been better said
by others. But I hope, at least, by a reasoned presentation of the case along my own lines, to do something
to remove misconceptions, to " stablish, strengthen,
settle " faith,[1] where that has been unduly shaken,
and to produce a stronger impression in some minds
than perhaps at present exists of the place which this
much-contested article holds in the organism of Christian truth.

I have said that the article of the Virgin Birth of
the Lord is being at the present time fiercely assailed.
I do not know that, since the days of the conflicts with
Jews and pagans in the second century, there has been
so determined an attack on this particular article of
the creed as we are now witnessing.[2] The birth of
Jesus from the Virgin has always, of course, been an
offence to rationalism. The attack on it had its place,
though a comparatively subordinate one, in the Deis-
tical controversies of the eighteenth century.[3] Avail-

---

[1] 1 Peter v. 10.

[2] The change is perhaps most clearly seen in the literature of
apologetics. One is struck by observing how, even in approved
text-books on the "Evidences," attention is concentrated on the
Resurrection—the great miracle at the *end* of our Lord's life—but
little or nothing is said of the Virgin Birth—the miracle at the
beginning.

[3] Cf. Paine's *Age of Reason*, Reimarus, etc.

ing himself of the Jewish slanders, Voltaire treated it with a scurrilous indecency.[1] In this form the attack perpetuates itself in the coarser unbelief of our own time—in Haeckel, for example.[2] The older rationalism, in all its schools, rejected the miracle, or explained it away. Paulus, in his insipid way, gave a " natural " explanation of the event, supposing Mary to be the victim of a deception practised upon her by her kinswoman Elisabeth.[3] De Wette, who has been followed by many since, saw in the stories poetic symbols of religious ideas. The attack of Strauss on the narratives left little unsaid that could be said, and prepared the way for all subsequent developments. A more recent turning-point was Renan's *Life of Jesus*, which opens in the bold style of assertion with which we are now familiar: " Jesus was born at Nazareth, a small town of Galilee, which before His time had no celebrity. . . . His father Joseph and His mother Mary were people in humble circumstances." [4] Direct attacks on the article of the Virgin Birth developed a little later in the Lutheran Church,[5] and the movement hostile to the article has gone on gathering in volume, and spreading its influence into other countries since.

[1] Cf. his *Examen Important de Milord Bolingbroke*, ch. x.

[2] *Riddle of the Universe*, ch. xviii. Cf. in criticism, Loofs, *Anti-Haeckel*, and see below, pp. 95, 146.

[3] Cf. Strauss's *Life of Jesus*, I, p. 18 (E. T.).

[4] Ch. ii.

[5] Cf. Schaff, *Creeds of Christendom*, I, p. 20.

A marked impulse was given to it in 1892 by the deposition of a talented young pastor, Herr Schrempf, in Würtemberg, for refusal to use the Apostles' Creed—a case which brought the redoubtable Prof. Harnack into the field, and gave rise to an enormous controversial literature. Now, in the wake of newer tendencies, has come the so-called " historical-critical " school, with its open repudiation of everything supernatural in the history of Jesus. The movement which this influential school represents is deeply penetrating Britain and America. The result in both countries is seen in a wide-spread tendency, if not to deny this article, at least to represent it as unessential to Christian faith; and the impression left on a still larger number of minds is that the case for the Virgin Birth must be a very weak one, when so many scholarly men reject the belief, and so many more hold themselves in an attitude of indifference to it. Thus the question stands at the present moment.

What now are the grounds on which this article of our old-world faith is so confidently challenged? It would be a poor compliment to pay to our opponents to deny that their grounds of objection, when boldly and skilfully stated, and set forth with some infusion of religious warmth—as they are, e. g., by a writer like Lobstein [1]—have not a measure of plausibility fitted to

---

[1] In his book on *The Virgin Birth of Christ,* translated in the Crown Theological Library.

produce a strong impression on minds that hear them for the first time. Briefly sketched, they are such as the following:—

The narratives of the miraculous birth, we are told, are found only in the introductory chapters of two of our Gospels—Matthew and Luke—and are evidently there of a secondary character. The rest of the New Testament is absolutely silent on the subject. Mark, the oldest Gospel, and John, the latest, know nothing of it. Matthew and Luke themselves contain no further reference to the mysterious fact related in their commencement, but mention circumstances which seem irreconcilable with it. Their own narratives are contradictory, and, in their miraculous traits, bear clear marks of legendary origin. All the Gospels speak freely of Jesus as the son of Joseph and Mary. The Virgin Birth formed no part of the oldest Apostolic tradition, and had no place in the earliest Christian preaching, as exhibited in the Book of Acts. The Epistles show a like ignorance of this profound mystery. Paul shows no acquaintance with it, and uses language which seems to exclude it, as when he speaks of Jesus as "of the seed of David."[1] Peter, John, the Epistle to the Hebrews, the Book of Revelation, all ignore it. If thousands were brought to faith in Jesus as the divine Redeemer in this earliest period, it was without reference to this belief. There is no proof that the

[1] Rom. i. 3.

belief was general in the Christian Church before the second century.[1]

On the other hand, it is alleged, the origin of this belief, and of the narratives embodying it, can be readily explained. It grew out of a mistaken application of Old Testament prophecy (Is. vii. 14), or from contact with, or imitation of, pagan myths; and is itself an example of the myth-forming spirit which ascribes a superhuman origin to great men or religious heroes. In any case, it is no essential part of Christian faith. Nowhere in the New Testament is anything ever based on it, and neither the sinlessness of Christ nor the Incarnation itself can be shown to depend on it. Why then, it is urged, burden faith with such a mystery? Why ask men to believe in that for which, in conscience, they do not think there is sufficient evidence? Why retain so doubtful an article as a binding part of the creed of the Church?

With such reasonings confidently put forward, can we wonder that many are swept along, overpowered,

[1] Mr. Campbell says: "The Virgin Birth of Jesus was apparently unknown to the primitive church, for the earliest New Testament writings make no mention of it. Paul's letters do not allude to it, neither does the Gospel of Mark. . . . Nowhere does Paul give us so much as a hint of anything supernatural attending the mode of His entry into the world. Mark does not even tell us anything about the childhood of the Master; his account begins with the Baptism of Jesus in Jordan. The Fourth Gospel, although written much later, ignores the belief in the Virgin Birth, and even seems to do so of set purpose as belittling and materialising the truth." (*The New Theology*, pp. 97-8.)

shaken in mind, and disposed to acquiesce in the question being left an open one? Especially when they are told, as they commonly are, that all the really competent scholarship has gone over to this side.

I shall immediately try to state the case from the other side, but, before doing this, there is one important remark which I feel it incumbent upon me to make. We are discussing the Virgin Birth, but it is necessary at the outset to point out that, in the present stage of the controversy, this is only a fragment of a much larger question. It is a fact we cannot ignore— it will appear more clearly as I proceed—that the great bulk of the opposition to the Virgin Birth comes from those who do not recognise a supernatural element in Christ's life at all. I do not state this as a reproach— the writers in question would not regard it as a reproach, but as a mark of their modernity—I call attention to it only that we may see exactly where we stand in the discussion. It is not with these writers, as we soon come to discover, a question of the Virgin Birth alone, but a question of the whole view we are to take of Jesus in His Person and work; not a question of this single miracle, but a question of *all* miracles. This of itself, I grant, does not prove the impugners of the Virgin Birth to be wrong. If the evidence for the narratives of the Nativity is weak, and the belief based on them erroneous, the fact that it is negative critics who bring the weakness to light

will not make the history again good and true. Nevertheless it is highly important, in entering on our inquiry, to keep in mind this general standpoint of the
opponents. We constantly hear it said—Even if the
Virgin Birth is given up, there is enough left in the
Gospels to furnish a secure basis for faith and hope.
My point is, that, with these writers, the rest of the
record does *not* stand—is not allowed to stand. They
work from a basis, and by a method, which will not
allow it to stand. If the Virgin Birth is attacked so
pertinaciously, it is because it seems to them the weak-
est of the Gospel facts in point of evidence, and because they feel instinctively that its overthrow would
mean so much. It would be like the dislodging of a
great stone near the foundation of a building, that would
bring down much more with it.

But is the case for the Virgin Birth really a weak
one? Let me now, having stated the position as fairly
as I can for the opponents, put before you an opposite
supposition. I state it at present only hypothetically:
the proof will come later.

Suppose, then, it can be shown that the evidence is
not what is alleged in the statement above given, but
that in many respects the truth is nearly the reverse:—
suppose it shown that the narratives in Matthew and
Luke are unquestionably genuine parts of their respective Gospels; that the narratives have come down
to us in their integrity; that the sources of their in-

formation were early and good; that they do not contradict, but, on the contrary, corroborate and supplement each other, and have every right to be regarded
as trustworthy narrations:—suppose it shown that the
alleged silence of Mark and John can be readily explained—*is* explained, indeed, by the fact that it does
not lie within the scope of these Gospels to narrate
the Lord's birth and infancy at all; [1] that the Apostolic
doctrine does not contradict or exclude a miraculous
birth, but immensely strengthens the grounds of our
belief in it; that so far as we can trace back the history
of the early Church, it was united in its testimony to
this truth—only the narrowest and most backward of
Jewish-Christian sects (the Ebionites), and a few of
the Gnostic sects (not all) denying it; that the fact
attested is not, as alleged, of minor significance, but,
as part of the deep "mystery of godliness," [2] stands
in close and inseparable relation with the other truths
about our Lord's Person (sinlessness, Incarnation):—
suppose it shown that the attacks of the critics on all
these points fail, and that the failure is witnessed to,
not only by the verdict of scholars of more believing
tendency, but by the inability of these writers to agree,
on almost any single point, among themselves; that

[1] Cf. e. g. Mr. Campbell's statement quoted above: "Mark does
not even tell us anything about the childhood of the Master; his
accounts begin with the Baptism of Jesus in Jordan" (p. 98). How
then can it be contradictory of a narrative which *does* tell us of the
Infancy?　　　　[2] 1 Tim. iii. 16.

their rival theories in explanation of the narratives are hopelessly at variance with each other, each effectually knocking the bottom out of the arguments of its neighbours:—suppose, I say, these things, or anything like these, to be established, there are few, I think, but will admit that the question stands in a very different light from that in which it is represented by opponents. Well, but this, in a word, is what I am to try to show is the actual state of the case, and you yourselves are to be the jury to decide whether I succeed or not. " I speak as unto wise men; judge ye what I say." [1]

I have stated thus briefly the issues we are to discuss: there are now one or two things it is necessary to say, in order to define more distinctly the limits of my argument. Here:—

1. My argument is not primarily, or in the proper sense at all, with those who rule out these narratives simply on the ground that a *miracle* is implied in them. I am not here, in other words, to discuss the general question of the possibility or probability of the miraculous. I am quite prepared to do that in its own time and place; but that is not my business at present. If, therefore, a man comes forward and says: " I do not believe in the Virgin Birth of Christ because it involves a miracle, and miracles *do not happen*! [2] I have no place for them in my intellectual scheme," I do not

[1] 1 Cor. x. 15.   [2] Thus Matt. Arnold, *Lit. and Dogma*, Preface.

profess to argue with that man. When he descends
from his *a priori* altitude to discuss the evidence, I
will hear him, but not before. It is evident that this
canon already rules out a great deal of objection of
a sort to the narratives of the Virgin Birth. Here,
e. g., is Prof. Foster, of Chicago, who, in his book on
The Finality of the Christian Religion, goes so far as
to declare that an intelligent man who now affirms his
faith in miraculous narratives like the Biblical as actual
facts—who believes, say, in the resurrection of Christ—
" can hardly know what intellectual honesty means." [1]
I say nothing of " honesty," but I do marvel at the self-
assurance of any intelligent man who permits himself
in these days to use such language. It is language that
might be justifiable on the lips of a Spinozist to whom
nature and God are one, but which surely is not justifiable on the lips of any one professing faith in the
living Father-God of Jesus Christ. For who is this
God? The Creator and Sustainer of the world—imma-
nent in all its forces, Cause in all causes, Law in all
laws—yet Himself not identified with the world, but
above it,[2] ruling all things in personal freedom for
the attainment of wise and holy ends. How great the
intellectual confidence of any man who undertakes *a
priori* to define what are and are not possibilities to
such a Being in His relations to the universe He has
made! Personally, I have only to say that I believe

----

[1] p. 132.   [2] Eph. iv. 6.

that God can reveal Himself in extraordinary as well as in ordinary ways,—that miracle enters deeply into the economy of revelation,—that Jesus Christ is the Person in whom the long course of historical revelation culminates. To me, therefore, it is in no way *a priori* incredible that God should make a new supernatural beginning in the entrance of His Son into humanity. The world knows many new beginnings. I do not think you can explain nature itself without taking such into account. Prof. Foster himself, I observe, admits that the consciousness of Jesus is " empirically inexplicable "—incapable of causal and psychological explanation—and that a " creative " element derived immediately from God must be discerned in it.[1] That is a large admission, and involves much more than perhaps Prof. Foster thinks. What bearing it has on such a miracle as the Virgin Birth will be considered after.

2. The second thing I have to say is, that I do not profess to argue with those who rule out as inadmissible *the higher aspects* of Christ's Person involved in the New Testament doctrine of the Incarnation. I say advisedly, " rule out as inadmissible," for I do not wish to exclude those who may be looking towards this truth, without having obtained clearness in regard to it; and I am ready, again, to hear any, whatever their standpoint, when they descend into the sphere of evi-

[1] pp. 265–7.

dence. All I mean is that my own standpoint is that
of faith in the Christian doctrine of the Incarnation,
and that I address myself primarily to those who share
with me in this belief. I can, therefore, naturally
entertain no argument which proceeds on the assumption of a purely humanitarian estimate of Christ,—
which concedes Him to be holy man, religious genius,
human revealer of God, but acknowledges no supernatural element in the constitution of His Person, or
the course of His life. I admit at once—there is no
need of any further argument about it—that if this
is all we can say of Jesus,—if there has been no such
life, or works, or claims, as the Gospels depict,—no
resurrection from the dead, no exaltation to glory,—
then there is no fitness or credibility in the idea of a
Virgin Birth. If there is no resurrection at the end,
there is no suitableness in a Virgin Birth at the beginning. It would be folly to argue for the supernatural
birth of Christ with those who take the naturalistic view;
for, to minds that can reject all the other evidence in
the Gospels for Christ's supernatural claims, such reasonings would be of no avail. The evidence for this
particular miracle goes down in the general wreck of
all evidence for the supernatural in the Gospels. This
obviously, as I remarked before, raises a much larger
question than the one immediately before us. I have
again only to say that I take here for granted the great
facts of Christ's life, death, and resurrection, as re-

corded in the Gospels, and the main outlines of the
Apostolic teaching on Christ's Person; and my argument is directed to the question: How, on this assumption, does it stand with the evidence for the Virgin
Birth of Christ? It may be true that, if there is no
resurrection at the end, there is no fitness in a Virgin
Birth at the beginning. But my question is a different
one. If there *has* been a resurrection at the end, what
of the fitness of the Virgin Birth *then*?

In brief, my argument will have special respect to
those who, accepting the general New Testament doctrine of Christ, are disposed to regard this as independent of the doctrine of the Virgin Birth, or who
think the evidence for the latter insufficient. With
such I desire to reason.

The way is now open for the direct discussion of the
subject, and in the remainder of this lecture I propose
to deal in a preliminary way with *the objection* that the
Virgin Birth is *not a vital part of Christian doctrine*,
and therefore may safely be omitted, or at least left
an open question, in the Church's public profession.
The full discussion of the doctrinal implications of this
article of faith necessarily comes later. But certain
considerations may here be adduced, which may suffice
to show, in starting, that the connection between fact
and doctrine is at least closer than many imagine.

The grounds on which objection to the Virgin Birth

is based have already been indicated, and the question is asked: How can that which was not essential to the faith of a Peter, a Paul, or a John, be an essential of faith for us? Prof. Harnack is very angry with a Lutheran official pronouncement in which it is declared: "That the Son of God is 'conceived by the Holy Ghost, born of the Virgin Mary' is the foundation of Christianity, is the corner-stone on which all wisdom of this world will shatter," and replies: "If that were the case, ill would Mark fare, ill Paul, ill John, ill Christianity." [1] This consideration undoubtedly weighs with many, even among those who do not themselves reject the fact. It seems to me, on the other hand, that, if the Virgin Birth be true, its connection with the other truths about our Lord's Person cannot be other than essential.

One thing which creates a strong presumption in favour of this connection is the fact already adverted to—the connection which experience shows actually to exist between belief in the Virgin Birth and adequate views of our Lord's divine dignity. The article is assailed because it is alleged to be indifferent doctrinally. I draw a very different inference. The very zeal with which it is attacked is to my mind a disproof of its slight significance. Men do not as a rule fight strenuously about points which they think of no importance. They concentrate their attack on points

---

[1] *Das apostolische Glaubensbekenntniss,* p. 39.

which they feel to have strategic value. The Virgin
Birth would not be assailed so keenly as it is, if it were
not felt to mean a great deal more than appears upon
the surface. I am strongly confirmed in this conviction when I look to the dividing-line of parties, and observe the almost invariable concomitance of belief in
the Incarnation with belief in the Virgin Birth, and of
denial of the one with denial of the other.

This is a point of so much importance that it de-
serves a little closer attention. From whom, as a rule,
do the attacks on the Virgin Birth of Christ come?
I find, of course, ranked on the side of the assailants,
as already said, the whole multitude of those who reject the supernatural nature and claims of Christ. But
what of the other side? There are exceptions, I know.
Meyer, the commentator, was one; [1] Beyschlag, who
occupied a half-way house theologically, but accepted
the resurrection, was another — and others might be
named. But that stage is practically past. I do not
think it will be doubted by any one who has looked
into the literature that the scholars and theologians
who accept the higher claims of Christ—who are *bona
fide* believers in His Incarnation and resurrection—
are nearly all—you could count the exceptions on your
fingers—likewise among the upholders of the Virgin
Birth. Does this, on the face of it, look as if there was

[1] Meyer accepted the Incarnation, but rejected the Virgin Birth—
an almost solitary exception of his class.

no connection? When in nature a nearly invariable concomitance is observed between two sets of phenomena, the scientific inquirer seldom hesitates to postulate some causal relation. Is the presumption of a hidden bond of connection not equally strong here?

I may illustrate this by reference to the remark one frequently hears about the weight of scholarship being cast preponderatingly on the side of the denial of the Virgin Birth. The assertion weighs with many who are not too deeply rooted in their own convictions, but it rests on an illusion which it is desirable at the outset to dispel. My reply to it is that the statement can only be accepted if you begin—as many do—by defining " scholars " as those, and those only, who take up the negative attitude already described to the supernatural claims of Christ. Thus regarded, it is a new proof of what I say on the dividing-line of parties. Take any list of the scholars who are best known and most frequently quoted as impugners of the Virgin Birth of Christ, and note who they are. Passing over Keim and Beyschlag, who represent an older strain, you have at the present hour such writers as Lobstein, Pfleiderer, Schmiedel, Harnack, Soltau, Usener, Gunkel, O. Holtzmann, Bousset, Percy Gardner, F. C. Conybeare, Prof. Foster, of Chicago, Prof. N. Schmidt, of Cornell University, and others of like standpoint. These writers, as I said before, do not regard it as any reproach, but boast of it as a mark of their intellectual maturity, that they are one and all rejectors of miracle in the life of Christ.

What now of scholars on the other side? I shall not dwell on the long roll of the older theologians— though, when I think of the devout faith and massive learning of these truly great men who pass before me in mental review—of men like Tholuck, and Lange, and Luthardt, and F. Delitzsch, and Rothe, and Dorner, and Martensen, and Oosterzee, and Godet, not to speak of many who might be named among our own country- men—I wonder, and ask myself what rich and ripe scholarship is, if they did not possess it. But I take scholars of our own time or of the immediate past— scholars of all types: New Testament scholars, Old Testament scholars, Church historians, theologians— some more conservative, some more liberal, some " higher critics," some non-higher critics—who accept this doctrine of the Virgin Birth, and they are so numerous that time would fail me to recount them fully. Were the late Bishop Lightfoot and the late Bishop Westcott, e. g., not scholars? Are Dr. Sanday, of Oxford, and Dr. Swete, of Cambridge, at the pres- ent time, not among the finest of our Greek scholars? Is Principal Fairbairn, of Mansfield, Oxford, not a scholar and thinker? Is Sir Wm. Ramsay, of Aber- deen, who has written one of the best defences of Luke's narrative of the Nativity, not a scholar? Are Bishop Gore, or Canon Ottley, both liberal in their

Old Testament views, or Dr. R. J. Knowling, or the writers who ably defend this belief in the recent volume of *Cambridge Theological Essays*, not to be classed as scholars? Canon Henson, in England, has been alarming his fellow-churchmen by his free views on many things; but Canon Henson holds stoutly by the Incarnation and the Virgin Birth.[1] Among the scholars in the Free Churches of Britain (I have already mentioned Principal Fairbairn), probably the names of Principal W. F. Adeney, of Principal A. E. Garvie, of Prof. Vernon Bartlet, of Prof. J. Denney, are as representative as any; but these are understood to accept, and some of them have written ably in defence of, the Virgin Birth.[2] You glance at the Continent, where rationalism so strongly prevails—though the forces are more evenly divided than many suppose—and you have on this side the great New Testament scholar, Th. Zahn, *facile princeps* in his own field; you have had the learned B. Weiss, of Berlin; you have leading theologians like Seeberg and Cremer, above all, Prof. M. Kähler, of Halle, who has, I suppose, more students in his classes than any other half-dozen theological professors put together. Against these you

---

[1] Cf. his volume, *The Value of the Bible and Other Sermons*, on these points.

[2] See specially Dr. Adeney's valuable essay on *The Virgin Birth and the Divinity of Christ* in the series "Essays for the Times," No. xi. Cf. Dr. Denney's article on "The Holy Spirit" in the *Dict. of Christ and the Gospels*, vol. i.

have, I grant, to place some even of the more positive Ritschlian theologians, as Kaftan, Häring, Loofs, who shy at this article; but in Germany as elsewhere the general fact is that full belief in the Incarnation and belief in the Virgin Birth go together. In America, among a multitude of others, mention should be made of the late Dr. Philip Schaff, a fine historical scholar, if ever there was one; and now Dr. Briggs, of the same Seminary,[1] one of the most advanced Old Testament scholars, has thrown himself into the strenuous defence of this article. A similar combination of standpoints is witnessed in England in Prof. W. E. Addis, a radical Old Testament critic, but a devout believer in the Incarnation, and upholder of the birth of our Lord from the Virgin. Many other names might be cited, but I forbear. If scholarship is to be the test, we need not be afraid to meet the adversary in the gate.

While this large consensus of opinion exists as to the reality of the Virgin Birth, it is right to notice that there are many who themselves accept the fact, who still, on the ground that it does not enter into the " foundation " of our Christian faith, are in favour of making this point of belief an " open " one in the Christian Church. One thing, it seems to me, too often forgotten in the discussions on this subject is, that the

---

[1] Union Theol. Seminary, New York. Cf. Dr. Briggs's work, *New Light on the Life of Jesus*, pp. 159*ff.*, and a striking article in the *North American Review* for June, 1906.

question we are dealing with is not, in the first instance, one of *theology*, but one of *fact*. What raises the question at all is that we have two evangelical narratives—the only two which relate the events of our Lord's Nativity—which circumstantially testify that this *was* the mode of His earthly origin. The first thing to do, plainly, is to try to ascertain whether this witness is true. If it is not, there is no more to be said. If it is, then we may sure that the fact it attests *has* some bearing on the constitution of our Lord's Person, whether at first we see it or not. It is here that the position of those who accept the fact of the Virgin Birth, but deny its essential connection with the other truths about our Lord's Person appears to me illogical and untenable. The one thing certain is: either our Lord was born of a Virgin, or He was not. If He was not, as I say, the question falls: there is an end of it. But if He was—and I deal at present with those who profess this as their own belief—if this was the way in which God *did* bring the Only-Begotten into the world—then it cannot but be that it has a vital connection with the Incarnation *as it actually happened*, and we cannot doubt, in that event, that it is a fact of great importance for us to know. In any case, we are not at liberty summarily to dismiss the testimony of the Gospels, or relegate the fact they attest to the class of " open questions," simply because we do not happen to *think* it is important. It is not thus that science stands before its facts. If an alleged fact is presented to science, it does not first ask: What is the importance of the fact? but, Is the fact real? If it is, the man of science is sure it will have some valuable light to throw on the department of knowledge to which it belongs, whether at first he perceives it or no. This is the spirit in which we should approach the subject now under consideration.

Still, the objection will be pressed that the Virgin Birth does not enter into the "foundation" of our Christian faith; hence cannot be regarded as an essential article of belief. It did not form part of the foundation of the faith of the Apostles, or of the earliest Christian teachers, so cannot be reasonably made part of the foundation of ours. It might be replied, for one thing, that our position is, after all, not quite that of the earliest believers; that for us the truth is now there, and that we have, whether we will or no, to take up some kind of relation to it, just as they would have had to do, had they been where we are. But, leaving the discussion of the faith of the Apostles to its own place, and without prejudging the degree of their knowledge of this mystery—a matter to be afterwards investigated—I should like to point out that a truth may not be the *foundation* of our faith, yet, once it is known, may be found to have very important bearings on our faith, to contribute to it, to be so closely related to what is vital in our faith, that our faith thenceforward may feel it to be indispensable, and would be greatly impoverished without it: moreover, that a truth may not be the foundation of my *faith* in a fact, yet may very well be part of the foundation of the *fact* itself. The law of gravitation, e. g., is no part of the foundation of my belief that stones fall. The world knew that stones fell before it ever heard of the law of gravitation. Yet the law of gravitation has much to do with a proper understanding of the fact that stones fall, and more, lies at the foundation of the fact itself, though not at the foundation of my belief in it. Shakespeare's authorship is no part of the foundation of my knowledge of the play of *Hamlet*, or of my appreciation of the genius displayed in it. Yet Shakespeare's authorship is not a matter of indifference either to the origin, or to the character of the play. No one I ever heard of has affirmed that the Virgin Birth was the original ground of the belief of the Apostles in the Incarnation or the sinlessness of Christ. These truths stood on their own broad evidence, of which the Virgin Birth may or may not have formed part; but it in nowise follows that the Virgin Birth, if a fact, does not stand in the most vital relations to both the one and the other.

This leads me to remark that there seems to me to be in these discussions a constant tendency to the confusing of two very different things—the foundation of my *faith* in the Incarnation, and the foundation of the *fact* itself. The proposition is first laid down, perhaps quite truly, though not necessarily so: " The Virgin Birth does not enter into the foundation of my *faith* in Christ's Incarnation and sinlessness." This is then immediately transformed into the other proposition: " It does not enter into the foundation of the *fact* of the Incarnation "—a very different thing. But where is the proof of this latter proposition? Is it sought in our ignorance or inability to see the connection? Need I remind you that there are a thousand things in nature you do not see the reason of, yet they are facts? There are organs in the body the uses or precise functions of which are obscure; but sound physiology does not doubt that they have their uses, and does not abandon the hope of yet discovering them. You go home at night to sleep, yet you would be hard put to it to explain why it should be necessary to spend so large a portion of your existence in this state of dormancy. You know, of course, that it *is* necessary for the recuperation and refreshment of the body, but you cannot tell why. Even, therefore, were it granted that we could in no degree penetrate the mystery of the connection of the Virgin Birth with the Incarnation and sinlessness of our Lord, it would be unwarrantable dogmatism on our part to declare that there was no connection. Only if we knew all the implications of these transcendent facts would we have the right to make such an affirmation. But that knowledge no one has, and our very ignorance is a reason why we should not belittle the historically recorded fact.

Thus far I have been arguing on the assumption of the opponent that no obvious relation subsists between the Virgin Birth, and the other elements of our faith in Christ. I desire now to say, however, that this, in my opinion, is far from being the case. The consideration of this connection belongs to succeeding lectures, but there is one thing, I think, which most fair-minded people will be willing to admit. It will hardly be disputed that, if the Incarnation is a reality, a miracle of some kind is involved in the constitution of our Lord's divine and human Person — even on the assumption of Christ's perfect sinlessness, so much may be conceded; and, on the other hand, granting the Virgin Birth, it will hardly be denied that the Person so born is, in some sense, superhuman in nature and dignity. We may, if we please, deny that the Incarnation necessarily involves the Virgin Birth; but few will question, at least, that, if Christ was born from the Virgin, there is a supernatural element in His Being.

Only one thing more I would say at this preliminary stage. It will scarcely be doubted, I think, that, if the Virgin Birth is true, it is a fact of great *historical value*. A chief worth of the narratives of the Infancy is just that, by showing how Christ actually came into the world, they incorporate Him, as nothing else could do, into the history of the world, give Him a real place

in the history of our humanity, and furnish the needful introduction to what is told us regarding Him by
the other Evangelists. The Gospel of Mark, e. g.,
brings Jesus before us at His entrance on His public
ministry without preface or explanation. Had this been
all that was told regarding Him, His history would
have hung, so to speak, in the air. It would have
had no beginning; just as, if the resurrection were
wanting, it would have had no suitable ending. We
shall see afterwards how, in the conflicts of the early
Church, the Fathers made effective use of these narratives in warding off, on the one hand, the Gnostic denial
of our Lord's real humanity, and, on the other, the
Ebionitic lowering of the divine significance of His
Person—thus preserving to the Church His true image
as at once Son of Man and Son of God.[1] These much-
assailed narratives have thus approved themselves as
possessed of a historical and doctrinal worth which
should make us very cautious how we join in any de-
preciation or thoughtless surrender of them. For some,
I know, this historic value of the narratives will only
aggravate their offence. Religion, we will be told, cannot be bound up with historic facts. I reply—Religion
abstractly may not be; but a religion like the Christian, which has its essence in the entrance of God into
history for man's redemption, cannot but be. This

[1] See good remarks on this in Rev. Louis M. Sweet's *The Birth
and Infancy of Jesus Christ*, pp. 14*ff*.

means that, if we are to gain the full benefit of the religion, we must believe in the facts on which it is based. We shall see, I hope, as we proceed, that among these Christian facts, not the least fruitful in help to mind and heart is the Virgin Birth.

LECTURE II

An inquiry into the historical reality of the Virgin Birth naturally begins with the documents from which the knowledge of the Virgin Birth is derived. These are, as every one knows, the two Gospels of Matthew and Luke—the opening chapters in each, with part of the third chapter of Luke, containing the genealogy.[1] I shall afterwards have to deal with the objection that the other two Gospels, Mark and John, do not furnish such narratives. Perfectly good reasons, I think, can be given for the omission; but this is a question to be investigated by itself. At present we are concerned, not with the silence of the New Testament, but with its speech; and here the salient fact before us is, that *in two of our Gospels out of the four*—the only two that narrate the birth of Jesus at all—we *do* have this circumstantial testimony regarding Christ's human origin, that He was conceived by the Holy Ghost, born of the Virgin Mary. This is a weighty fact, if there were no

[1] Matt. i., ii.; Luke i., ii.; iii. 23–38.

30

other, and we do well to consider it closely and carefully.

My starting-point, then, is this, that we have these
narratives of the two Gospels, both bearing witness
that our Lord was born of a Virgin. To set this fact
of the witness of the Gospels in its true light, there
are certain things which it is important to notice regarding it.

1. I would ask you to observe, what I have just
noted, that this is *the only account of Christ's birth* we
possess. You may think you see indications in other
parts of the Gospels that our Lord was not born as
these opening chapters describe: that can be discussed
after. What I wish at present to impress is that, if this
account which the Evangelists give is parted with, you
have no narrative at all of how or where Christ was
born, or of anything about Him prior to His baptism.
You read, e. g., in books like Pfleiderer's *Christian
Origins*, or in " modern " Lives of Jesus like Bousset's
or Oscar Holtzmann's, that Jesus, the son of Joseph
and Mary, was born at Nazareth.[1] But there is no
historical corroboration for that categorical statement.
The Gospels are our only authorities on the subject,
and the same Evangelists who tell us that Jesus was
" brought up " [2] with Joseph and Mary at Nazareth,

[1] Pfleiderer, p. 83; Bousset's *Jesus*, p. 2; O. Holtzmann, *Leben
Jesu*, p. 68. Cf. Renan, quoted above, p. 5.   [2] Luke iv. 16.

tell us that He was *not* born at Nazareth, but was born
at Bethlehem, and that it was after His birth that
Joseph and Mary settled in Nazareth. It is made a
contradiction between Matthew and Luke that Matthew is said to know nothing of Joseph and Mary's
previous residence in Nazareth, which Luke, on the
other hand, relates.[1] But Luke is as explicit as Matthew that it was not at Nazareth, but at Bethlehem, that
Jesus was born. As it is with the *place*, so it is with
the *time* of Christ's birth. It is usual to say that Jesus
was born shortly before the death of Herod the Great
(4 B.C.); but, if the birth-narratives are rejected, there
are, as Wellhausen seems to admit,[2] no reliable data on
which to found so precise an assertion.

It may be argued, indeed, that, because parts of the
narratives are rejected, we are not bound to reject the
whole; some true elements of tradition may be preserved in them. One writer—the only one I know—
who tried this plan was Beyschlag. Beyschlag thought
he could pick and choose; take some parts and leave
others. He very justly argued that, at the time when
Matthew and Mark wrote, any free invention of the
stories of the Infancy would have met with instant contradiction from the family of Jesus. He sought, therefore, to save some fragments of the narratives—the
birth at Bethlehem, the visit of the shepherds, etc.—

[1] Luke i. 26; ii. 4. See below, pp. **34, 99**.
[2] *Das Evang. Lucae*, p. 6.

while rejecting the fact which is the kernel of the whole, the Virgin Birth.[1] It is agreed on all hands, however, that this arbitrary procedure of Beyschlag's is quite inadmissible. The cycle of narration in both Evangelists is too firmly connected to be thus broken up; and the authority for one part of the story, as we shall immediately see, is the same as the authority for the rest. I repeat, then, that, if these narratives are rejected, we really know nothing of the circumstances of Christ's birth at all.

2. The only accounts of the birth of Jesus we have declare that He was born of a Virgin. My next point is that we have *two* such accounts, and that the accounts are *independent*. There are two evangelical witnesses, not one; and, as the most cursory inspection of the narratives shows, their testimony is independently given. Attempts have been made, I know, by one or two scholars to show some kind of dependence of one narrative on the other, or of both on some common source.[2] These isolated attempts have met with no

[1] *Leben Jesu*, I, pp. 159*ff* (3d Ed.). See below, p. 76.

[2] E. g., the writer Conrady (*Die Quellen der kanonischen Kindheitsgeschichte Jesu*) seeks to derive the narratives from the apocryphal *Protevangelium* of James (the relation is really the reverse); another writer, Reitzenstein, derives from an earlier Gospel supposed to be indicated by a poorly preserved Egyptian fragment of the 6th cent.; Resch (*Texte und Unters.*, x. 5, p. 208) derives from a purely imaginary *Book of the Generations of Jesus Christ*, etc. See a good account of these and cognate theories in papers by J. Gresham Machen, in *The Princeton Theol. Review* for Oct., 1905, pp. 648–9; Jan., 1906, pp. 39–42.

favour, and need not here detain us. The favourite method of dealing with the narratives is rather to seek to discredit their trustworthiness by pitting one against the other, and declaring them to be divergent and contradictory. I shall immediately endeavour to show that the two narratives, so far from being contradictory, in reality remarkably corroborate and supplement each other. In proof that the alleged discrepancies are not really serious, I might appeal to one of the latest of these critical writers, Oscar Holtzmann, who, in his recently published *Life of Jesus*, tells us: " A contradiction between these narratives of Matthew and Luke does not exist; even in regard to the places of residence there is no need for assuming one." [1] The difficulty about the places of residence has already been referred to. Matthew does not mention the former residence of Joseph and Mary at Nazareth, and speaks as if, after Christ's birth, they went to Nazareth for the first time.[2] Suppose, however, that Matthew did not know of this earlier residence, but, in writing his Gospel, kept faithfully to the information he had, without adding or inventing—is this a contradiction, or a reason for distrust? But I do not think we need assume even this. A writer like Soltau, indeed, permits himself to say: " We learn from Matthew that Bethlehem was the real native place of Joseph and Mary." [3] But there is not an atom of foundation for this statement.

[1] *Leben Jesu*, p. 65.   [2] Matt. ii. 23.   [3] *Op. cit.*, p. 30 (E. T.).

Matthew says nothing in his first chapter as to where the events he narrates happened; it is not till the second chapter that he mentions Bethlehem of Judæa as the place where Christ was born. When, therefore, he tells of the withdrawal of Joseph and Mary to Nazareth after the return from Egypt, he naturally names the place for the first time.

There is, therefore, no necessity for assuming real contradiction; but the point I would urge, as it has often been urged before, is, that the very existence of these so-called discrepancies is a proof of the entire independence of the narratives. It is the complete independence of the accounts, in truth, which is the cause of any superficial appearance of discrepancy which they present. They tell their story from different points of view—what these are will be seen afterwards; they group their facts from a different motive, and for a different purpose. They evidently have different sources. Yet in the great *central* fact, viz.: that Jesus, conceived by the Holy Ghost, was born of Mary, a Virgin betrothed to Joseph, with his full knowledge of the cause—in this they are altogether at one: this stands out sun-clear in the narratives, and was never, so far as we know, challenged in the Church from the time it was made public, save by the insignificant Ebionitic fraction already mentioned.[1]

[1] On the fewness of the Ebionites, cf. Salmon, *Introd. to N. T.*, p. 173 (2d Ed.).

3. The independence of the narratives is a guarantee of their *worth*. It shows that they are not inventions of either of the Evangelists, but are drawn from an outside source—nay, from *two* sources, which are distinct, yet agree in their testimony to the essential fact. I desire now to take a further step, and to show that the narratives are not only not contradictory, but in a singular degree are *mutually corroborative and complementary*. This is evidently a point affecting closely the value of their testimony.

The critics speak of the discrepancies of the narratives. Much more remarkable, it seems to me, are their *agreements*, and the subtle harmonies that pervade them. The agreements, if we study them carefully, prove to be far more numerous than may at first strike us. Here, e. g., is a list of twelve points, which lie really on the surface of the narratives, yet give very nearly the gist of the whole story. (1) Jesus was born in the last days of Herod.[1] (2) He was conceived by the Holy Ghost.[2] (3) His mother was a Virgin.[3] (4) She was betrothed to Joseph.[4] (5) Joseph was of the house and lineage of David.[5] (6) Jesus was born at Bethlehem.[6] (7) By divine direction He was called Jesus.[7] (8) He was declared to be a Saviour.[8] (9) Joseph knew beforehand of Mary's condition and its

[1] Matt. ii. 1, 13; Luke i. 5.
[2] Matt. i. 18, 20; Luke i. 35.
[3] Matt. i. 18, 20, 23; Luke i. 27, 34.
[4] Matt. i. 18; Luke i. 27; ii. 5.
[5] Matt. i. 16, 20; Luke i. 27; ii. 4.
[6] Matt. ii. 1; Luke ii. 4, 6.
[7] Matt. i. 21; Luke i. 31.
[8] Matt. i. 21; Luke ii. 11.

cause.[1] (10) Nevertheless he took Mary to wife, and assumed full paternal responsibilities for her child—was from the first *in loco parentis* to Jesus.[2] (11) The Annunciation and birth were attended by revelations and visions.[3] (12) After the birth of Jesus, Joseph and Mary dwelt in Nazareth.[4]

This, however, is not the whole. For here a fact emerges about these narratives to which we cannot give too much attention. There is this common basis of agreement of which I have spoken. But careful inspection of the narratives shows that, even in the respects in which they are divergent, so far from being discrepant, they are really, in a singular way, *complementary*; that where a careless glance suggests contrariety, there is really deep and beautiful harmony. The full illustration of this belongs to a later stage;[5] but, at the risk of anticipating what is to come after, let me take a single crucial example. Is it not strange that Luke's Gospel, while giving us such full accounts about Mary, should tell us next to nothing about Joseph, and specially about his state of mind when he first learned of the situation of his betrothed wife? It is implied in Luke's narrative, as in Matthew's, that

[1] Matt. i. 18–20; Luke ii. 5.
[2] Matt. i. 20, 24, 25; Luke ii. 5*ff.*
[3] Matt. i. 20, etc.; Luke i. 27, 28, etc.
[4] Matt. ii. 23; Luke ii. 39.
[5] See below, pp. 83*ff.* It will be found that Matthew's narrative is told throughout from the standpoint of Joseph; Luke's from that of Mary.

Joseph came to know that Mary was about to become a mother, and, when he did know it, the fact must have profoundly staggered him. Yet in Luke, as in Matthew, he appears later with Mary at Bethlehem, takes Mary to wife, and assumes parental responsibilities for Mary's babe. What had happened in the interval to clear his mind of any doubts or perplexities he had entertained, and to induce him to act as he did? Luke has not a syllable in explanation, but Matthew tells it all. Matthew, again, tells us fully of Joseph's difficulties and perplexities. But what of Mary? What did she say or think of this wonderful thing that had happened to her? How did she come to learn the truth about herself? Matthew has not a word on this subject, but Luke tells it all. In a most real sense, therefore, the narratives are shown to be complementary. Neither is complete in itself; both are needed to tell the whole story. And subtler harmonies still will reveal themselves when we come to look more closely into the character of the narratives.

This, then, is my first fact—the existence of two distinct, yet mutually complementary narratives of the Virgin Birth of our Lord. I come now to discuss a *second*—closely connected with the foregoing—the evidence we have for the *genuineness* and *integrity* of these narratives as parts of the Gospels to which they belong.

This is a question which I must argue with some care, for it has been contested. It is evident that if, from dislike of miracle, or any other cause, these records containing the story of our Lord's birth are to be got rid of, it is necessary in some way to break down their credit as early and authentic productions. If these sections are really genuine parts of the original Gospels of Matthew and Luke—assuming the latter, as I here do provisionally, to be themselves genuine documents of the Apostolic Age—most will feel that a long step is taken to establish the historical truth of the Virgin Birth which they narrate. It is, therefore, almost a vital point for the opponents to disprove their original and authentic character. Can this be done? I am here to affirm with some confidence that it cannot. My second fact—as I call it—which I oppose to their contention is, that *these chapters containing the narratives of the Virgin Birth are attested by all available evidence as indubitably genuine parts of their respective Gospels.*

What are the means of proof which it is usual to apply in such cases? A first source of evidence is *Manuscripts*. It is here to be remembered that the wealth of MS. authority for the Gospels, as for the New Testament generally, is without a parallel in literature. We can see this most easily by comparison with the MS. authority for the works we call the classics. Of some important classical works only one MS. is in exist-

ence—Nestle reminds us, for instance, that all we possess of Sophocles depends on a single MS. of the eighth
or ninth century;[1] ten or fifteen is thought a large
number for others; and few of these go beyond the
tenth century, or are even so old. In contrast with
this, the MSS. of the Gospels, whole or parts, are reckoned by scores; if you include cursives, by hundreds;
and some of these, as is well known, are of great age
and authority. The great Uncials, e. g., go back to
the fourth and fifth centuries, with, as their peculiarities show, a long textual history behind. Another chief
source of evidence is *Versions*, to which have to be
added quotations, and all the other indirect means by
which the existence and genuineness of a book can be
ascertained. The net result of the application of these
tests in the present case can be readily stated. Is there
a single unmutilated MS. of the Gospels—older or
younger—from which these chapters in Matthew and
Luke are absent? *Not one.* Are these sections absent
from any of the Versions? So far as our evidence
goes—No.

The case, however, is too important to be thus summarily dismissed, and I propose to take up the evidence
under these heads more particularly.

1. I have said that the opening chapters of our two
Gospels are found in all unmutilated *MSS.* That
broad fact will not be disputed. But let me try to

[1] *Textual Criticism*, p. 33 (E. T.).

emphasise the moral of the fact by contrast. You are aware of the doubt which attaches to the last twelve verses of Mark's Gospel. In the margin of the R. V., you will find this note opposite ver. 8: " The two oldest Greek MSS., and some other authorities, omit from ver. 9 to the end. Some other authorities have a different ending to the Gospel." Here is very strong evidence that these last verses did not belong to the original Gospel, but were supplied to take the place of the lost original ending. So again with the episode of the woman taken in adultery in John vii. 53 to viii. 11. These verses are bracketed in the R. V., and the note is added that most of the ancient authorities omit them. But there is no lacuna or omission of a similar kind in regard to the opening chapters of Matthew and Luke. Take the oldest Uncials. The Sinaitic MS. [א] —the chapters are there. The Alexandrian MS. [A] —this is mutilated down as far as Matt. xxv., but Luke i., ii., are there, and nobody doubts that the first chapters of Matthew were there also. The Vatican MS. [B]—there. The Codex Ephraemi [C]—there. The Codex Bezae [D], representing an independent (Western) text—there. Uncials and cursives generally —there in all.

2. That is MSS.: glance now at *Versions.* It was very early in the history of the Church that translations of the Gospels and of other New Testament writings began to be made into the languages of the coun-

tries into which Christianity had spread. Hence, beginning with the second century, we have the rise of Syriac, Latin, Egyptian, and other Versions, the MSS. remains of which throw light on the kind of Scriptures circulating in these sections of the Church. And what do they tell us? The chapters containing the birth-narratives are as little absent from the Versions as they are from the Greek MSS. They are there in all the Latin Versions; in the Vulgate of Jerome, of course, but also in the Old Latin Versions, going back as far as the days of Tertullian. They are there in all the Syriac Versions—in the Peshitta, in the Curetonian, in that very old Syriac Version discovered by Mrs. Lewis in the convent at Mt. Sinai in 1892. They are there in all the Egyptian (Coptic) Versions—in a word, are there in all. In that famous old Syriac Harmony of the Four Gospels made by Tatian about 160 or 170—the *Diatessaron*—recently so strikingly recovered, the chapters are present, though the genealogies are dropped, probably as unsuitable for the author's purpose. The Harmony is now translated, and any one can consult the book, and read the narratives for himself. Other sources of evidence yield the same result. The quotations and allusions in Justin Martyr, Tatian's master, show that these chapters were in the " Gospels " or " Memoirs of the Apostles " which he tells us were read week by week in the assemblies of the Christians.[1] Even the Epicurean Celsus, the bitter

[1] 1 *Apology,* 66, 67; *Dial. with Trypho,* 10, 100, 103.

heathen opponent of Christianity in the second century, draws freely in his attacks on the Gospels from the incidents in the birth-narratives—the genealogies, the star in the East, the flight into Egypt, the Virgin Birth itself.[1]

3. There are three special recensions of the Gospels, however, respecting which we have information, on which, in this connection, I must make a few remarks.

(1) There is the *Gospel of the Hebrews*, an Aramaic version of the Gospel of Matthew in use among that more liberal section of the Jewish Christians whom Jerome calls Nazarenes—those who, while retaining their Jewish customs for themselves, accepted the mission of Paul, and did not seek to impose circumcision and the Jewish law upon the Gentiles. It was an idea formerly sometimes mooted—Jerome himself seems at first to have entertained it—that this *Gospel of the Hebrews* was the original of our present Gospel of Matthew. But that opinion has long since been abandoned.[2] The Gospel in question was dependent on our Matthew, not the original of it, and, while there must have been a general resemblance, it had a good many apocryphal additions. Unfortunately we only know it in extracts. The point of interest for us is that this Jewish-Christian Gospel likewise had the chapters re-

---

[1] Origen, *Against Celsus*, i. 38–40; ii. 32.

[2] Cf. Stanton, *The Gospels as Historical Documents*, I, pp. 258*ff*. Meyer, *Com. Introd.*; Salmon, *Introd. to N. T.*, etc.

cording the birth and infancy of Jesus. Harnack, I know, disputes this. But he stands almost alone in doing so, and the reasons against his opinion seem conclusive. We have the direct attestation of Eusebius that the section of Jewish Christians using this Gospel were distinguished by their accepting the Virgin Birth of our Lord.[1] We have the testimony of Epiphanius that the Gospel used by the Nazarenes was a complete one;[2] we can be certain that Jerome, who knew and translated the Gospel, would not have failed to mention so serious an omission, had it existed; finally, what appears decisive, we have actual allusions in Jerome to the contents of these early chapters in the Hebrew Gospel. Thus he notices that it had the peculiar reading "Bethlehem of Judah" for "Bethlehem of Judæa" in Matt. ii. 5; also the citations of prophecy, "Out of Egypt have I called my Son," and "He shall be called a Nazarene"—both unmistakably from Matthew.[3]

(2) This, however, was not the only form of the Gospel of Matthew in circulation among the Hebrew Christians. There was a version in use among that narrower section known commonly as the Ebionites— the descendants, formerly alluded to,[4] of those anti-

---

[1] Eusebius, iii. 27; cf. Origen, *Against Celsus*, v. 61.

[2] Cf. Westcott, *Introd. to Gospels*, p. 465.

[3] Cf. Stanton, *op. cit.*, p. 258.

[4] See above, pp. 11, 35. It should be noted that the name Ebionites was often given by the Fathers to all Jewish Christians. The different classes were then distinguished by their Christological and other peculiarities.

Pauline Judaizers we read of in the Acts and the Epistles, who contended for the imposition of the Mosaic law upon the Gentiles. These held Jesus to be merely a man, chosen by God on account of his legal piety. We do not know much about the Gospel used by this party—the so-called *Gospel of the Ebionites*—but it is described to us as not "entire and perfectly complete, but falsified and mutilated'; [1] and we do know that it omitted the first two chapters of Matthew, and commenced: "It came to pass in the days of Herod, King of Judæa, that John came baptizing with a baptism of repentance in the river Jordan, who was said to be of the race of Aaron the priest, a son of Zachariah and Elisabeth, and all went out to him." [2] Of course, a Gospel of this kind, which puts the baptism of John in the days of Herod of Judæa, and otherwise falsifies its text, is absolutely worthless. But it will be observed how, even in rejecting the narratives of the Infancy, it is forced unwittingly to bear testimony to them; for where else does it get the date, " in the days of Herod, King of Judæa," [3] and the information about Zachariah and Elisabeth, the parents of John? [4] Most probably the Gospel was simply a badly corrupted version of *The Gospel of the Hebrews,* with the first two chapters left out.

Why have I spent so much time on this obscure

---

[1] Westcott, *op. cit.*, p. 467.   [3] Matt. ii. 1; Luke i. 5.
[2] *Ibid.*, p. 466.   [4] Luke i. 5.

Gospel of a backward and reactionary sect? Simply because, as I hinted before, this is the *solitary* instance within the Church of any sort of party who rejected the narrative of the supernatural birth. I say within the Church, though we see from Justin Martyr that already by the middle of the second century this sect was coming to be regarded as hardly a part of the true Church.[1] Surely, however, it requires hardihood on the part of any one to hold that this reactionary party—this mere side-eddy in the stream of the Church's development—represented the true, original Christianity, and that their Gospel was the genuine *Gospel of the Hebrews*, instead of being, as has always been believed, a corrupt and mutilated form of that Gospel.[2] In any case it is certain that it was not the original Gospel of Matthew, any more than the *Gospel of the Hebrews* itself was.

(3) I have to notice still a third non-canonical recension—the *Gospel of Luke used by Marcion*. Marcion was a Gnostic teacher (c. 140), who held that the God of the Old Testament was an inferior, imperfect Being, in contrast with the good God of the New Testament, and who believed in the essential evil of matter. He could not, therefore, in consistency with his principles, allow that Jesus was, I do not say supernaturally born,

---

[1] *Dial. with Trypho*, 47; cf. Ritschl, *Altkathol. Kirche* (2d Ed.), p. 253.

[2] Keim actually bases on this Gospel an argument for the omission of chs. i., ii. from the original Gospel of Matthew.

but born at all. Marcion drew up for himself a Canon which included one Gospel—that of Luke—and ten Epistles of Paul. But his Gospel of Luke had not the first two chapters. It began at the third chapter: " In the fifteenth year of the reign of Tiberius," then passed to ch. iv. 31; " He came down [i. e., from heaven] to the Galilean city of Capernaum." [1]   Here, again, the attempt was formerly made by certain writers to show that Marcion's Gospel represented the original Luke. But the attempt met with no success. Ritschl, who at first advocated this view, afterwards gave it up. Dr. Sanday gave it its death-blow in England when revived by the author of the book called *Supernatural Religion.* I do not know of any scholar who now holds it.[2]   The discussion on Marcion's Gospel thus really turned round into a new evidence that the genuine Luke *had* these two chapters.

I have thus surveyed the field of MSS. and Versions, and have sought to show you how absolutely unbroken is the phalanx of evidence that these first chapters of Matthew and Luke are genuine parts of the Gospels in which they are found. Well, but, I have no doubt you are long ere this asking in surprise: If the facts are thus undeniable, what do the objectors say to them? How are they dealt with? One characteristic example

---

[1] Cf. Tertullian, *Against Marcion*, iv. 7.
[2] Cf. Plummer, *Luke*, p. lxviii.

of how they are dealt with may perhaps suffice. Here
are two recent publications of the great Old Testament
critic Wellhausen—*The Gospel of Matthew, Translated
and Explained*, and *The Gospel of Luke, Translated and
Explained*.[1] I take up his version of the Gospel of Matthew, and what do I find? It begins with ch. iii. 1.
What has become of the first two chapters? They
are simply dropped out. For what reason? There is
not a word of note or comment to explain. The critic
thinks they should not be there, so, MSS. and Versions
notwithstanding, out they go. It is the same with the
Gospel of Luke. I open it as before, and find it begins
with ch. iii. 1. Where have the first two chapters gone
to? Again they are simply dropped out, and again without note or explanation. Here, however, is a third work
from the same author—an *Introduction to the First
Three Gospels*. Perhaps we shall find what we want
there. But no. There is a minute and destructive
criticism of the Gospels; much about Q, the alleged
common source of Matthew and Luke; but not a word
in explanation of why these chapters are dropped from
what professes to be—and in the main is—a version
of our existing Gospels. It is no doubt easy enough
to get rid of the evidence for the Virgin Birth in this
way. But is it scientific? Is it right? Would a similar treatment be tolerated of any classical work?

[1] *Das Evangelium Matthaei, uebersetzt und erklärt* (1904). *Das
Evangelium Lucae*, etc. (1904).

It is the case, then, that there is no external warrant for dropping these chapters out of the two Gospels. If they are rejected, it must be for some internal reason which the critic thinks justifies him in setting aside all this mass of external evidence. So it has been held by some—not by many—critics, that these chapters cannot be original parts of their Gospels, since—(1) They lie outside the limits of the original Apostolic preaching; and (2) show marks of being additions in their looseness of connection, and in their difference of character from the rest of the Gospels. I might almost be excused, in view of what has been advanced, from dealing with these subjective and arbitrary reasons for rejection, but, as they really, when fairly considered, redound to the strengthening of my position, I give them a brief consideration.

(1) The first objection turns on the limits of the *oldest Apostolic tradition.* That oldest tradition, assumed to be represented by the common parts of the first three Gospels, and thought to be preserved most nearly in the Gospel of Mark, had no narrative of the Nativity. It began, as we learn from Acts i. 22, with the baptism of John, and ended with the ascension. But, granting this, how can it prove that these two Evangelists—Matthew and Luke—may not have gone beyond the common tradition, if they felt that they had information enabling them to do so? Or how can it disprove the worth of their information? Matthew

and Luke have both elsewhere large sections not found
in Mark, and Luke has some six chapters wholly his
own. Why should it not be so here? The facts about
Christ's birth and childhood, surely, were matters about
which there would be a desire for information; why,
if these Evangelists had the knowledge, should they
not impart it? I cannot, therefore, allow that any
weight attaches to this objection.

(2) The second objection, drawn from *internal
marks* showing the narratives to be additions, is more
to the purpose, if it can be made good, which, however,
it certainly cannot be. Keim, e. g., among older writers, argued that the connection is loose between the
first two chapters of Matthew and the third chapter.[1]
It needs a keen vision to see the force of his arguments,
but in any case the facts of the case are against him.
Ch. iii. begins with the words—" In those days."
What days? The very form of the expression points
to something preceding. So ch. iv. 13 speaks of Jesus
as " leaving Nazareth." But this has obvious reference
to ch. ii. 23, the only place where Nazareth is previously mentioned—" He [Joseph] came and dwelt in
a city called Nazareth."

It is futile to point in this connection, as Wellhausen
does, to the genealogy in Luke iii. 23*ff.* as proof of
separate authorship,[2] or, with others, to Matt. xiii. 53
or Luke iv. 22, where Jesus is spoken of by the people

[1] *Jesus of Nazara*, I, p. 82 (E. T.).   [2] *Das Evang. Lucae*, p. 6.

as Joseph's son; for this in no way proves that the
Evangelists held Jesus to be the son of Joseph, which
certainly they did not.[1] On the other hand in such
allusions as " John the son of Zacharias " in Luke iii. 2,
and " came to Nazareth, where he had been brought
up "—mark the carefully chosen phrase " brought
up " (τεθραμμένος), not " born " [2]—in ch. iv. 13, one
cannot help seeing clear glances backward to the previous narratives (cf. Luke i. 5*ff*.; ii. 51).

The clearest evidence, however, of the unity of these
sections in Matthew and Luke with the rest of the
Gospels is found in their stylistic character. As respects Matthew I simply quote the words of one of the
latest and most learned writers on this subject, Mr. F.
Crawford Burkitt, in his work on the Syriac Gospels.
He says:

" The Greek style of Matthew is marked: he has
a fondness for certain words and phrases, so that
almost every passage of considerable length contains
some of them. . . . When we come to Matt. i., ii., and
ask ourselves whether these chapters belong to the rest
of the Gospel, or whether they are to be regarded as a
later insertion, we find that the internal literary character is extraordinarily strong in their favour. The
two chapters contain no less than five of the Old Testa-

[1] See below, pp. 99, 100.

[2] Mr. Sweet, in his book on *The Birth and Infancy of Jesus
Christ*, remarks on the " skilfully chosen" character of this phrase
(p. 195).

ment quotations, accompanied by the regular **Mat-
thean** formula,[1] etc. . . . We may say, in fact, that
if the Nativity story (Matt. i. 18–ii. 23) be not an
integral part of the First Gospel, it must be counted
one of the cleverest adaptations: a verdict that is not
likely to be passed on it by a sane criticism." [2]

The case for the unity of the sections in Luke is
perhaps even stronger. Harnack's recent brilliant vindication of the Lucan authorship of the Third Gospel
turns in part on this very point—that the unmistakable
marks of Luke's Greek style in the rest of the Gospel
and in the Book of Acts are found also in the first two
chapters. The argument is not original to Prof. Harnack. Among recent writers Dr. Plummer has ably
developed it in the Introduction to his *Commentary on
Luke*; but Harnack has brought to it fresh and weighty
corroboration.[3]

We may, therefore, rest with confidence in the view
expressed by J. Weiss in a recent article, borne out by
all the external evidence, that " there never were forms
of Matthew and Luke without the Infancy narratives." [4]

The *genuineness* of these chapters of the Gospels
may be regarded as established, but there remains the

---

[1] Cf. e. g., outside these chapters, Matt. viii. 17; xii. 17; xiii. 14, 35.
[2] *Evangelion Da Mepharreshe*, pp. 258–9.
[3] Cf. his *Lukas der Arzt*, p. 73, and Appendix II.
[4] *Theol. Rundschau*, 1903, p. 208 (quoted by Machen).

question of their *integrity*. If the chapters cannot be excised in whole, may they not be in part? To a sufficient degree, at least, to destroy the evidence of the Virgin Birth? The method of mutilation has seldom been attempted in Matthew [1] (the disputed reading in ch. i. 16 will be referred to later [2]); but it *is* attempted by a considerable number of recent scholars,[3] including Prof. Harnack himself, in the case of Luke. Remove certain verses, it is ingeniously contended, from Luke's narrative—principally ch. i. 34, 35, the verses which record Mary's question to the angel: "How shall this be, seeing I know not a man?" and the angel's answer: "The Holy Ghost shall come upon thee, and the power of the Most High shall overshadow thee," etc.—and the evidence for the Virgin Birth disappears. The story becomes one of the promise of a son, like the promise of Isaac, or Samson, or Samuel, or John the Baptist, to be born in the ordinary way. So, *mirabile dictu*, it turns out that we have in Luke no story of a Virgin Birth at all! [4]

[1] On the theories of Schmiedel, who makes Matt. i. 18–25 later than ch. ii., and of Charles, who makes the genealogy a later addition (against him F. C. Conybeare), see article by Machen in *Princeton Theol. Review*, Jan., 1906, p. 63.

[2] See below, p. 102.

[3] Thus, e. g., Pfleiderer, Schmiedel, Usener, Hillmann, J. Weiss, Cheyne, Conybeare, etc. Other critics, as Hilgenfeld, Clemen, Gunkel, and in part Wernle, Weinel, etc., oppose. See below, p. 56.

[4] Wellhausen thinks there is no Virgin Birth in Luke ii., but sees it in ch. i.

On what grounds, we naturally ask, is this omission
of Luke i. 34, 35 made? First, it is emphatically to be
said: On no good textual grounds. Here again the evidence of MSS. and Versions is decisive. Apart from
a few various readings, such as occur in all texts, the
chapters in Luke are vouched for as coming down to
us in their original form, with ch. i. 34, 35 as part of
them. The only partial exception to this statement
is that, for ver. 34 (Mary's question), one Latin MS.
(*b*), for an obvious reason, substitutes the words in the
first part of ver. 38: "Behold the handmaid of the
Lord: be it unto me according to thy word." For the
excision of ver. 35—the crucial verse—there is no authority at all. The change, if made, has to be made
wholly on internal grounds—as that the critic thinks
that ver. 35 breaks the connection, is not consistent
with the Davidic descent, is irreconcilable with Mary's
after behaviour, etc.[1] Even so, the Virgin Birth is
implied in many ways in the context; so, to suit the
theory, further changes have to be made. "Betrothed" in ch. ii. 5, has to be altered into "wife"—
a change which has some MS. support,[2] though the
overwhelming weight of authority is against it; above

[1] Harnack has *ten* such reasons.

[2] The reading "wife" appears in two or three Latin and one
Syriac MSS., and with "betrothed" or another word in several
others. Nothing would be seriously affected even were the change
into "wife" made, for Matthew, too, speaks of Joseph as the
"husband" of Mary, and of Mary as his "wife" (i. 19, 20), when
as yet they were only "betrothed."

all, ch. i. 27, which tells how the angel was sent " unto a virgin betrothed to a man whose name was Joseph," has to be disposed of—this time without any authority —by deleting the word " virgin," which occurs twice, and likewise the word " betrothed." The way is then open for Harnack to pronounce: " After these few and easy deletions, . . . the narrative is smooth, and nowhere presupposes the Virgin Birth "! [1]

This, I submit, may be magnificent, but really it is not war. It is not serious criticism. Is any one so simple as to imagine that these changes would ever have been thought of, but for the previous desire to get rid of this particular feature of the Virgin Birth? Even then trouble is not over, for, as another critic—Usener—is quick enough to perceive, if these deletions are made, one would expect to find some notice of a marriage of Joseph and Mary. Usener, however, is equal to the occasion. It is naturally as easy to put in as to take out. So he courageously writes: " We are in a position to infer with certainty" [I always prick up my ears when one of these writers speaks of something he can " infer with certainty "; I am sure it will be something peculiarly doubtful] " from Luke ii. 5 that in the original form of the narrative after i. 38 stood the further statement, hardly to be dispensed with (even though judged inadmissible by the redactor who inter-

---

[1] Cf. his discussion in *Zeitschrift für die neutest. Wissenschaft*, 1891, pp. 53*ff.*

polated i. 34, 35), that Mary was then taken to wife
by Joseph, and that she conceived by him!"[1]   Comment on such criticism is needless.

A few other critics think they can get rid of the
Virgin Birth by expunging ver. 34, without sacrificing
ver. 35;[2] Gunkel more justly dismisses all these interpolation theories as baseless.[3]   Dr. Chase says of
them in a recent paper: "I cannot think there is a
shadow of justification for regarding Luke i. 34, 35 . . .
as an addition to the original document, inserted either
by St. Luke himself, or by some unknown interpolator,
and for thus eliminating the idea of the Virgin Birth
from the genuine Gospel. . . . The arguments brought
forward against them are wholly subjective; and I hope
that it is not arrogant to say that these arguments appear to me both far-fetched and mechanical."[4]   This
opinion I entirely endorse.   How strange that MSS.
should be so universally silent on these alleged interpolations; that no Father of the Church should ever
have heard of them; that the whole Church should have
understood the narrative of Luke in a way contrary
to its real sense!   The thing would be incredible
enough, if Luke stood alone.   But we have to remember that, when all is done, it is only one of the narratives that is got out of the way.   The narrative of

[1] Article "Nativity" in *Ency. Biblica.*
[2] Thus, e.g., Kattenbusch, Weinel.
[3] *Zum religionsgeschichtlichen Verständniss des N. T.*, p. 68.
[4] *Cambridge Theol. Essays*, p. 409.

Matthew, which cannot be operated on in this fashion, remains as a second corroborative witness.

I come now to my last point in this part of the discussion. I am entitled to assume that these narratives of the Virgin Birth are genuine parts of their Gospels, and that they have come down to us in their integrity. But what of the Gospels themselves, and of their value as witnesses to such transcendent facts? The Gospels, we are told, are late; we do not know for certain who are their authors; they are at least far removed from the events which they relate. What credit, therefore, can be attached to them?

The full answer to this question cannot be given here, for much depends on the internal evidence, which falls to be discussed in a succeeding lecture. Neither can I enter into the intricacies of what is called the Synoptical problem; but I may endeavour to show briefly how the question stands as regards external attestation, and what grounds we have for believing that our two Gospels are, as I have taken them to be, *unquestionably genuine documents of the Apostolic Age.*

On this subject it will be generally admitted, I think, that we are in a better position for meeting objections than we have been for a long time. Of late years, as Harnack has been reminding us,[1] we have been in

----

[1] See the Preface to his work on Luke.

a current moving strongly backward towards tradition, and there is coming to be very general agreement among sober-minded scholars that the first three Gospels lie well within the limits of the Apostolic Age, that Matthew is at least older than Luke, and that this Gospel is an undoubtedly genuine composition of Luke the physician, the companion of Paul. And this is nearly all I need to have admitted for my present purpose.

Take first *Luke*. The great bulk of scholarship in the Church has never seriously doubted the tradition which ascribed the Third Gospel and the Book of Acts to Luke, the companion of Paul. This has been the view defended by such writers as Keim, Beyschlag, Meyer, Godet, and most English scholars, though it has been strongly contested in the extremer critical schools. Now Harnack has thrown his powerful advocacy into the same scale in his work, *Lukas der Arzt*, and the authorship of Luke may be regarded as more firmly established to-day than it has ever been before. With what careful accuracy Luke went about his work, we know from his own prologue, ch. i. 1–3.

As regards the *date* of the origin of the Gospel, more difference of opinion prevails. Harnack, in his dating of the Gospels, puts Mark between 67 and 70 A.D., Matthew between 70 and 75, and Luke between 78 and 93. But these dates, in the opinion of many, are still too late. Luke is put by not a few about 70

A.D. or earlier;[1] the late Prof. Blass put it as early as 59 or 60.[2] This is not the whole; for even those who give Luke the later dates agree that his Gospel is based on documents much older, and, in regard to chs. i. and ii., it is very generally recognised that the Evangelist uses an earlier Aramaic source. I return to this in next lecture.

The Gospel of *Matthew,* though older than Luke, is in somewhat different case. The point of difficulty about Matthew is this: All ancient writers tell us that Matthew composed his Gospel in Hebrew, i. e., in Aramaic; on the other hand, our existing Gospel of Matthew is in Greek, and bears no marks of being a translation. Moreover, from the fact that the oldest notice we have of the Gospel—that of Papias—speaks of the work which Matthew composed under the name of " Logia," or " Oracles," many have concluded that what Matthew wrote was not a Gospel in the strict sense, but a collection of Sayings or Discourses of the Lord, and they are confirmed in this view by noticing that Matthew and Luke evidently drew from a common source of this kind. On this theory, which is at present the prevailing one, our Greek Gospel of Matthew is not from Matthew's own pen, but is based on Matthew's " Logia," and, along with this, on the Gospel of Mark; the same is true of the Gospel of Luke. The

---

[1] Cf. Plummer on dates for Luke, later and earlier.
[2] *Philology of the Gospels,* p. 35.

point of this, as it bears on our present discussion, can be readily seen. Matthew's Gospel, it is urged, so far as it was based on Matthew's " Logia,"—i. e., was really Matthew's—had no birth-stories; so far, again, as it was based on Mark, it had no birth-stories. Chs. i. and ii. of our Gospel, therefore, are due to the Greek Evangelist, and have no Apostolic authority.

This is the case against the historic worth of these chapters, from the point of view of criticism of the Gospels, and my reply to it is the very simple one that, supposing it all granted, the conclusion does not follow. It does not touch Luke, whose authorship we do know; but it does not really touch Matthew either; for the Greek Evangelist, whoever he was, was evidently a man who stood in closest relation with the Apostle as coadjutor or disciple,[1] as is evident from the fact that his Gospel passed ever afterwards as Matthew's Gospel—in any case, was a man possessed of full information, who wrote with a strong sense of responsibility, and with scrupulous care in the use of his materials, as can be proved by comparison with the corresponding sections in the other Gospels.

Harnack, as we saw, dates the Gospel of Matthew shortly after the destruction of Jerusalem, but others, again, put it before that event. Even so critical a writer as Holtzmann put it about 68 A.D.;[2] and the

[1] Cf. Godet, *Biblical Studies* (N. T.), p. 20; and see article "Matthew" by Dr. V. Bartlet, in Hastings' *Dict. of Bible*, III, p. 297.

[2] Cf. Godet, *Ibid.*, p. 22.

great scholar Zahn puts the supposed original Aramaic Matthew, of which more immediately, as early as 61–66.[1] The sources, on the " Logia " theory, are, of course, earlier still.

I have thus stated the views currently held; but, having made this explanation, I desire now to say for myself—it is only due to myself that I should say it— that I am not at all personally convinced of the truth of this so-called " Two-Source " theory of the Gospels of Matthew and Luke,[2] and see much reason for agreeing with those, including Zahn, who think that the Apostle Matthew's connection with the First Gospel, not excepting the first two chapters, was much more direct than the prevailing theory assumes. I speak with diffidence, and must not unduly prolong the discussion. I would therefore only in closing draw attention to the following points, which seem to me of much weight:—

1. The tradition of the early Church was that " the Gospels containing the genealogies [i. e., Matthew and Luke] were written first," and that Matthew was the earliest of all.[3]

[1] *Einleitung*, II, p. 263.

[2] It seems to me, e. g., in the highest degree improbable that Luke intended in his prologue to include the Gospel of Mark among the many attempts at composing Gospels which his own better-ordered work was to supersede. The difficulties of the theories of dependence are very great, and I prefer to think of the Gospels as drawing from more or less common sources, oral or written, but as independently originating.

[3] Clem. of Alex., in Eusebius, vi. 14; Keim, I, pp. 69, 97; Meyer, *Matthew*, I, p. 25; Zahn, *Einleitung*, II, pp. 177, 263, 322, etc.

2. The tendency has been increasingly to recognise in the so-called " Logia " of Matthew a modicum of narrative matter as well as discourses. This has been ably advocated by B. Weiss, Klostermann,[1] and others. The " Logia "-Source thus approaches more nearly to the nature of a Gospel.

3. The testimony of the ancient Church is unanimous as to the identity of our existing Greek Gospel with the Gospel that Matthew wrote. The early Fathers knew no other Gospel of Matthew, and they attributed it unhesitatingly to the Apostle. It follows that, if an Aramaic Gospel ever existed, it must, as Meyer says, " apart from the language, have been, in contents and form, in whole and in part, substantially the same as our Greek Matthew.[2]

4. The statement, first met with in Papias, that Matthew wrote his Gospel in Hebrew, must, in that case, be due either (1) to a confusion with the *Gospel of the Hebrews*, which Papias, no great judge, may easily, like others, have supposed to be the original of our Gospel; or (2) to the fact that Matthew *did* write his Gospel originally in Aramaic, and that this was subse-

---

[1] Godet, *Luke*, I, p. 44. See also Salmon's newly published *Human Element in the Gospels*, pp. 70, 403.

[2] *Com. on Matt.*, I, p. 11; cf. p. 44. Westcott says: "All early writers agree that Matthew wrote in Hebrew. . . . At the same time all equally agree in accepting the Gospel of Matthew without noticing the existence of any doubt as to its authenticity" (*Introd. to Gospels*, pp. 223–4). Cf. also Zahn, *op. cit.*, II, p. 259.

quently replaced, by his own hand, or that of another, by our Greek Gospel. This is the view of Zahn,[1] as it was earlier that of Westcott, and of others. It is the view which commends itself to my own mind. There is nothing more wonderful in Matthew reproducing his Gospel in Greek, or having it done for him, than in Calvin, e. g., publishing his *Institutes* in Latin and in French.

5. Matthew's Gospel, on this view, may have been produced shortly after 60 A.D. I strongly incline also to an early date for Luke. Luke's Gospel was written before the Book of Acts, and it has always been borne in upon me that the latter must have been written before Paul's death, else there would surely have been somewhere some allusion to that fact.

If these conclusions are just, we find in them new evidence of the early date, and, in Matthew's case, direct Apostolic attestation, of the narratives of the Virgin Birth.

[1] *Com. on Matt.*, II, pp. 259, etc. Cf. Salmon, as above.

LECTURE III

In last lecture I tried to show that the narratives of
the Nativity were genuine parts of their respective Gospels. To-day I am to be engaged in discussing the external and internal credibility of the narratives considered in themselves. This is an important branch of the
argument. These narratives of the birth of our Lord
are not, like the pagan stories of the sons of the gods
to which they are sometimes compared, vague, formless
myths, but are rooted down to time and place, under
definite historical conditions, by reference to which they
can be tested. In Marcion's Gospel, to which I formerly
referred,[1] Jesus came down from heaven in the 15th
year of Tiberius; in our Gospels, He was born of a
human mother in Bethlehem, in the last days of Herod,
the King of Judæa. In this sense also " the Word became flesh," that He has His definite place in the history
of the world in a known age. He was born of a definite
race, in an ordained line of descent, at a particular point

[1] See above, p. 47.

64

of time, and in definite circumstances, which give a concrete reality to His appearance.

But, besides this *historical* side, our narratives have an *internal* character by which their credibility can be tested, and some reliable light thrown upon their sources. I here remind you only that internal evidence is a powerful factor in determining the trustworthiness of any narrative. A fabulous or apocryphal narration betrays its false character by many signs—we have only to think of the grotesque puerilities of the Apocryphal Gospels [1]—while a truthful record bears in itself many subtle indications of its authentic origin and essential credibility. I hope to make it clear that few narratives sustain a test of this kind more successfully than these accounts of the birth of our Lord.

One thing and one only I feel it necessary to premise in this inquiry: I postulate the *honesty* of the writers. I recall a sentence of Godet's at the end of the Preface to his Commentary on Luke, which will bear quoting. " If I am asked," he says, " with what scientific or religious assumptions I have approached this study of the third Gospel, I reply, with these two only: that the authors of our Gospels were men of *good sense* and *good faith*." These are my assumptions also in this discussion. I do not see how any one can read these simple, straightforward records, and not feel that the writers are

[1] See below, pp. 85, 88–90.

at least honest in their purpose—that they are faithfully setting down what they themselves believed to be true, and what they expected their readers to accept from them as true. They were not romancers, spinning their stories out of their own brains, but were narrators, who had their information from sources which they believed to be credible, and wrote with a certain sense of responsibility. Many, I am aware, go on an opposite assumption. They credit the Evangelists with incredible stupidities, and ascribe to them a freedom in concoction, and artful manipulation in the use of their materials, not readily distinguishable from knavery. Réville, e. g., quoted by Godet, thinks that Matthew did not even perceive the incompatibility between the miraculous birth and the genealogy ascribing to Jesus (according to him) a human father; while Luke did " perceive very clearly the contradiction, nevertheless he writes his history as if it did not exist." " In other words," as Godet comments, " Matthew is more foolish than false; Luke more false than foolish." [1]　I hold that, in the sobriety which characterises the Gospels as a whole, we have abundant reason to ascribe to the Evangelists " good sense," and a serious purpose in what they wrote.

I should like to press this point for a moment longer, that, if the narratives of the supernatural birth are rejected, the real alternative by which we are confronted

[1] *Com. on Luke*, I, p. 203.

is that of *deliberate fiction*—for unconscious myth and legend, as we shall by and by see, are here quite out of place. It is easy to say, with writers like Keim and Lobstein, that the idea of the miraculous birth grew up as an attempt at the explanation of the origin of so remarkable a personality as Jesus was; but it is to be remembered that it is not the bare *idea* of the miraculous birth we have to deal with, but the translation of that idea into long and detailed narratives, comprising, both in Matthew and in Luke, a whole cycle of connected incidents. It is easy to suggest again that the Evangelists picked up floating legends which had already begun to attain a certain cohesion and acceptance in the Church. But not to speak of the difficulty which this raises in connection with the very different character of the two narratives, it is directly contradictory of a chief point in the mythical theory, which is that the Church, in the early time, had no knowledge or story of a miraculous birth, but got it from these very Gospels. I think we may hold it for certain that our two Gospels are the sources of any *public* knowledge the Church ever had of the circumstances of the birth of Christ; and, if the Evangelists did not obtain their knowledge of the incidents they record from some reliable authority, there is no escape from the conclusion that the narratives are, in the main, their own creation. But this is an alternative from which, when it is fairly faced, I am sure most reverent minds will shrink.

This being premised, let us look first at the *historical
setting* or framework of these narratives of the Infancy.

In both Evangelists, the date of Christ's birth is fixed
as falling shortly before the death of Herod the Great,[1]
which we know to have taken place in the year of Rome
750, or 4 B.C. Jesus was born, according to these narratives, at least within two years—more probably within
a few months—of that event: say provisionally in 751,
or 5 B.C.

In the case of Luke, however, a more precise deter-
mination is given, which, as it has been made the ground
of serious objection to the narrative, must here receive
attention. Luke tells us, in ch. ii. 1 of his Gospel:
" Now it came to pass in those days "—the days of the
previous events, dated under Herod (i. 5)—" there
went out a decree from Cæsar Augustus that all the
world [i. e., the Roman Empire] should be enrolled,"
and he adds in ver. 2: " This was the first enrolment
made when Quirinius was governor of Syria." Now it
happens that we know a good deal incidentally from
other quarters about this Quirinius. Quirinius *was*
governor of Syria, and he *did* carry out an enrolment
in Judæa; but this, according to Josephus, who is our
authority for the fact, and may here be depended on,[2]
was not before Herod's death, but in 6 A.D., ten years

---

[1] Matt. ii. 1; Luke i. 5; ii. 1.

[2] *Antiq.*, xviii. 1. Zahn thinks that Josephus is here mistaken,
and that Luke gives the correct date (*Einleitung*, II, pp. 397–8).
Acts v. 37 is, however, against the idea of a mistake.

later. Here then, it is contended, is an obvious error
on the part of the Evangelist, who unhistorically dates
the governorship of Quirinius and his census ten years
before the actual time. His story of the enrolment at
the birth of Christ, and so his whole narrative, is thus
discredited.

In dealing with an objection of this kind, the high
character of Luke for conscientiousness and accuracy as
a historian, which Sir Wm. Ramsay has done so much
of late years to establish, has to be kept in mind. Specially in dealing with governors and their titles Luke's
minute accuracy is proverbial. A new instance has recently been furnished in the vindication of the correct-
ness of his mention in ch. iii. 1 of Lysanias as " the
tetrarch of Abylene," which formerly was disputed.[1] In
addition, it was early pointed out (1) that Luke himself
refers to this later census of 6 A.D. in Acts v. 37—" *the*
enrolment," as he calls it [2]; and (2) that in the Gospel
he expressly distinguishes the census at the birth of
Christ as " the *first* enrolment," in contrast, evidently,
to a second he knew of. Whatever blunder Luke per-
petrates, therefore, it is clearly not that of confusing
these two enrolments.[3]

---

[1] Cf. article by Dr. Knowling on "The Birth of Christ" in Hastings'
Dict. of Christ and the Gospels, I, p. 206; with Schmiedel's and
Schürer's admissions noted there.

[2] Cf. Ramsay, *Was Christ Born in Bethlehem*, p. 127.

[3] Schürer acknowledges that Luke knew of the enrolment in 6 A.D.,
yet thinks he mistakes it for one occurring at the birth of Christ
(*Jewish People*, etc., II, pp. 131, 143).

The whole subject, however, took on a new aspect, and Luke's credibility received fresh confirmation, from the important discovery of the German antiquarian scholar Zumpt that Quirinius must have been *twice* governor of Syria, and that the earlier governorship must have fallen between 4 A.D. and 1 A.D.—a conclusion in which most scholars now acquiesce, and which is corroborated by a fragment of an inscription believed to relate to Quirinius.[1] To this has recently been added the discovery of actual census papers in Egypt establishing the fact of periodical enrolments in that country, and creating the high probability that Augustus *did* ordain periodical enrolments of his subjects in the provinces of the empire.[2]

I do not affirm that all difficulties are removed by these discoveries, for the date given for the first governorship of Quirinius — not earlier than 4 B.C., after Herod's death—is still at least about a year too late. The governor when Christ was born cannot, it is evident, have been Quirinius, but was probably his predecessor Varus. Still, most sensible people felt that, by this discovery of Zumpt's, the back of the objection to Luke was broken; for, even if the census was begun under Varus, it is conceivable, and indeed probable, that, owing to the troubles which we know broke out in Judæa at

[1] Cf. Ramsay, *op. cit.*, pp. 227–8, 273.

[2] The details about the enrolments may be studied in Prof. Ramsay's book above named. For the general facts, cf. Schürer, I, pp. 351*ff*.

Herod's death,[1] it was not completed till the time of
Quirinius, with whose name it is accordingly officially
connected. If, on the other hand, the earlier governorship of Quirinius was not, as some, including Ramsay,
have thought, an ordinary, but an extraordinary one,
which may have included this very matter of the census, the difficulty disappears altogether. Even the particular mode of conducting the enrolment — each one
going to his own city [2]—to which some ·have taken exception, is entirely consonant with what we might expect
in a subject kingdom like Judæa, where naturally respect would be paid to Jewish usages and ideas, as far
as possible.[3]

I need not wait on the other objections derived from
the history of the period, as, e. g., that drawn from the
silence of historians on the slaughter of the infants at
Bethlehem. The story connects itself with the other incidents in the narrative, and is in perfect keeping with
the jealous, crafty, cruel spirit of Herod, and with his
ready resort to massacre, as history discloses it. But it
would be too much to expect that, with so many greater
crimes to record, historians would deem the murder of
a few babes in Bethlehem worthy of their notice. To
be perfectly exact, a late pagan writer, Macrobius, *does*

[1] Tacitus, *Hist.*, v. 9. Cf. Josephus, as above. It is to be remembered that the census would be under Herod himself as long
as he lived.

[2] Luke ii. 3, 4.

[3] Ramsay lays stress on this.

seem to allude to it,[1] but I attach no importance to the
reference.

I now come to a subject which has always occasioned
a real difficulty—I mean the *two genealogies*. These
are found in Matt. i. 1–17, and in Luke iii. 23–38.
In Luke, it will be observed, the genealogy occurs, not
in the introductory chapters, but in the body of the Gospel—a fact which connects the one part with the other.
I do not, of course, enter into the details of the discussion, but confine myself to the principles involved, so
far as they bear on the credibility of the chapters.

On two points there is very general agreement with
regard to these genealogies:—

1. That the genealogies formed an original part of the
Gospels.[2] The female names and artificial arrangement
into three fourteens, along with grounds of style,[3] prove
this for Matthew: the *ascending* order of the genealogy
proves it for Luke.[4]

2. That nevertheless they are not free inventions of
the Evangelists, but were *found* and used by them. As
Lobstein puts it: " Our Evangelists evidently found
these genealogies in older documents." [5]

[1] Cf. Ramsay, p. 219.

[2] Dr. Charles is an exception in making the genealogy of Matthew
a later addition. F. C. Conybeare controverts him in the *Academy*,
Dec. 8, 1894.

[3] Cf. on style, Burkitt, *Evang. da Mepharreshe*, p. 258.

[4] Cf. Godet, *Luke*, I, p. 197.

[5] *The Virgin Birth*, p. 46; cf. Godet, p. 203. Burkitt dissents on
this point (p. 260).

3. A third point may be added in which most agree, viz. : that, in form at least, the genealogies are both genealogies of Joseph—not one of Joseph, and one of Mary.

As respects aim, the object of Matthew is obviously to establish or confirm the Davidic descent of Jesus : i. e., the aim is legal or theocratic. The genealogy of Luke, on the other hand, carries back the lineage of Jesus beyond David and Abraham to Adam, " the son of God " —i. e., it appears to give the natural descent.

Certain preliminary objections need not detain us, as that it is unlikely that family genealogies of this kind would be preserved. We are not without some evidence to prove that they were. Luke may be supposed at least to know something of the customs of the Jews ; and when he speaks of every one going " to his own city " for the enrolment, and of Joseph going with Mary to Bethlehem " because he was of the house and lineage of David," [1] he takes it for granted that people did have some knowledge of their tribal and family descent. That tribal knowledge was in certain cases preserved we see from such instances as Anna the prophetess, who is described as " of the tribe of Asher," [2] and Paul, who was " of the tribe of Benjamin." [3] Josephus was able to give his own genealogy as he " found it described in the pub-

---

[1] Luke ii. 3, 4. It may occur to us that the genealogies in the Gospels would not themselves have been produced, unless such things as genealogies were known to exist.

[2] *Ibid.*, ii. 36.   [3] Phil. iii. 5.

lic records " [1] (there *were* public records then) ; and he
speaks of the great care with which the pedigrees of the
priests were preserved, not only in Judæa, but in Egypt,
Babylon, and " whithersoever our priests are scattered." [2] If, however, there was any family of which
careful pedigrees would be preserved, it would assuredly
be that of David, and we know that, in some cases at
least, such registers existed.[3] Even in Domitian's time
there were relatives of Jesus who were known to be of
David's race, and on that account were brought before
the emperor.[4]

The real difficulty about the genealogies is that which
lies upon the surface, viz., that, while both profess to be
genealogies of Joseph, they go entirely apart after
David—one (Matthew's) deriving the descent from
Solomon, the other (Luke's) deriving it from Nathan,[5]
the lines only touching at one or two points (e. g.,
Zerubbabel). From Celsus down [6] this alleged contradiction of the genealogies has been urged as an objection
to the Gospels. The fact of the divergence is not ques-
tioned; how is it to be explained ?

One solution, as I have hinted, is to suppose that the

---

[1] *Life*, i.

[2] *Against Apion*, i. 7. Cf. Plummer, *Luke*, p. 102; Godet, I, p. 204.

[3] Cf. Dalman, *Die Worte Jesu*, I, pp. 265–6; Godet, as above.

[4] Eusebius, *Ecc. Hist.*, iii. 20.

[5] This is an interesting corroboration of the connection of the
house of Nathan with that of David in Zech. xiii. 12 (cf. Dalman,
I, p. 265).

[6] Origen, *Against Celsus*, ii. 32.

genealogy in Matthew's Gospel is that of Joseph, and
that the other, in Luke's Gospel, is Mary's. The idea
is a modern one, but while influential names may be
quoted for it, it has not, in this form, generally commended itself. Yet probably in reality, if not in form,
as many also admit, this explanation comes very near
the true one. We shall see, when I come to speak of the
Davidic descent,[1] that there is strong reason to believe
that Mary was a descendant of David, as well as Joseph;
that they were near relations; and that their betrothal
was an inter-tribal one.[2] This also, it will appear, was
the persistent tradition of the early Church, though the
Church did not directly apply either of the genealogies
to Mary. If this be so, it is to be expected that at a
point near the end of the genealogies the two lines will
coalesce, and they probably do so in Matthan (Matt. i.
15), called by Luke Matthat (iii. 24), two removes
from Joseph. This view harmonises with the character
of Luke's Gospel, which has been happily described as
" the woman's Gospel," [3] and in its opening chapters is
certainly *Mary's* Gospel: which does not concern itself,
like Matthew's, with theocratic descent, but, as already
indicated, traces back the lineage of Jesus to Adam, the
father of the *race*. For the various ways in which the
combination of the two lines may be conceived to be

[1] See below, p. 104.
[2] Cf. article "Genealogies" in *Dict. of Christ and Gospels,* I, p.
639.
[3] Thus Sanday, Ramsay, etc.

effected, I must refer you to the books dealing with the subject.[1] So far from the genealogies reflecting on the credibility of the narratives of the Virgin Birth, it seems to me more correct to say, with Godet, that it is really the peculiarity of Christ's birth which furnishes the key to the striking divergence of the genealogies.[2]

Leaving these external questions, I advance to what is the main subject of my inquiry to-day: the *internal credibility* of the narratives, and the light cast by their character and contents on their probable *sources* and *origin*.

There is one fact about these narratives to which I would, at the outset, solicit your careful attention. It is that, in each of the Gospels, the cycle of incidents goes together as a whole. Beyschlag, as I remarked before, in his poetic way, thought he could pick and choose in these birth-narratives. He would retain the birth at Bethlehem, the pious shepherds, the visit of the astrologers to Christ's cradle—most of the accessories of the narratives, in short, without the fact round which they all gather, the Virgin Birth itself. But, as every one else admits, this attempt to save portions of the narratives as historical, while rejecting their most essential feature, is an impossible one. The nucleus of the narrative—the fact which dominates all the rest—is, in

[1] Cf. Lord Hervey in Smith's *Dict. of Bible*; Andrews, *Life of Our Lord*; Godet, etc. See further below, pp. 104–5.

[2] Godet, I, pp. 201, 204.

each case, the conception by the Holy Ghost and the Virgin Birth. The centre of the story in Luke, e. g., is precisely that verse, ch. i. 35, which Harnack and others would expunge—" The Holy Ghost [*lit.* " Holy Spirit," no article is used] shall come upon thee, and the power of the Most High shall overshadow thee ; wherefore also that which is to be born shall be called holy, the Son of God." With this the other incidents are connected in inseparable relation. The story of Zacharias and Elisabeth leads up to the Annunciation to Mary ; the birth of the forerunner prepares for that of Jesus ; the shepherds are guided to the manger by the songs of the angels ; Simeon and Anna in the temple hail the Lord's Christ. It is not otherwise in Matthew. Here again the central fact is the miraculous birth at Bethlehem. The Magi are led by a star to Christ's cradle, and the subsequent events form a series arising out of that visit. With this is to be taken the other fact, commented on in last lecture, that the two narratives, while independent, are not contradictory, but are really complementary. Matthew supplements Luke's silence about Joseph and the removal of his difficulties ; Luke supplies what is lacking in Matthew about the thoughts and feelings of Mary. We must treat the series of incidents in both Gospels, therefore, together ; they stand or fall as one set of facts.

But let us look more closely at these narratives—particularly at the singularly beautiful and delicately told story in Luke's Gospel. Luke incorporates these narratives of the birth of John the Baptist and the birth of Jesus; but where did he get them? Now there are two features in these narratives which practically all scholars are agreed in recognising. (1) They are in Greek—and in Luke's Greek; and (2), they exhibit unmistakable marks of dependence on a Hebraic or Aramaic source. It may be regarded as demonstrated that the narratives bear the marks of Luke's distinctive style.[1] The contrast is not less evident between the pure Greek of Luke's Preface (vers. 1–4)—one of the finest pieces of Greek in the New Testament—and the sections that follow, steeped in Hebraic sentiment and idiom.[2] Prof. Harnack acknowledges the fact, though he strangely thinks it may be due to a deliberate change of style in Luke himself.[3] Plainly Luke is using in these sections an Aramaic source; the only question that can arise is, whether this source was oral or written. Prof. Ramsay inclines to the former view; most scholars prefer the latter. Gunkel, who has a good feeling in these matters, says the chapters are probably a translation from a Hebrew original, described by him as " a genuine document of a very primitive Jewish-Christian type." [4]

[1] Cf. Harnack, *Lukas der Arzt*, p. 73 and Appendix.
[2] Cf. Sanday, *Critical Questions*, pp. 129–35; Plummer, *Luke*, p. 7; Swete, *Apostles' Creed*, pp. 49–50; Ramsay, etc.
[3] *Op. cit.*, p. 73.
[4] *Zum religionsgeschichtlichen Verständniss des N. T.*, p. 67.

With this view of the Aramaic character of the source, the contents of the sections entirely agree. We are transported in these narratives into the midst of a purely Hebrew circle—of that holy company " that were looking for the redemption in Jerusalem " [1] — and never once throughout the chapters do we leave the Old Testament standpoint, or transcend the Old Testament horizon. We see the aged pair, Zacharias and Elisabeth, both of Aaronic descent, " walking in all the commandments and ordinances of the Lord blameless"; [2] we wait with Zacharias at his altar; we hear the promise of a son, on whom, as in the case of Samson, the Nazirite vow is to be laid; we are greeted with the last refrain of Old Testament prophecy in Malachi: [2] we listen to holy canticles in the old style of Hebrew parallelism; the long-sealed fountain of prophetic inspiration begins again to flow. But the language used, the salvation looked for, the predictions given, are all genuinely Old Testament in character and outlook. " When we look at the *Benedictus* at all closely," says Dr. Sanday, " how intensely Jewish it is! And not only is it Jewish, but Jewish of the period to which it is ascribed." [4] It would, indeed, be strange if a Hellenist like Luke, imbued with the universalistic spirit of Paul, and writing a Gospel intended to bring out the universal note in Christ's sayings and acts, could, from amidst his Gen-

[1] Luke ii. 38.   [2] *Ibid.*, i. 6.   [3] *Ibid.*, i. 17.
[4] *Critical Questions*, p. 132.

tile surroundings, throw himself thus completely back into the atmosphere, thoughts, and speech of a purely Old Testament circle, at a time when Christ had not yet come, but was only hoped for, or rather at the transition-point when the day-spring from on high was just breaking, and its first beams were illuminating the sky! All this attests that we are here dealing with material of a very primitive kind, reproduced by Luke, yet preserved by him with its essential characters unchanged.[1]

It is fitting that I should refer in this connection to the interesting studies of Dr. Briggs, who finds in Matthew and Luke evidence of the existence of Hebrew poems—probably of " two original poems "—giving accounts of the birth and infancy of Jesus.   Matt. i. 20–21 is taken from a longer poem.   " This piece has the parallelisms and measures of Hebrew poetry."   The story of Luke, he notices, " is composed of a number of pieces of poetry "—seven in all.   " These seven pieces of poetry are a series of annunciations and of songs of gratitude and praise, all with marked characteristics of Hebrew poetry, not only in form, but in the style and substance of the thought."   Six of them are trimeters; " one of them is a pentameter, like the pentameter preserved in Matthew."   " So far as Luke is concerned, his

---

[1] Principal Adeney says in his essay on *The Virgin Birth*: "The infancy narrative in this Gospel is extremely Jewish.   Even the language at this part is very Hebraistic—a sign that the Evangelist was drawing on Hebrew or Aramaic sources, and that without very materially altering them."   ("Essays for the Times," No. xi, p. 24.)

story of the Infancy is nothing more than a prose setting for these seven poetic pieces given by him." He says: " Making every allowance for the poetic form, style, and conception, these poems are sources of the highest value, and of the first degree of historic importance "; and, generally, he claims for this Gospel of the Infancy: " There is no sound reason to reject it as merely legendary in its material. There is every reason to accept it as giving a valid and essentially historic account of the Infancy of our Lord, so far as it could be reasonably expected in poetic forms." [1] I am not competent to judge of Dr. Briggs's metrical theories, but his investigations afford at least strong corroboration of the Hebraic character of this source as a whole—not only of its poetic parts, but of its prose portions as well. It will be observed that Matthew as well as Luke is involved in Dr. Briggs's investigations, and other scholars have pointed out indications of the Hebraic form of Matthew's narrative.

There are two ways, I would now ask you to consider, in which this fact we have ascertained of the Hebraic and primitive character of these early sections in Matthew and Luke bears on their historic trustworthiness. One is that they give us very early, and to all appearance first-hand, evidence of the events to which they relate. I shall come back to that immediately. The other is, that they leave no place for a late and legendary

[1] *New Light on the Life of Christ,* pp. 161–6.

origin of the idea of the Virgin Birth.   I do not wish
to anticipate, but there is a point here which I should
like for a moment to emphasise.   With all that is said
of the facility with which legend can grow up, it is very
certain—I should say almost demonstrable—that this
is not a kind of legend which would naturally grow up
on Jewish soil, especially in such intensely Hebraic surroundings as are here pictured.   The idea of a Virgin
Birth, as has often been shown, and will hereafter be
proved more in detail,[1] was one entirely foreign to Jewish habits of thought, which honoured marriage, and set
no premium on virginity.   Hence, indeed, the zeal of
most recent theorists to seek for it a Gentile origin.[2]
There was no precedent for such an idea in the Old
Testament.   The children of promise there — Isaac,
Samson, Samuel—were in every case children born in
marriage.   The prophecy in Is. vii. 14, as we shall see,
could not, despite Lobstein and Harnack, suggest it;
for, apart from the ambiguity of the Hebrew word, of
which more hereafter, it is certain that no Jew of that
age applied the prophecy to the Messiah.   The very
severity of the Hebrew idea of God was unfavourable to
the notion of a divine paternity.   How then could this
conception originate in the bosom of the simple, pious-
minded, conservative community that gave rise to these
stories and hymns, saturated with the purest Old Testament feelings and hopes?   Even if the narrators had

[1] See below, pp. 125–6.   [2] See below, pp. 125, 132.

been ever so much given to romancing, this was not the kind of romancing they would have indulged in. On this ground also we are compelled to deal with the narratives on the assumption of the honesty of the narrators, and of their belief that what they recorded was true.

And so I am brought to the last important stage in the present part of my argument. We have seen that these narratives bear in themselves the signature of their primitive and genuine character. But now one thing is certain. If the stories are true at all, there are, in the nature of the case, only two persons from whom they *can* ultimately have come in their details, viz. : Joseph and Mary themselves. This also, as we saw before, is precisely the conclusion to which we are pointed by the internal structure of the narratives. When we look carefully into the two narratives, we find that they have just this character—that this, indeed, is the most remarkable thing about them—that the narrative of Matthew is given throughout from the standpoint of Joseph, and the narrative of Luke from the standpoint of Mary. This is undoubtedly the fact about the two histories, explain it as we may. Romancists could hardly have kept up so perfect a distinction; yet, apparently without design, it is kept up here. In Matthew, as I showed, the whole story is concerned with Joseph. It tells of his shock at the discovery that Mary was about to become a

mother; of his perplexity and proposed action, of which
no one could have known but himself; of the divine dis-
closure to him in a dream; of his taking Mary to wife,
his naming of Jesus, and his subsequent conduct as the
guardian of mother and child. Mary, as I said, has no
independent place in the narrative. She appears only
in her relation to Joseph, and as the mother of the babe
whose protector Joseph became. Even the birth of Jesus
is not narrated in an independent sentence, but in subor-
dination to the statement of Joseph's relation to his
wife.[1] In the incidents that follow Joseph takes the
lead. This is the more striking that, quite evidently, it
is the miraculous conception and Virgin Birth of Christ
which is the pivot on which the whole narrative turns.

In Luke's narrative, as I likewise before indicated,
these relations are precisely reversed. Joseph does not
appear in Luke's story except incidentally, as the person
to whom Mary is betrothed. The story, led up to by the
account of Zacharias and Elisabeth, is all about Mary.
We are told of the Annunciation to Mary by the angel,
and of her reply; of her visit to her kinswoman Elisabeth, and of what passed between the friends; of Mary's
Magnificat; of the birth of Jesus; of the visit of the
shepherds; of how Mary "kept all these things, and
pondered them in her heart."[2] It is she that Simeon
specially addresses in the Temple; she who, when Jesus
is found in the Temple, with the doctors, speaks the gen-

[1] Matt. i. 24, 25.   [2] Luke ii. 19.

tle word which drew from Him the answer: " Wist ye
not that I must be in my Father's house ? " [1] And
again it is recorded that she " kept all these sayings in
her heart." [2] In these chapters, in short, we seem looking through a glass into Mary's very heart. Her purity
of soul, her delicate reserve, her inspired exultation, her
patient committing of herself into God's hands to vin-
dicate her honour, her deep, brooding, thoughtful spirit
—how truth-like and worthy of the fact is the whole
picture; how free from everything sensational; how far
removed from the legendary Mary of the Apocryphal
Gospels, pictured as dancing when three years old on the
steps of the Temple, fed by the hand of an angel till she
was twelve, etc.

What shall we say is the explanation of all this?
What explanation can be given but the one which most
believing scholars—practically all who do not dispute
the good faith of the records—do give: that Joseph himself is ultimately the informant in the one case, and
Mary in the other ? The narratives, on this view, come
from the holy circle itself: secondary agencies may be
considered after. This accounts for their circumstan-
tiality, their delicate reserve, their primitive standpoint,
their literary peculiarities, as nothing else can do.

Is not this, I might further ask, exactly what we
might expect on the supposition that these things did
actually happen ? Consider. Every one, I think, will

[1] Luke ii, 49.   [2] *Ibid.*, ii. 51.

feel that, while these were things that would not, and could not, be gossiped about, but that would be long kept by Mary as a secret buried deep in her own heart; yet both she and Joseph must have realised that they were not things that could be treated as entirely private to themselves—that it was necessary, both for the clearing of Mary's honour and for the right understanding of Jesus Himself, that the facts of His birth should at some time become known—and that a sacred responsibility rested on them both to see that the knowledge of events so transcendent did not pass away with themselves. This could only be done by solemn deposition, or other form of communication made to some person or persons in their lifetime. For myself, I confess I cannot form a conception of how these narratives in the Gospels obtained the unchallenged reception in the Church they did, unless it was understood or believed that such was their origin.

Against this account of the sources and credibility of the history objections drawn from the *supernatural character* of the occurrences seem to me vain. The Incarnation, in whatever way we conceive of it, is a stupendous miracle—" the mystery of godliness "—and the astonishing thing would have been, had such an event taken place, and nothing of the nature of miracle been associated with it.

The narratives, I grant, are steeped in the super-

natural. But look to the form of that supernatural. It
is not the supernatural of the puerile, extravagant kind
you find in the Apocryphal Gospels of the Infancy,
or in the birth-stories of the Buddha—late products of
imagination. It is the kind of supernatural which connects the Old Testament with the New—a revival of the
spirit of prophecy, sacred hymns, men and women filled
with the Holy Spirit, monitions by dreams, angelic ap-
pearances. Oh, but, you say, these very things—especially the angels — are sufficient to relegate the narratives to the domain of poetry and fiction. Is it so?
The presence of these elements does imply that there is
a divine idealism in the story. It does imply that there
exists a spiritual world which may manifest itself. It
does imply that the shepherds on that first memorable
Christmas night were not dreaming when they heard
those celestial voices telling them of Christ's birth, and
singing, " Glory to God in the highest." [1]   But, seriously, is this incredible in the beginning of the life
of Him who said: " Thinkest thou that I cannot be-
seech my Father, and He shall even now send me more
than twelve legions of angels ? " [2]   Is it not too much
to find a world, which at this hour is busily engaged in
investigating scientifically the border-region between the
natural and the supernatural—instituting " Psychical
Research " societies, and the like, to explore and test
the phenomena of apparitions, of telepathy, of spiritism

---

[1] Luke ii. 14.   [2] Matt. xxvi. 53.

—too much to find it asking us to reject a narrative of the greatest supernatural event of time, because it records that, for a few brief moments, the veil was drawn aside, and that heavenly forms were seen, and voices from heaven heard, by men on earth?

When this fundamental objection is set aside—and I grant that the root of the matter is here—not much difficulty of a serious kind remains. Why, it is asked, knowing all she did, did Mary wonder at His wisdom? Why did she join His friends, when they sought to lay hold of Him, because they thought He was beside Himself? It is all very human, if we only think of it; though it is not said, and is hardly to be believed, that Mary joined in the thought that Jesus was mad.[1] She may well have had other reasons for being there, and, in her maternal anxiety for His safety, for trying to get Him to come away.[1] The difficulty, remember, is the same, if we suppose Mary to have believed in the divine mission of her Son at all, which I think we may assume beyond question that she did. Who ever said of Mary, as it is said of the brethren of Christ—" Neither did His mother believe in Him "?

I have just spoken of the contrast between the supernaturalism of the Gospels, and the false, tinselly supernaturalism of the Apocryphal Gospels. A word may be said on these in closing, as showing in the clearest way

[1] Mark iii. 21, 31. John's Gospel shows that Mary had a belief in Christ's supernatural powers from the beginning (ii. 3–5). See below, p. 112.

the difference between a true and a merely legendary history. Here is seen at a glance what the legendary spirit can do, when it takes up work like this, even with stories like those of our Gospels as models to go upon. The chaste delicacy, the reserve, the long thirty years' silence, broken only by one incident, the restraint and sobriety of tone, of the canonical Gospels—all is gone. Instead you are in the midst of prodigies of the crudest and most puerile kind. As I have written about these elsewhere: " Time, place, propriety, even ordinary consistency, are recklessly disregarded. Jesus has and exercises from His cradle all divine powers—is omniscient, omnipotent, etc.—yet plays with children in the street, and amuses Himself by making pools of water and moulding clay sparrows. When challenged for breaking the Sabbath, He claps His hands, and the sparrows fly away. He is the terror of the place in which He resides. If man or boy offends, injures, or contradicts Him, He smites the offender dead, or otherwise avenges Himself. He confounds His teachers, and instructs them in the mysteries of the Hebrew letters. When His pitcher breaks, He carries home the water in His lap. He aids Joseph in his carpentry by lengthening or shortening the pieces of wood at pleasure." [1]   Look on

---

[1] *Apocryphal Writings of the N. T.* ("Temple" Series), p. xii. Cf. Ignatius (*Eph.* 19) on the star at Christ's birth. "A star shone forth in heaven above all the other stars, the light of which was inexpressible, and all the rest of the stars, with the sun and moon, formed a chorus," etc.

this picture and on that, and the proof of the veri-similitude of our Gospels will be nearly complete!

Why is there nothing of all this puerility in the Gospel narratives? Why no attempt to fill up the vacuum of the long period of Christ's boyhood and early life? Is it not simply because the truth was already there to forestall the error, and check its entrance? To adapt a phrase of Sabatier's, used by him for a different purpose, they "had something better." The ground was already occupied: weeds had no room to grow.

LECTURE IV

I COME now to deal with an objection to the credibility of the narratives of the Virgin Birth which perhaps weighs more with many minds than any I have
yet touched—I mean the alleged silence of the rest of
the New Testament with regard to this mystery of our
Lord's earthly origin. Why, it is asked, if the miraculous birth is a fact pertaining to the essence of the Gospel, do we never hear any more about it? Matthew and
Luke themselves are silent about it after the first chapters; the other Gospels, Mark's and John's, are devoid
of all trace of it; there is no whisper of it in the Book
of Acts; Paul and Peter, the Epistle to the Hebrews,
the Book of Revelation, all are silent about it. More
even than this—I am stating the case at present for the
opponent—there are many things in the Gospels and
Epistles which look in an opposite direction. Jesus is
freely spoken of as the son of Joseph; the genealogies
manifestly go on this assumption; the Davidic descent

91

depends on Joseph's parentage, etc. It was necessary, Paul and the other Apostles tell us, that Jesus should die; necessary that He should rise again; but there is no hint that it was necessary that He should be born as the Gospels say He was.

This, one must confess, is a formidable indictment —to look at. It may, perhaps, not appear quite so formidable when we take it to pieces, and reduce it to its proper dimensions. It may even be found that there are elements in it which, properly regarded, turn round into a confirmation of our view.

One important question I should like the objector to face at the outset is: What are we entitled to *expect* in the way of mention of this event by the sacred writers? Without discussing the opinions of others, let me briefly state how the case presents itself to my own mind.

Supposing, then, the fact to be true, exactly as related, how far, or how quickly, would the knowledge of it be likely to travel? Who knew of it to begin with? Here, let me say, I am not sure that we are right in assuming that *nothing* was known in the circles immediately about Jesus of at least some of the wonders connected with His birth. Joseph and Mary, of course, alone knew the facts fully and intimately. They alone could give authentic and complete narratives regarding them such as we possess. But we cannot quite stop here. There was at least one other who knew of the facts in some degree—I mean Mary's kinswoman, Elisabeth, the mother of the Baptist. You remember that, shortly after the angel's announcement to herself, Mary paid Elisabeth a visit in the hill-country of Judæa, when that holy woman was herself six months on the way to motherhood—mark how all the dates in this narrative are woman's dates!—and that Elisabeth, in an access of inspiration—" filled with the Holy Ghost," the text says—greeted Mary as the blessed among women, and mother of her Lord.[1] She went on: " Blessed is she that believed; for there shall be a fulfilment of the things which have been spoken to her of the Lord." Mary, moved by a like inspiration, responded in the hymn we call the *Magnificat*. Here, then, we have one person who certainly did know that Mary was, by divine power, to be the mother of the Christ; and we cannot doubt that, during the three months that these holy women abode together, the closest confidences would be exchanged between them. Whether Zacharias was admitted to any share in these confidences we cannot tell.

But we must widen the circle a little further. The shepherds who visited the new-born Saviour naturally knew nothing of the secret of His miraculous birth. But they had at any rate the knowledge that the child born was " Christ the Lord," and that extraordinary signs

[1] Luke i. 43.

attended the birth. They knew it as a birth miraculous
in its accompaniments, if not in its origin; and, filled
with wonder, they did not refrain from spreading
abroad the things they had heard and seen, or from
glorifying and praising God on account of them.[1] Further still, there was the holy circle in Jerusalem who
heard from the lips of Simeon and Anna at the presentation in the Temple how the babe born was " the Lord's
Christ," " set for the falling and rising up of many in
Israel." [2] These also knew, and would not conceal the
fact, that a birth in some sense supernatural had taken
place.

What may we infer from these facts? Not, indeed,
that Joseph and Mary divulged to the world their personal experiences—we are expressly told of Mary that
she did not [3]—but that, nevertheless, it was known in
the circle most intimately associated with the holy
family, and by some outside of it, that this birth had
not been an ordinary one, and that divine wonders had
attended it. It is unlikely that this tradition would ever
wholly fail in the innermost circles of those about Jesus,
and later events would from time to time revive it.

There is another fact which should here, I think, be
taken into account. It is quite certain that, in the city
of Nazareth, to which Joseph and Mary returned, the
mystery of Christ's birth would not be publicly talked
about by them. The people of Nazareth did not know

---

[1] Luke ii. 20.   [2] *Ibid.*, ii. 25–38.   [3] *Ibid.*, ii. 19, 31.

—I don't suppose it ever entered their minds to think of — Jesus as other than the naturally born son of Joseph and Mary. It is hardly possible, however, accepting the facts as told by Matthew and Luke, that one thing can have escaped their notice earlier, viz.: that Mary was about to become a mother when her marriage with Joseph had not yet taken place. The fact which perplexed and staggered Joseph could hardly be unobserved by others. Jesus was actually born away from Nazareth, and in wedlock, but there would be those who, after their return, would remember the old malicious talk; and we are perhaps not unjustified in seeing in this the real germ of those later Jewish slanders and Talmudic fables which it is usual to trace to the Gospel narratives—narratives which, when they came, doubtless gave the slander a more definite shape, and would be interpreted as a cover for a dishonourable birth.[1] " We be not born in fornication," was perhaps a taunt that rose only too readily to Jewish lips.[2] If so, Mary meekly bore the misconstruction as her cross—part of the pain of the sword which should pierce through her soul also.[3]

Joseph and Mary would not talk of their peculiar experiences in Nazareth. Would they be talked about to the other children in the house—the brothers and sisters of Jesus, or however else we define the relation-

[1] Zahn supposes Matthew's narrative to be written in an apologetic interest in view of these slanders.

[2] John viii. 41.   [3] Luke ii. 35.

ship? We may say, I think: Assuredly not. A more difficult question is: Did Jesus Himself know of this miracle of His origin, or did He ever hear it from Mary's lips? That He did in some way—natural or supernatural—know the essential fact, I am persuaded. It seems to me to furnish the key to certain of His utterances.[1] But, if He did, we have no knowledge of the when, or where, or how, of His becoming acquainted with it. This only we can safely say: such a mystery would form no part of His public preaching, or of His private communications to His disciples, or to any, at a time when even His Messiahship was not openly disclosed. After the resurrection it was different. Joseph was dead; Mary had been committed to the care of the disciple John. There was no longer the same occasion for secrecy. But it would be rash to assume that, even then, Mary would feel at liberty to speak publicly of the things that lay so near to her heart; and it may be regarded as certain that, while she lived, others, even if they knew the facts, would be very reticent about them. Yet the circle around her may well have been aware that there was a mystery surrounding the birth of their Lord, though they had not the precise knowledge of its nature.

How, then, did the facts ever become known? This brings me back to the point I ended with in last lecture. I there indicated that, in my judgment, both Mary and

---

[1] E. g., John viii. 14, 23, etc.

Joseph must have felt that this knowledge was a sacred trust which they dare not keep wholly to themselves—that it was due to Jesus, to Mary herself, and to the world, in some suitable way to make it known—that an obligation, therefore, rested on them to provide in their lifetimes for the secure and authentic transmission of this knowledge. I likewise endeavoured to show from the narratives themselves that this is no mere conjecture: that the thing was actually done. *How* it was done we can never certainly know. A favourite theory is, that Mary's confidant is to be sought for in that group of holy women that companied with Jesus, and ministered to Him; possibly in Joanna, the wife of Chuza, Herod's steward.[1] Without, however, disputing that Joanna, or some other of this circle, may have been Luke's informant, I would suggest that the form of the records points to an origin much nearer the beginning. Both Joseph and Mary, if I am right in the view I have taken, must have felt this to be an obligation pressing on them from a very early period. Joseph might die—*did* die: Mary had no security for a prolonged life. Where, in these circumstances, shall we look so naturally for the origin of these records as just in that holy circle in Jerusalem in which the spirit of prophecy had anew manifested itself, and which, as we saw, was already in possession of some knowledge of these things —the circle to which Zacharias and Elisabeth and

[1] Luke viii. 2, 3. Sanday, Ramsay, Gore, etc., favour this idea.

Simeon and Anna the prophetess belonged? The narrative of Luke, in particular, in its primitive and Hebraic character, its intimate knowledge of the facts about Zacharias and the birth of the Baptist, its hymns, points to this circle as its source, through whatever hands or tongues the information was subsequently transmitted.

I have indicated that I find a strong corroboration of the views here put forth in the unanimity with which these Gospels, when they appeared, were accepted by the Church. How account for the apparently unchallenged reception of these narratives, unless there existed a preparation for them in something already known, in an expectancy which awaited their appearance—we cannot suppose that nobody knew that Matthew was writing a Gospel, or that Luke, whose inquiries had been so diligent, was writing a Gospel—based on the tradition of something mysterious in the birth of Jesus, in a knowledge which the churches that received them possessed, that the narratives rested on adequate authority, and conveyed authentic testimony?

We are now prepared to deal with the case as it presents itself from the side of the objector, and here, before considering the argument from silence, I would glance at the facts which are supposed to *contradict* the testimony of the chapters in our Gospels on the Virgin Birth.

Some of the statements made under this head are sufficiently reckless.   Take, e. g., the following from Soltau on the *birthplace* of Jesus: " Several passages in the Acts of the Apostles also," says this writer—six are named—" now mention Nazareth as the place where Christ was born." [1]   Of course there are no such passages.   The sole proof is that Jesus is spoken of in the places cited—for instance, in the healing of the lame man in Acts iii. 6—as " Jesus of Nazareth."   There is not a word of His being " born " there.   The same writer informs us: " We learn from Matthew that Bethlehem was the real native place of Joseph and Mary." [2] I showed before that we learn from Matthew nothing of the kind: that Matthew says nothing whatever of Joseph and Mary's native place.[3]   It will be felt that a case that needs to be bolstered up by such assertions has not much substance.

I pass, however, to instances that are of more importance.

1. A first fact on which stress is laid is, that Joseph and Mary are sometimes spoken of in the Gospels as *the father and mother* of Jesus.   It is desirable to observe with some care the exact range of this evidence.   Outside the birth-narratives, there are only four instances —one in Matthew, one in Luke, and two in John.[4]

[1] *Geburtsgeschichte*, p. 10 (E. T., p. 18).

[2] p. 30 (E. T.).   [3] See above, p. 34.

[4] Matt. xiii. 55; Luke iv. 22; John i. 45; vi. 42 (on Mark, see below, p. 106).

What these tell us is, that the people of Nazareth, Bethsaida, Capernaum — we may suppose of other places — spoke of Jesus as "the carpenter's son," "Joseph's son," "Jesus of Nazareth, the son of Joseph," "the son of Joseph, whose father and mother we know." They could not do otherwise, unless they had, what it is certain they had not, a knowledge of the actual mystery of the Lord's birth. But now note this other fact. The only other place in the Gospels besides these four where language of this kind is used—the only place where it is *not* used by outsiders—is in Luke's own narrative of the Infancy. Luke, who has just narrated the birth from the Virgin, himself uses this phraseology, and even puts it into the mouth of Mary. Three times he employs the expression, "the parents" or "His parents," in speaking of Joseph and Mary, and once he makes Mary say, at the finding of Jesus in the Temple, "Thy father and I have sought thee sorrowing." [1] Here is the clearest proof that the Evangelist did not regard this form of speech as in the least conflicting with the fact of the supernatural birth. How, indeed, could it? Joseph, acting on the monition of the angel, had taken Mary to be his wife. By that act, he had assumed full paternal responsibilities for Mary's child. Jesus was born into Joseph's house, grew up as one of his family, stood to him in every outward respect in the relation of son: in the household doubtless called

[1] Luke ii. 27, 41, 43, 49.

him " father." Say, if you will, that the relation was
only a " putative " one: still no other name was appropriate to describe it. To neighbours and townsfolk Jesus
was simply " Joseph's son."

2. Next, the *genealogies* are brought in as witnesses
that the relation of Joseph to Jesus was really a natural
one. " It is beyond dispute," says Lobstein, " that in
the mind of both genealogists Jesus is the son of Joseph." [1] That can hardly be " beyond dispute " which
is, in point of fact, widely disputed. I for one do dispute it. For (1) here again we are confronted by the
fact that the Evangelists, who knew the meaning of
plain terms, saw no contradiction between these genealogies and their own narratives of the Virgin Birth;
indeed, Matthew introduces his genealogy for the very
purpose of showing that Jesus had the legal rights of a
son of Joseph. And (2) it is not the case that the
genealogies have the meaning put upon them. It is not
the genealogies as we have them in our Gospels, but the
genealogies in their supposed original form—what the
critics take to be their original form—which affirm the
paternity of Joseph. The Evangelists are very careful
in the language they use. Matthew has a periphrasis
expressly to avoid this idea: " Jacob begat Joseph, the
husband of Mary, of whom was born Jesus, who is
called Christ." [2] Luke carefully inserts the clause, " as
was supposed "—" being the son, as was supposed, of

[1] *Virgin Birth*, p. 46.   [2] Matt. i. 16.

Joseph " [1]—a clause found in all the texts. The case would be a little altered, though not seriously, if the reading in the recently discovered Sinaitic Syriac Version of Matt. i. 16 could be accepted: " Jacob begat Joseph: Joseph, to whom was betrothed Mary the Virgin, begat Jesus, who is called the Christ." This reading has been eagerly seized on by certain critics; but, in the opinion of the best textual scholars, it has no claim to be regarded as original.[2] Partially resembling readings are found in certain Latin codices, and in one or two late (12th or 14th cent.) Greek MSS.,[3] but even these all fail in the vital point: " Joseph begat Jesus." The reading is not found in any early Greek MS.; it is not supported in the essential point by the other Syriac versions; [4] the texts of the Latin versions are in great confusion. Above all, the reading itself is contradictory, for in the same breath in which it affirms that " Joseph begat Jesus," it names Mary " the Virgin "; and it stands in connection with the narrative of the Virgin Birth in the succeeding verses. The leading textual critics, therefore, as I say, reject it; [5] the R. V., which

---

[1] Luke iii. 23.

[2] Cf. the discussions in Burkitt (see below); Gore, *Dissertations*, pp. 192*ff*.; Wilkinson, *Hibbert Journal*, Jan., 1903, etc.

[3] The "Ferrar" group. See specially Kenyon, *Textual Criticism*, pp. 112*ff*., 131.   [4] Cf. Gore, p. 299.

[5] Cf. Bartlet on Matthew in Hastings' *Bible Dict.*, III, p. 203; but specially Burkitt, *Evang. da Mepharreshe*, pp. 263–4. Burkitt, as said before, regards the genealogy as the Evangelist's own composition (p. 260).

had all the material, except this one codex, before it, does not so much as refer to the variants. Setting this reading aside, the ground vanishes for saying that the genealogies affirm a natural paternity of Joseph. It appears to me very probable that the genealogies were originally genealogies of Joseph, not of Jesus; Luke's, perhaps, a genealogy of Heli;[1] and that the clauses connecting the tables with Jesus are the work of the Evangelists themselves. It is certain, in any case, as shown already, that the genealogies, if found by the Evangelists, were recast by them into their present form.[2]

3. This leads me to another point of real interest— the question of Christ's *Davidic descent*. Everywhere in the New Testament it is recognised that Jesus was " of the house of David," " of the seed of David " " of David's loins," " the son of David." [3] This fact, as Meyer,[4] Dalman,[5] and others have shown, stands fast quite apart from the genealogies; was, indeed, the fact which gave occasion for the genealogies. But just here, it is alleged, we have a conclusive proof of the real paternity of Joseph, since it is always through Joseph, not through Mary, that the Davidic descent is traced. " Fear not, Joseph, thou son of David," we read in Matt. i. 20. " Betrothed to a man whose name was Joseph, of the house of David," says Luke in ch. i. 27.

---

[1] Cf. Godet.　　　　　　　　[2] See above, p. 72.

[3] Rom. i. 3, etc.; Matt. ix. 27; xii. 23; xxi. 9, etc.

[4] *Com. on Matt.*, I, p. 61.　　　　[5] *Die Worte Jesu*, I, pp. 202*ff.*

The reply that may at once be given to this is, that the inference cannot be a correct one, since it is the very Evangelists who lay this stress on Jesus being " of the house and lineage of David " [1] who narrate for us in the same context the Virgin Birth. It is directly as part of the narrative of the Virgin Birth that these statements occur. If the Davidic descent was only through Joseph, then " son of David " to the Evangelists could mean no more than that the relationship to Joseph conveyed to Jesus the legal claim to David's throne—not that He was naturally Joseph's son.

But this now raises another question: Is it so certain that Jesus derived His connection with David only through His relationship to Joseph? I seriously doubt it. I confess I have never been able to read these birth-narratives without feeling that there runs through them all the tacit implication of Mary's Davidic descent, equally with Joseph's. This is specially the case in Luke's Gospel, which, as I showed, is, in these opening chapters, peculiarly Mary's Gospel. No doubt in Luke's Gospel also stress is laid on the fact that Joseph was of the line of David (ii. 4). But it is not to Joseph, but to Mary, that, in the very act of announcing the miraculous conception, the angel says: " The Lord God shall give unto Him the throne of His father David." [2] It is difficult also, I think, not to read this signification into the statement about Joseph going up to Bethle-

[1] Luke ii. 4, 5.   [2] *Ibid.*, i. 32; cf. ver. 69.

hem, " to enrol himself with Mary, who was betrothed to him," " because he was of the house and lineage of David." [1] That Mary was of Davidic descent was, as I mentioned formerly, the consistent tradition of the Church of the second century, as attested to us by the fathers of the time—Justin, Irenæus, Tertullian, and others.[2] The view is one which leading writers have largely favoured.[3] If accepted, it bears out the suggestion previously made that Luke's genealogy, while in form a genealogy of Joseph, is in reality the line of descent through Mary, to whom Joseph was nearly related.

I now proceed to the direct consideration of the argument on which so much is built from the alleged *silence* of the remaining New Testament books. It may, on closer inspection, be found that the argument is not nearly so convincing as it appears at first sight. That there is no direct mention of the Virgin Birth may be at once admitted. But mere silence, if it can be satisfactorily accounted for, does not carry us far in proving either lack of knowledge or denial; and indirect indications may often be shown to be present, where direct

[1] Luke ii. 4, 5.

[2] See the evidence in Meyer, *Com. on Matt.*, I, p. 61 (Meyer himself rejects Mary's Davidic descent). Cf. Knowling, *The Virgin Birth*, pp. 32, 33.

[3] Thus, e. g., Lange, Godet, Ebrard, B. Weiss, Edersheim, Andrews, etc.

testimony is wanting. But let us see what the facts
are.

1. I begin with the Gospel of *Mark*. Here, it is
said, is absolute silence: obvious ignorance of the Virgin
Birth. For, if Mark had known of so remarkable an
occurrence, is it conceivable that he would not have
recorded it? Mark, therefore, is claimed as a witness
against us.

One curious circumstance in connection with this Gospel may be noted in passing. It was the singular contention of the older Tübingen critics—of Baur, Hilgenfeld, and others of the school, but also of a scholar like
Bleek—that Mark *did* know of the Virgin Birth, and
a point was even made of the fact in proof that his
Gospel was later than, and presupposed, the Gospels of
Matthew and Luke. It will be remembered that in
Matthew's Gospel the people of Nazareth are represented as saying: " Is not this the carpenter's son? " [1]
In Mark this saying appears in the simpler form: " Is
not this the carpenter, the son of Mary? " [2] Which of
these forms is the original? Most critics will say the
former. How then, these older scholars argued, do you
account for Matthew's form, " the carpenter's son," get-
ting toned down into this milder utterance, " the carpenter, the son of Mary "? Can it be from any motive
except the desire to avoid the impression that Jesus was
really the son of Joseph—a precaution the *more* neces-

[1] Matt. xiii. 33.   [2] Mark vi. 4.

sary that Mark's Gospel does not contain an account of the birth ? " Mark," says Hilgenfeld, " does not tolerate the paternity of Joseph, even in the mouth of the Nazarenes." [1] The argument is an ingenious illustration of how readily facts can be turned about to suit the exigencies of hypotheses.

Apart from such precarious reasonings, however, the general answer to the objection from the silence of Mark seems to be very simple. Before we can fairly urge an objection of this kind, we must ask: What is the scope and design of the Gospel in question ? Did this scope include the narrative of the birth of Christ ? Now in the case of Mark plainly it did not. Mark had a definite object in his Gospel — viz.: to narrate the events of Christ's ministry within the limits of the common Apostolic testimony, which, as we know, began with the baptism of John, in Christ's thirtieth year, and ended with the ascension.[2] He therefore gives no account of Christ's birth at all. How then can his Gospel be held to contradict the testimony of the other Gospels, which *do* give circumstantial information on this subject.[3]

How much or how little Mark knew of the mysterious

[1] Cf. Meyer on Mark vi. 4.

[2] Cf. Acts i. 22. Mark assuredly knew that Jesus *was* born, though he does not mention it.

[3] Dr. Swete says: "Much has been made of the silence of St. Mark, but the argument *ex silentro* was never more conspicuously misplaced; it is puerile to demand of a record which professes to begin with the ministry of the Baptist, that it shall mention an event which preceded the Baptist's birth" (*Apostles' Creed*, p. 48).

events connected with the birth of Christ, we cannot, of course, definitely tell. He was the son of that Mary of Jerusalem in whose house the Church met in early days for worship.[1] There he must often have met the mother of Jesus and others of her company; and it seems to me more probable than not that he *would* know something of the facts which the other Evangelists record. At least from his silence we are not entitled to infer the contrary. His Gospel opens with the words: " The beginning of the Gospel of Jesus Christ, the Son of God." But why or how the Son of God? Who will say what explanation he would have given of this title, had he been asked to do it? Or will venture to affirm that his answer would have been different from that which the other Gospels afford?

2. I turn in the next place to *John*. Here the same remark has to be made to begin with, that John's Gospel can be no contradiction of Matthew's and Luke's, for the plain reason that John does not narrate the earthly origin of Jesus at all, but contents himself with the divine descent. " The Word became flesh," [2] he tells us: but *how* he does not say. His words assuredly do not exclude—as some have strangely imagined—an exceptional mode of birth; rather the assertion of so transcendent a fact creates a presumption in favour of the truth of what is narrated in the other Gospels. It would be as reasonable to argue that John meant to deny that

---

[1] Acts xii. 12.   [2] John i. 14.

Jesus was born at all, as that he meant to deny that His birth was such as the Gospels describe.

There is a good deal more than this, however, to be said about John. The case stands here quite differently from what it did with Mark, where it was possible to doubt whether the Evangelist knew anything of Christ's supernatural origin. No doubt of this kind is possible about John. John had unquestionably the Gospels of Matthew and Luke in his hands; he wrote, as we shall see, at a time when the Virgin Birth was already a general article of belief in the Church; it is generally understood that one part of his design, at least, was to supplement the other Gospels with material from his own recollections. What then is John's relation to the narratives of the birth of Christ in these earlier Gospels? He knew them. Does he repudiate them? Or contradict them? Or correct them? If he does not— and who will be bold enough to affirm that he does?— what remains but to believe that he accepted and endorsed them? Remember that Mary had been placed under John's guardianship by Jesus Himself, and probably lived in his house till she died.[1] Remember also that these stories, if not true, could only be interpreted in a way which implied a slur on Mary's good name. Is it conceivable that, if he knew them to be false, the Evangelist would have met them with no word of indignant denial?

[1] John xix. 26, 27.

There is another fact to be mentioned in this connection. One of the best-attested traditions of the early Church about John—it comes to us through Irenæus, on the authority of Polycarp, John's own disciple [1]—is that he was in keenest personal antagonism to the Gnostic teacher, Cerinthus, his contemporary at Ephesus. We know very well about the errors of Cerinthus. He taught that the earthly Jesus was the son of Joseph and Mary by ordinary generation, and that the heavenly Christ descended on Him at the Baptism, but subsequently deserted Him. He is the earliest known impugner of the Virgin Birth. The story of John fleeing from the bath-house because he perceived Cerinthus within, may be legendary, but the abhorrence of the tenets of Cerinthus which it enshrines is doubtless historical. Is it to be supposed, then, that John and the arch-heretic were at one on the very point in which Cerinthus came into sharpest conflict with the belief of his time ?

Does John's Gospel contain any clue to his knowledge of the wonderful facts of Christ's birth ? Not directly, perhaps, but indirectly, I should say—yes. Let me refer to only one *doctrinal* point, with which an interesting textual question is connected. John has often been accused of idealising Jesus. But this is a one-sided view. The Jesus of John is no unreal, super-earthly, transcendental being—no Gnostic æon, or spectral ab-

[2] Iren. iii. 4.   Cf. Gore, *Dissertations*, pp. 49–51.

straction—but true man in every sense of the word. The supreme heresy to John was the denial that Jesus had " come in the flesh." [1]   To him the declaration, " the Word became flesh " was weighted with tremendous emphasis. Jesus " came in the flesh "—had a true human beginning—but how? Recall that saying of Jesus to Nicodemus—" That which is born of the flesh is flesh: that which is born of the Spirit is spirit." [2]   Man in his natural condition, that is—as born simply of the flesh— cannot enter the kingdom of God. Did John then suppose that Jesus was ever by nature excluded from the kingdom, or needed a spiritual regeneration in order to enter it? If not, by what constitution of Person did He obtain that exemption? If even of believers it is said that they " were born, not of blood [Gr. " bloods "— male and female?], nor of the will of the flesh, nor of the will of man, but of God," [3] what is to be said of Him who never needed to be born anew, but came into the world holy from the first—" the only begotten of the Father "? [4]   This brings me to the textual question I spoke of. There is a curious reading of this verse, John i. 13, found in some of the Fathers, which, changing the " which were " into " who was," applies the whole passage to Christ — " Who was born, not of bloods," etc. I do not think of accepting as correct this

---

[1] I John iv. 2, 3.   [2] *Ibid.*, iii. 6.   [3] *Ibid.*, i. 13.
[4] What precisely is the connotation even of this expression—*only begotten* of the Father"?

reading, which, however, is defended by the late Prof. Blass,[1] and, with slight modification, is looked favourably on by Zahn; but I agree at least with these scholars that the reading is on the track of a right idea. It is the mode of Christ's birth which is in view, and which furnishes the type of the (spiritual) new birth of believers. As Paul in Eph. i. 19, 20 takes God's mighty power in raising Christ from the dead as the type of the quickening of believers—" According to the working of the strength of His might which He wrought in Christ when He raised Him from the dead ";[2] so John here takes as a pattern the divine begetting of Christ in His conception by the Holy Ghost.

This is a doctrinal point, but take now one or two that are *historical*. We saw that one objection to the narratives of the Virgin Birth is that, in the after history, Mary shows no consciousness of the divine greatness of her Son. But this at least is not true of the Gospel of John. There, as the incident of the marriage of Cana plainly shows, Mary regarded Jesus from the beginning as endowed with supernatural powers.[3] It is the irony of this mode of criticism that the only Gospel which shows clearly this consciousness on the part of Mary should be one challenged for ignorance of the Virgin Birth! Another point on which objection has been taken is, that none of the Gospels, outside the birth-narratives,

[1] *Philology of the Gospels,* pp. 234, etc.
[2] Eph. i. 19, 20.   [3] Cf. John ii. 3, 5.

show a knowledge of the birth at Bethlehem. Is that true of John? In ch. vii. 41, 42, John represents the multitude as saying: " What, doth the Christ come out of Galilee? Hath not the Scripture said that the Christ cometh of the seed of David, and from Bethlehem, the village where David was?" The opponents of the Virgin Birth—Schmiedel,[1] Soltau,[2] Usener,[3] and others—turn this round into a proof that John did not believe that Jesus was born in Bethlehem, seeing that he did not correct the misapprehensions of the multitude—Soltau even sees in it a polemic against that idea. Usener, on his part, thinks that the text " reveals the hidden path by which Bethlehem had found its way into the Gospel tradition." This, however, is a missing of the point. It might as well be argued—indeed Soltau does argue it—that John did not believe that Jesus was of the seed of David. We may take it that John accepted the prophecy that Christ should come out of Bethlehem, just as he did the fact of the Davidic descent, and we know that it was an axiom with him that " the Scripture cannot be broken." [4] He must therefore have believed that Bethlehem was Christ's birthplace, as the other Gospels attest. Prof. Bacon correctly says: " The author presupposes the birth in Bethlehem." [5]

[1] *Ency. Bib.*, article "Mary," III, p. 2959.
[2] *Op. cit.*, p. 19 (E. T.).
[3] *Ency. Bib.*, article "Nativity," III, p. 3347.
[4] John x. 35; xix. 36, 37.
[5] Article "Genealogy," Hastings' *Dict. of Bible*, II, p. 138.

From Mark and John I pass to a weightier count of
the indictment in the alleged silence of *Paul* on this
mystery of our faith.   That Paul, in his numerous writings, shows no trace of acquaintance with the Virgin
Birth is held to be a powerful evidence against the
reality of the fact.   I shall ask you to consider how far
this silence of Paul extends, and whether there are not
counter-indications of the Apostle's belief in the Lord's
supernatural origin.

It is first to be observed that, even were Paul's silence
as great as is alleged, it would not justify the conclusion
which the objectors draw from it.   It is to be remembered that Paul is not in the habit of alluding to, or re-
calling, the incidents in Christ's life—incidents which
must have been perfectly familiar to him from the common preaching.[1]   His whole interest in the Epistles
centres in the great facts of Christ's death and resurrection.   It is granted that Paul nowhere expressly mentions the Virgin Birth, but there is nothing strange in
the fact.   The Incarnation for Paul rested on its own
broad evidence in the Person and work of Christ, and
was attested by the great public fact of the resurrection.
On that, therefore, he uniformly builds, and not on a
fact of so essentially private a nature (the Gospels had
not yet publicly divulged it) as the birth from Mary.

---

[1] Cf. I Cor. xi. 23*ff.*; Acts xiii. 23*ff.*, etc.   It might as well be
argued that Paul did not believe in the *existence* of Mary, since he
never once mentions her.

Did Paul, therefore, know nothing of this mysterious fact of Christ's origin? It is not essential to my position even to assume that he did know of it, though, as I shall show immediately, there is a strong presumption that he did. There is certainly not a word in any of his Epistles which *excludes* such knowledge—not even the mention of Jesus as " of the seed of David," [1] which some bring forward, for precisely the same language is used by the Evangelists who record the Virgin Birth. In estimating the probability of Paul's knowledge, we have to take into account the fact that, during a large part of his journeyings, he had Luke—the author of the Third Gospel—as his travelling companion; and we may be very sure that everything that Luke knew on this subject of the birth of Christ, Paul knew likewise. I do not mean that Luke's Gospel was already written; though from such a passage as I Tim. v. 18, where Paul quotes as Scriptural the two sayings: " Thou shalt not muzzle the ox when he treadeth out the corn," and " The labourer is worthy of his hire "—the latter found only in Luke x. 7—I might argue that it was at least published before Paul's death.[2] But it does seem certain to me that Luke, while he was with Paul, was already engaged in those researches which yielded him the material for his Gospel (cf. ch. i. 1–4), and I should be extremely surprised if these

[1] Rom. i. 3.

[2] I myself see no difficulty in this supposition.   (See above, p. 63.)

did not include the chief facts recorded in his first chapters.[1]

But look now at Paul's own Epistles. If, as Paul affirmed, Jesus, the Son of God, was " of the seed of David, according to the flesh," He must have been humanly born. How did Paul conceive of that birth? You remember how strongly in Rom. v. he affirms the solidarity of the whole race with Adam, and how emphatically he declares: " Through one man sin entered into the world, and death through sin; and so death passed unto all men, for that all have sinned." . . . " Through the one man's disobedience the many were made sinners; "[2] and how he sets forth Jesus, in contrast with Adam, as the new Head of the race, the Righteous One, through whom all this evil condition was to be reversed. Now Paul's was a logical mind. How did he explain to himself this appearance of a Sinless One —a Redeemer—in the midst of a sinful humanity? How did he account for this exemption of Christ from the common lot of sin and death? Could he do it, consistently with his own principles, on the view that Christ's was a birth simply in the ordinary course of nature—that a miracle of some kind was not involved in it?

If we look to the Epistles for an answer to this question, I do not think we are wholly disappointed. Christ's entrance into our world, in Paul's view, was no ordinary

[1] Cf. below, pp. 119–121.   [2] Rom. v. 12, 19.

act. He was " the second man from heaven," [1] who took our nature upon Him by voluntary condescension,[2] and I have been much struck by observing that there is hardly an allusion to Christ's entrance into our humanity in the Epistles (I do not think there is any) which is not marked by some significant peculiarity of expression. I do not say that the peculiarities are such as would of themselves prove the Virgin Birth; but I think it may be affirmed that they are such that the Virgin Birth, assuming a knowledge of it on Paul's part, would furnish a simple and natural key to them.

Let me give a few illustrations of my meaning.

Leaving over Rom. i. 3, 4, for the present, take two other passages relating to Christ's earthly origin, and note the periphrastic character of the language employed. In Rom. viii. 3, we read: " God, sending His own Son in the likeness of sinful flesh [" flesh of sin "], and as an offering for sin, condemned sin in the flesh "; and in Phil. ii. 7: " He emptied Himself, taking the form of a servant, being made [R. V. Marg. " becoming "] in the likeness of men." Is this, I ask, how one is accustomed to speak of a natural birth? God " *sends* " His Son " *in the likeness* of flesh of sin* "; Christ " *empties* " Himself, " *taking the form of a servant,*" is made or " *becomes* " " *in the likeness* of men." The Son of God voluntarily enters our nature, yet there is suggested a distinction. He is one of us, yet not *of* us. He

---

[1] I Cor. xv. 47.   [2] Cf. II Cor. viii. 9; Phil ii. 5–8.

is distinguished from us (" in the *likeness* "), specially in the point of sin. He is, in Luke's phrase, " that holy thing that shall be born," [1] because a higher Power is concerned in His origin.

Or take the well-known passage, Gal. iv. 4, " God sent forth His Son, born of a woman, born under the law," and mark the peculiarity of the expressions. It is not simply that Paul uses the phrase, " born of a woman." We are told, even by Bishop Lightfoot, that this has no special meaning, since the phrase was a usual one to denote simply human birth; and we are referred in illustration to Matt. xi. 11 (= Luke vi. 28), where Jesus says, " Among them that are born of women there hath not arisen a greater than John the Baptist." I should like to point out, however, that the word for " born " in this passage in Matthew is not that used by Paul, and that Paul's phrase is not, so far as I know, exactly paralleled anywhere. This introduces us to an interesting comparison. The Greek word used in Matthew is the word properly denoting " born " ($\gamma\epsilon\nu\nu\eta\tau\delta\varsigma$). The same word is used in the two cases where the phrase occurs in the Septuagint—Job xiv. 1; xv. 14. But in Paul, here and elsewhere, we have the employment, in application to Christ, of a more characteristic term— " becoming " ($\gamma\epsilon\nu\delta\mu\epsilon\nu\sigma\varsigma$). Thus in Rom. i. 3, " was born [lit. " became "] of the seed of David," and in Phil. ii. 7, " being made [R. V. Marg. " becoming "] in

[1] Luke i. 35.

the likeness of men." So in this passage in Gal. iv. 4. It reads: "God sent forth His Son, born [lit. "become"] of a woman," etc. It may be thought that this is simply a case of Paul's peculiar usage; that it was his habit to use this, and not the more ordinary Greek term. But Paul knew the ordinary Greek term very well. In this very chapter in Galatians he uses its verb no fewer than three times in reference to Ishmael and Isaac (ch. iv. 23, 24, 29). But when he speaks of Jesus, he employs the more general term, more appropriate to one of whom John likewise says—" The Word *became* flesh." [1] In such a connection, it may be felt that the expression, " born of a woman," derives a new significance.

I now go back to Rom. i. 3, 4, and ask your attention to one or two points of interest in connection with these verses. Prof. Pfleiderer had a curious theory about this passage which he has since abandoned. He actually thought he saw in these words of Paul about Jesus " being born of the seed of David according to the flesh," and " declared to be the Son of God with power, according to the Spirit of holiness, by the resurrection of the dead," the origin of Luke's narrative of the Virgin Birth. [2] The idea is, of course, untenable, yet there is a gleam of insight in it. I confess it is difficult for me to read this passage in Romans, and rid my mind of the impression that there is a relation between it and what

[1] John i. 14.
[2] See his *Urchristenthum*, 1st Ed., pp. 420-1.

we find in Luke i. 35.[1] Look at the words in the Gospel.
The angel announces to Mary that she shall conceive in
her womb, and bring forth a son, and that " the Lord
God shall give unto Him the throne of His father
David " (vers. 31, 32).   Then, when Mary inquires
how this shall be (ver. 34), the answer is given : " The
Holy Ghost shall come upon thee, and the power of the
Most High shall overshadow thee ; wherefore also that
which is to be born shall be called holy, the Son of God "
—or, " the holy thing which is to be born shall be called
the Son of God " (ver. 35).   In the Greek, however,
and always throughout these chapters, except in ch. ii.
26, 27, the words rendered " the Holy Ghost " are
simply " Holy Spirit "—the article is wanting.   Turn
now to Romans.   Here Paul announces, first, that Jesus
was born " of the seed of David according to the
flesh " ; then that He was declared (not " constituted,"
but " defined ") by the resurrection " to be the Son of
God, with [or " in "] power, according to the Spirit of
holiness."   The last is a peculiar expression.   It also is,
literally, " Spirit of holiness," without the article.   The
contrast indicated is commonly taken to be between
Christ's human and His higher or divine nature ; but
it seems to me more in keeping with the context to interpret it of origin.   " Of the seed of David, according to
the flesh "—on the side of fleshly origin ; " Son of God,

[1] The narrative at the basis of the Gospel may have been known
to Paul through Luke.   (See above, p. 115.)

with [or " in "] power, according to the Spirit of holiness " on the side of higher spiritual origin. The words
are then almost an echo of Luke's—" Give unto Him
the throne of His father David "—" Holy Spirit shall
come upon thee"—"Power of the Most High shall overshadow thee "—" *Wherefore* also that which is to be
born shall be called . . . the Son of God " (or, " the
holy thing which is to be born," etc.).[1]

To allude to only one other passage, it is a fair
exegetical question, I think, whether, in the light of its
context (" For Adam was first formed, then Eve," etc.),
the phrase in I Tim. ii. 15, " Saved through the child-
bearing," should not be taken, with Ellicott and others,
as an allusion to the promise in Gen. iii. 15, and its fulfilment in the birth of the Saviour.

I hope I have said enough to show that Paul is not a
witness that can be relied on to disprove the Virgin
Birth.[2]

In the remaining books of the New Testament, the
only passage I need advert to is the description in Rev.

[1] The suggested parallels may be exhibited as follows:

Luke	*Paul*
"bring forth a Son"	"born"
"His father David"	"of the seed of David"
"Holy Spirit"	"Spirit of holiness"
"Power of Most High"	"with [or "in"] power"
"Wherefore called . . . the Son of God"	"Son of God, according to Spirit of holiness"
"holy"	[implied in above]

[2] See further on Paul's relation to this truth in Lects. VII and VIII.

xii. of the woman with child, " arrayed with the sun, and the moon under her feet, and upon her head a crown of twelve stars " [1]—but the discussion of this passage I postpone till we come to the theories which derive the idea of the Virgin Birth from heathen mythology.[2] It is the newer theorists themselves who bring this Apocalyptic description into connection with the Virgin Birth, supposing both to be of Babylonian origin. Suffice it to say at present that, if there is any relation, and I am disposed to believe that there is, it is the Apocalyptic picture which is dependent on the story in the Gospels, not the other way.[3] In that case it is an additional attestation of the Gospel narratives.

[1] Rev. xii. 1–6.
[2] See below, p. 180.
[3] Cf. Gore, *Dissertations*, p. 9.

LECTURE V

IT is obviously not enough for the objector to deny
the historical character of the narratives of the Virgin
Birth: he must find some method of explaining how the
narratives come to be there. One such method very
commonly employed has been to represent the narratives
as myths or stories arising out of the application of Old
Testament prophecies—or what were taken to be such—
to Jesus. Strauss was the great master of this method
in the past. He carried it rigorously through the Gospel
history, developing from it his well-known " mythical
theory " of the life of Jesus. The Jews, he reasoned,
entertained certain notions of the Messianic character
and office. The Messiah, for instance, was to be a Son of
David, was to be born at Bethlehem, was to do great
signs and wonders, was to come to Jerusalem riding on
an ass. But Jesus, His disciples believed, was the Messiah. Therefore these things must have happened to
Him. So stories grew up, or were invented, showing
that they *did* happen to Him.

This theory of Strauss's, as a general theory of the

life of Christ, could not maintain itself. Apart from other objections, it assumed a unity in Jewish conceptions of the Messiah which we know did not exist, and broke down on the absurdity of supposing a multitude of minds evolving from a miscellany of Old Testament predictions a picture of such coherence and harmony as that of Jesus in the Gospels.

While, however, Strauss's theory had to be abandoned as a general explanation of the Gospel history, the method of finding in Old Testament prophecies the germ of Gospel narratives was still retained *in certain cases*—particularly in the derivation of the story, or "myth," of the Virgin Birth from the prophecy in Is. vii. 14, "Behold a virgin shall conceive, and bear a son," etc., with which it is associated in Matthew. This prophecy, it was thought, lay so aptly to hand that there was no need of going further in search of an explanation. As Lobstein puts it: "The new faith, in quest of arguments and illustrations furnished by the Old Testament, hit upon a prophetic passage which furnished religious feeling with its exact and definite formula." [1] This is the view, accordingly, formerly taken by such writers as Keim and Beyschlag, and now favoured by Lobstein, Harnack, and many more.

But just here a deep cleft in the opposing camp reveals itself; for, as has already been indicated, the newer

---

[1] *The Virgin Birth*, p. 73. This is what Harnack euphemistically describes as "enriching the life of Jesus with new facts"! (*Hist. of Dogma*, I, p. 100.)

school, represented by such writers as Schmiedel, Soltau, Usener, Gunkel, Cheyne, declare emphatically that a derivation from Isaiah's oracle is impossible, and that the origin of the idea of the Virgin Birth must be sought, not in Hebrew prophecy, or from Jewish sources of any kind, but outside—in *paganism*. The subject will come up again,[1] but the reasons urged against a Jewish origin of the idea may here be briefly given:

1. There is no reason to believe that the prophecy in Is. vii. 14 was ever applied by the Jews to the Messiah. We know, indeed, that it was not. Edersheim gives a list of all the passages—some 456 of them[2]—which were Messianically interpreted by the Jews, but this is not among them.

2. The Hebrew word used in the prophecy, 'almah, does not, scholars tell us, properly mean " virgin," but denotes in strictness only a marriageable young woman. I shall return to this presently. Meanwhile, it is certain that no expectation of the birth of the Messiah ever obtained among the Jews [3]—not even after the translation of this word in the Greek version by $\pi\alpha\rho\theta\acute{e}\nu o\varsigma$, which does mean virgin.

3. The idea of birth from a Virgin was, as stated before,[4] one wholly foreign to the Jewish mind. The Jews honoured marriage and family life, and children were regarded by them as a heritage from the Lord. There

---

[1] See below, pp. 154–5.   [2] *Jesus the Messiah,* App. vii.

[3] On Mr. Badham's assertions to the contrary, cf. Gore, *Dissertations,* pp. 289*ff.*   [4] See above, p. 82.

were cases of children given by promise, as Isaac, Samson, Samuel, and now John the Baptist; but the birth was always in the estate of marriage.[1]

4. In Luke's narrative there is no hint of connection with Is. vii. 14, or with any prophecy. Harnack, as we saw, evades this by declaring that ch. i. 34, 35 is an interpolation, and that Luke had not originally the story of a Virgin Birth. But I sought to show before that there is not the least good ground for this assertion.[2]

5. To these reasons it may be added that, even if the idea of a Virgin Birth had occurred to the mind of any Christian reader of this prophecy, there was the strongest reason why such a story as that which we have in the Gospels should *not* have been spun out of it. A story like that of Matthew—if not true—could only have one result: to provide material for such slander of Mary and Jesus as we shall see did afterwards arise in the Jewish Synagogue.

Dr. Cheyne and his friends, therefore, must be allowed to have good reasons for rejecting Is. vii. 14 as the explanation of the narrative in Matthew. Whether their own theory is in any better case I shall consider in next lecture.

---

[1] Cf. Neander, *Life of Christ*, p. 15: "Such a fable as the birth of the Messiah from a *virgin* could have arisen anywhere else easier than among the Jews; their doctrine of the divine unity placed an impassable gulf between God and the world; their high regard for the marriage relation," etc.

[2] See above, pp. 53*ff*.

Do I then, it will now be asked, deny the reality of Messianic prophecy in connection with the birth of Jesus? Or do I question the legitimacy of the Evangelist's application of this prediction in Is. vii. 14? I reply: By no means. I am dealing in what I have said with the hypothesis that the story is a fiction, evolved from Isaiah's words; but I in no way doubt the Evangelist's right to regard the birth of Jesus as a fulfilment of this prophecy, once the event itself had thrown back light upon the meaning of the oracle. To see, however, how the question precisely stands, it is necessary to take a wider and more systematic view of Matthew's use of prophecy in the narrative of the Lord's birth.

Observe then first, generally, that Matthew's is the *theocratic* Gospel, evidently penned with the design of showing that Jesus is the Messiah of the Old Testament. Jesus had already taught His disciples to see the fulfilment of Old Testament prophecy in Himself; to regard Him as the goal of all Old Testament revelation; to think of everything in the Old Testament as pointing forward to Him. It is in this light that Matthew looks always at the life of Christ. It is not, as Strauss thought, that the incidents in the Gospel are evolved from the prophecies; but, the incidents being given, it is sought to be shown how much of the Old Testament is fulfilled in them. The Evangelist, with this aim, is ever on the outlook to find suggestions, preludings, forecastings, prophecies, of the things he is narrating—some-

times actual predictions, sometimes only applications, or
what we would call " illustrations." [1]   I confine myself
to the instances in the sections on the Infancy.

1. Take the case in which it is said that the residence
of Jesus at Nazareth fulfilled that " which was spoken
by the prophets, that He should be called a Nazarene." [2]
There is no such specific prediction in any of the
prophets. Nor does Matthew say there is. He speaks
generally of " the prophets." What then is the explanation ? Simply, I think, this. It was made a reproach to Jesus that He came from so small and despised
a place as Nazareth.[3] His disciples were contemptu-
ously named " the Nazarenes." [4]   The Evangelist sees
in this the fulfilment of a whole series of prophecies
about the lowly and despised origin of the Messiah—
especially of the prophecy in Is. xi. 1, which speaks of
Him as a *Nezer*, or shoot, out of the stump of Jesse,
then decayed to its roots. The application was the more
natural, that, as there seems ground for affirming, the
name " Nazareth " is derived from this very word.[5]

2. Take next the case in which the Evangelist sees
in the return from Egypt a fulfilment of the word of
the Lord by the prophet, " Out of Egypt did I call my

---

[1] Mr. Sweet has valuable remarks on this point in his volume on
The Birth and Infancy of Jesus Christ, ch. ii, etc.

[2] Matt. ii. 23.   [3] Cf. John i. 46; vii. 41.   [4] Cf. Acts xxiv. 5.

[5] For authorities, see Hengstenberg, *Christology*, II, p. 106. It
is stated that in the Talmud the name *Ben Nezer*, i. e., the Nazarene,
is given to Jesus. Cf. also Meyer *Com. on Matt.*, I, p. 98.

Son." [1]   Egypt had been the place of refuge of Israel
for a time; afterwards, when oppression overtook Israel,
God, in a wonderful way, brought His people out, to
give them their own land. " When Israel was a child I
loved Him," it is said in Hosea xi. 1, " and called my
son out of Egypt." The Evangelist reads this passage,
and sees in it a dealing of God which had a new and
higher fulfilment in the calling back of Him who was
the Son—Immanuel, God with us—out of Egypt. It is
quite clearly the incident that suggests the application
of the prophecy here, not *vice versa*.

3. Again, take the passage about Rachel weeping for
her children, suggested by the slaughter of the infants
at Bethlehem.[2] In its original connection in Jer. xxxi.
15, the passage refers to the carrying off of the exiles
to Babylon, and the scene is laid in Ramah, in Benjamin. " A voice is heard in Ramah, lamentation and
bitter weeping, Rachel [the ancestress of the Benjamin-
ites] weeping for her children; she refuseth to be com-
forted for her children, because they are not." The sole
point of connection with Bethlehem is that, according to
Genesis (xxxv. 19; xlviii. 7[3]), Rachel's tomb was in the
neighbourhood of that city. All this the Evangelist is
quite aware of, for he, too, makes the lamentation and

[1] Matt. ii. 15.   [2] Matt. ii. 17, 18.
[3] On the apparent contradiction of this site with that suggested
by I Sam. x. 2, see Delitzsch, *Genesis, in loc.* Probably the "city" in
which Samuel was at the time was not Ramah. Cf. article "Ramah"
in Smith's *Dict. of Bible.*

weeping in the prophetic passage to be at Ramah; but, by a bold figure, using Rachel, whose grave was in the vicinity, as representative of the motherhood of Bethlehem,[1] he finds a new application of the prophetic words in the wailing that filled city and neighbourhood at the slaughter of the babes. It is again clear from the fact that the prophet's words had no original application to Bethlehem, that it is not from the prophecy the incident is evolved.

4. I come now to a passage which differs from the preceding in that it *is* Messianic and directly prophetic —I refer to the prophecy in Mic. v. 3, which predicts the coming forth of the ruler of Israel from Bethlehem. " But thou, Bethlehem Ephrathah, which art little to be among the thousands of Judah, out of thee shall one come forth unto me that is to be ruler in Israel, whose goings forth are from of old, from everlasting." There is no doubt that this passage was accepted as Messianic by the Jews. We know this from Jewish sources themselves,[2] and we see it in the Gospels. The scribes at once put their finger on this passage when asked by the wise men where Christ should be born;[3] and John vii. 42 shows that it was a current belief that the Christ should come out of Bethlehem. Given, then, a faculty or disposition for invention, it may be thought easy to explain

[1] The massacre included the surrounding district, no doubt also the part where Rachel's tomb was situated.

[2] See Edersheim, as above.

[3] Matt. ii. 5, 6.

how a birthplace was sought for Jesus in Bethlehem.
But there is one obvious difficulty. The passage might
suggest a birth in Bethlehem, but it would certainly not
suggest the *kind* of birth we have described in Matthew
and Luke. The prophecy in Micah speaks of a prince, a
ruler, going forth from David's city. How different the
picture in the two Evangelists of the lowly Babe, cradled
in a manger, because there was no room for Him—not
to speak of a palace—even in the common inn! The
prophecy was fulfilled, in God's good providence, as
Matthew notes; but it was not fulfilled in the way that
human imagination, working on the prophet's words,
would have devised. Is the story one that human imagination, granting it a free rein, would naturally have
devised at all for the advent of the Messiah? Here
again it is to be noted that Luke, who gives the most
detailed account of the birth at Bethlehem, has no suggestion of a connection with prophecy.

I now return by this somewhat roundabout road to
the prophecy in Is. vii. 14, with which we set out. The
Jews may not have given this prophecy a Messianic application,[1] but the Evangelist, looking back upon it with
the facts before him, rightly saw its Messianic import.
That therein he displayed a true discernment, a brief
inspection of the passage will, I think, make clear.

First recall the circumstances in which the prophecy

[1] See above, p. 125.

was given.[1] The throne of Ahaz was threatened by a
coalition of the kings of Ephraim and Syria, which had
for its object to depose Ahaz, and set up a creature of
their own, a certain son of Tabeel, in his stead. Isaiah
was sent to Ahaz to assure him that the conspiracy would
not succeed. A sign was offered to the king " either in
the depth (Sheol), or in the height above." But Ahaz,
who had designs of his own of an alliance with Assyria,
in mock humility declined the sign. Who was he, that
he should " tempt the Lord " ? The indignation of the
prophet then broke forth upon him. " Hear ye now, O
house of David, is it a small thing for you to weary men,
that ye will weary my God also ? " The Lord Himself,
the prophet announced, would give Ahaz a sign ; and,
after the king's refusal of a sign in the depths of Sheol
and the heights of heaven, we are justified in expecting
that the sign the Lord would give would be no ordinary
one. What was the sign ? I quote from the R. V.:
" Behold, a virgin shall conceive and bear a son, and
shall call his name Immanuel," etc. How are we to understand these words ?

The first point relates to the word rendered " virgin "
—the word 'almah. This word, Hebrew authorities tell
us, no doubt correctly, does not strictly mean " virgin,"
but simply a young woman of marriageable age. There
is another word—bethulah—which does express virginity in the strict sense. Even this word, it is worth

[1] Cf. Is. vii.

noticing, is once used (in Joel i. 8) of a bride lamenting over her bridegroom. The objection from the meaning of 'almah was, as we learn from Justin Martyr,[1] Origen,[2] and other fathers,[3] one urged by the Jews against the Christian interpretation of the passage from the earliest times. But it may fairly be replied now, as it was then, that, if the word does not necessarily bear this meaning of " virgin," it may, and indeed usually does, bear it. In fact, in all the six places in which, besides this passage, the word occurs in the Old Testament, it may be contended that this *is* its meaning.[4] The Septuagint renders it here by παρθένος, and even the R. V. retains the translation " virgin," while giving in the margin " maiden." It is true that the word means, as stated, a marriageable young woman; but it is not less true that in its use in the Old Testament it means an *unmarried* young woman; and we may repeat the challenge of Luther: " If a Jew or Christian can prove to me that in any passage of Scripture 'almah means ' a married woman,' I will give him 100 florins, although God alone knows where I may find them." [5]

---

[1] *Dial. with Trypho*, 43, 66–7.   [2] *Against Celsus*, i. 34.

[3] Cf. Iren. iii. 21; Tert. *Against the Jews*, 9; *Against Marcion*, iii. 13, etc.

[4] The passages are, Gen. xxiv. 43 (LXX translates παρθένος); Exod. ii. 8; Ps. lxviii. 26; Song of Sol. i. 3; vi. 8; Prov. xxx. 19. Cf. Hengstenberg, *Christology*, II, pp. 45–47. Prof. Willis Beecher says: "There is no trace of its use to denote any other than a Virgin" (*Prophets and Promise*, p. 334).

[5] Cf. Hengstenberg, II, p. 45.

This maiden, then, in the prophet's oracle, is figured (the tenses are present) as conceiving, as bearing a son, and as giving Him the name Immanuel, " God with us." Here is a sign indeed, and with it agrees the scope of the prophecy as a whole. For observe carefully, next, that the Immanuel prophecy does not end with these verses. Its refrain is heard through the next chapter in connection with the Assyrian invasions: " He shall overflow and pass through; he shall reach even to the neck; and the stretching out of his wings shall fill the breadth of thy land, O Immanuel " [1]—" Take counsel together, and it shall be brought to nought; speak the word, and it shall not stand; for *immanu El,* God is with us "; [2] till it culminates in ch. ix. 6, 7, in that magnificent prediction: " For unto us a child is born, unto us a Son is given; and the government shall be upon His shoulder; and His name shall be called Wonderful, Counsellor, Mighty God, Everlasting Father, Prince of Peace. Of the increase of His government and of peace there shall be no end, upon the throne of David, and upon His kingdom, to establish it," etc.

The import of the prophecy can now be readily grasped. The thing at stake was the perpetuity of the house and throne of David. Ahaz had refused a sign, and God now takes the matter into His own hands. And the guarantee He gives for the perpetuity of the house of David is this child Immanuel. The vision of the

[1] Is. viii. 8.   [2] Ver. 10.

prophet sweeps far beyond present events—beyond the
defeat of Syria and Ephraim; beyond even the devasta-
tions of the Assyrian invasions; and he beholds in this
Son that should be born, this child that should be given
—who can be no other than the Messianic King—the
security for the fulfilment of the promises to David, and
the hope for the future of the world.

The other elements of the prophecy fall naturally into
their places on this interpretation—even the time-ele-
ments, provided allowance is made for the character of
prophetic vision. To the prophet's view the maiden's
child is already there; is already conceived; is about to
be born; he can speak as if the period of its arrival at
the discernment of good and evil defined the limit of
this confederacy of Syria and Ephraim (ver. 14). But
again his vision stretches far beyond that limit into the
time of the Assyrian invasions, then, leaving even these
behind, sees this child of David's line, of the wonderful
names, firmly established on His throne.

Taking the prophecy in this light, we cannot, I think,
but see that Matthew's use of it is entirely justified.
The whole character of the prophecy leads us to expect
an exceptional and wonderful origin for the child that
should be born. All theories which see in this " maiden "
a person already married—e. g., Isaiah's own wife—or
one who is first to marry, then become a mother, break
on the meaning of the words and force of the context.
The idea of a peculiar birth for the Messiah does not

stand quite alone in Isaiah; it seems hinted at in Isaiah's contemporary, Micah, in the prophecy about the ruler from Bethlehem—" until the time come when she that travaileth hath brought forth." [1]   If any one chooses to think that there was some lower or nearer fulfilment, as in the distinct incident recorded in the next chapter (viii. 1–4) of the birth of a son to the prophet with a significant name,[2] accompanied with like promises of the overthrow of Syria and Ephraim, there is nothing to hinder.   But that does not fill up the meaning of *this* prophecy of Immanuel, nor did the latter ever receive its fulfilment till, as Matthew narrates, Jesus was born in Bethlehem of Judæa.

It seems a long step from the study of Old Testament prophecy in its relation to the Virgin Birth to the place of this belief in the early Church; but the transition is natural for the reason that it was chiefly by prophecy that Apologists and Church Fathers sought to establish the Messiahship of Jesus, and it was precisely on this point of the Virgin Birth that they were most keenly assailed by Jewish and heathen opponents.   The subject is one which requires investigation, for it is a main count in the opposing argument that the belief in the Virgin Birth grew up late, and did not form part of the early tradition of the Church.   I hope to convince you of the contrary.

[1] Mic. v. 3.   [2] Not this name, however.

One thing, I think, is plain at the outset. If this story of the miraculous birth is of late and gradual origin, then it is hopeless to look for any consensus about it in the Church of the earliest period. If, on the other hand, we find it, as I believe we shall, to be a firmly established and generally accepted article of faith as far back as we can trace it, then the inference is irresistible that it goes back to Apostolic times, and must have been believed from the first to have Apostolic authority and sanction. To see this, you have only, I think, to put yourself in the situation of the Church of that period,—to remember that even at the close of the first century the Church was not yet 70 years distant from the Lord's crucifixion,—that the Gospels containing these narratives had already appeared, and been received, some 30 years earlier than this,—that during this period the Church had a continuous history, and successions of office-bearers,[1] as well acquainted with the facts of its past, as we are with the prominent events in our respective Churches during the last half-century, or longer, —that the Churches of Apostolic and post-Apostolic times were in constant communication with each other, —that the Apostolic Churches, especially, felt a responsibility for the maintenance of a pure Apostolic tradition,[2]—you have only, I say, to put yourself in this situation to see the impossibility of foisting a late and baseless legend on these Churches, so as to secure

[1] Cf. II Tim. ii. 21.   [2] Cf. Tertullian, *On Prescription*, 36.

general acceptance of it, and how vital it is for those who hold the narratives to be late and legendary to show that the Church was not at first, or for long, agreed in this belief. That, however, I am persuaded, it is impossible for them to do. I feel that I am on peculiarly sure ground here, and take up the challenge offered us with all confidence.

First, generally, as against all assertions of a late acceptance of this doctrine, I lay down this position—the character of which I have already outlined—that, *apart from the Ebionites, or narrower section of Jewish Christians, and a few Gnostic sects, no body of Christians in early times is known to have existed who did not accept as part of their faith the birth of Jesus from the Virgin Mary*: while, on the other hand, we have the amplest evidence that *this belief was part of the general faith of the Church.* I shall give the proof immediately; but, for the general fact, I do not need to go beyond the admission of leading impugners of the doctrine themselves. Here is one testimony from Prof. Harnack. " It is certain," says this authority, " that already in the middle of the second century, and probably soon after its beginning, the birth of Jesus from the Holy Ghost and the Virgin Mary formed an established part of the Church tradition." [1] Another is from an able Ritschlian writer, A. Hering, who, in a long article on the subject, says: " It is a constant, and we may truly

[1] *Das apostol. Glaubensbekenntniss*, p. 24.

say, universal element in the doctrinal tradition of the post-Apostolic age, for of any important or fruitful opposition to it, the history of doctrine knows nothing." " The opposition to it," he adds, " was limited to the narrow circle of the Jewish Ebionites," and " even among the Jewish Christians the denial was not general, for the Nazarenes confessed the Virgin Birth of the Messiah, and at a later time even the remains of the old Ebionites appear to have shared this view." [1] This is what I have been affirming.

Let us now look more closely at the facts. I begin with the *opposition* to the belief.

1. The characteristics of the *Ebionites* (the " Pharisaic Ebionites," as some name them)—the narrow, legal, anti-Pauline section of the Jewish Christians —I formerly described to you. These rejected the supernatural birth. Regarding Jesus as a mere man, chosen to be Messiah for His legal piety, they affirmed Him to be naturally born of Joseph and Mary,[2] and cut out from their Gospel the chapters which narrate His birth from the Virgin.[3] Their action, we must admit, was perfectly logical. An Ebionitic Christ has no need of a supernatural origin. As we saw, however, this extreme party in no way represented the whole of Jewish

[1] *Zeitschrift für Theol. und Kirche*, V, p. 67.

[2] Cf. Justin, *Dial.*, 48; Iren. i. 26; Tert., *On Flesh of Christ*, 14; Euseb. iii. 27. On Christ's acceptance for His piety, cf. Hippol. vii. 22.

[3] See above, pp. 44–5.

Christianity. What we must regard as the main body of Jewish Christians—those whom Jerome calls the Nazarenes—were at one with the general mind of the Church in their acceptance of the Virgin Birth.

2. The other exception to the general acceptance of this doctrine is in certain of the *Gnostic* sects. These never were regarded as properly within the Church at all. Denying, as they usually did, the true humanity of Christ, or else, like Cerinthus, representing the earthly Jesus as a man on whom the heavenly Christ descended at the Baptism, the Gnostics were again logically bound to deny the supernatural birth, though it is a strong testimony to the hold of this belief upon the Church that, in fact, only certain of the sects—and these not the most influential—seem to have done so. It is attested, e. g., that the Valentinians,[1] the followers of Basilides,[2] some even of the *Docetæ* [3] (deniers of the real humanity), and others,[4] accepted in a fashion of their own the Virgin Birth. Those who did reject it were Cerinthus, spoken of already in connection with the Apostle John, the Carpocratians, one of the most licentious of the Gnostic sects, some of the Ophites, who revelled in a crude mythology, and Marcion, who, as I told you before, mutilated the Gospel of Luke in the interest of his theory, and made Jesus descend directly

[1] Hippol. vi. 30.
[2] *Ibid.*, vii. 14.
[3] viii. 2.
[4] Iren. xi. 3.

from heaven to Capernaum.[1] To these fantastic specu-
lators the Fathers of the time, in name of the Church,
with one voice, opposed themselves.

I come now to the main stream of tradition and belief
in the Church of the second century, and here the broad
fact that meets us—in harmony with all that has been
said—is the universal acceptance of the Virgin Birth,
not simply as a truth believed in, but as an article of the
highest doctrinal importance, by the acceptance of which
a genuine Christianity is distinguished from a spurious.
The testimony I have to produce is a single and undi-
vided one; you can judge of its weight for yourselves
when I set it before you.

1. The first witness I adduce is naturally *the Apostles'
Creed* itself in its older form and varying ecclesiastical
shapes. The history of this ancient symbol is now tolerably well known, thanks largely to the recent controversy
in Germany on the subject; and it is interesting to have
it acknowledged by a writer already quoted, A. Hering,
that it was, at bottom, about this article of the Virgin
Birth that the controversy turned.[2] The Apostles' Creed,
it is commonly recognised, is simply an expansion or en-
largement of the older baptismal confession—that, Harnack says, is the thing to be held fast [3]—and the oldest

---

[1] See above, p. 47.
[2] *Zeitschrift für Theol. und Kirche*, V, p. 58.
[3] *Op. cit.*, p. 19.

form in which it is known to us—the Old Roman form
—is dated by Harnack about 140 A. D.,[1] by Zahn about
120, and by Kattenbusch, a high authority, about 100.[2]
But in the forefront of this Old Roman Creed stands,
without dispute, the article: " Who was born of the Holy
Ghost and the Virgin Mary."

The Old Roman Creed, however, is not the whole.
We have very full information as to the forms which
these baptismal confessions, embodying the " Rule of
Faith," as it came to be called, assumed in the different
Churches: in Gaul, Carthage, Alexandria, and other
places; and their testimony on this point is again absolutely consentient. The importance of this is seen when
we remember that it was on this constant and steadfast
tradition of the Churches as embodied in the " Rule of
Faith," that the Fathers were wont to fall back in their
controversies with the Gnostics and others. I give you
two illustrations—one from Irenæus, and one from Tertullian. *Irenæus* (c. 175), in Gaul, thus writes: " The
Church, though dispersed throughout the whole world,
even to the ends of the earth, has received from the
Apostles and their disciples this faith. [She believes] in
One God, the Father Almighty, Maker of heaven and
earth . . . and in One Christ Jesus, the Son of God,
who became incarnate for our salvation; and in the

---

[1] *Hist. of Dogma*, II, 21. Elsewhere, "before the middle of the
2d century" (I, p. 157), "not before Hermas, about 135" (I, p.
159), etc.

[2] Cf. Schmiedel, article "Ministry" in *Ency. Bib.*, III, p. 3122.

Holy Spirit, who proclaimed through the prophets the dispensations of God, and the advent, and the birth from a Virgin, and the passion, and the resurrection from the dead,[1] etc. He enumerates as uniting in this faith the Churches of Germany, Spain, Gaul, the East, Egypt, Libya, etc. *Tertullian*, of Carthage, a few years later, declares the unity of the Churches in Africa with the Church of Rome in their confession of faith, including the article of the Virgin Birth,[2] and elsewhere gives the contents of the common Confession. " The Rule of Faith," he says, " is altogether one, sole, immovable, and irreformable—namely, to believe in One God Almighty, the Maker of the world, and His Son, Jesus Christ, born of the Virgin Mary," etc.[3]

2. When we pass from the united testimony of the " Rule of Faith " (or Apostles' Creed) to individual witnesses, we get fresh confirmation of the universality and constancy of this belief in the Virgin Birth. One of the oldest writers is *Ignatius*, about 110 A.D.—a few years after the death of the Apostle John—and no one will question the stress which Ignatius lays on the birth from the Virgin. " We find," Harnack says, " that Ignatius has freely reproduced a *Kerugma* [or preaching] of Christ, which seems, in essentials, to be of a fairly definite historical character, and which contained, *inter*

---

[1] Iren. i. 10; cf. iii. 4; iv. 35.

[2] *On Prescription*, 36.

[3] *Veiling of Virgins*, 1; cf. *On Prescription*, 13; *Against Praxeas*, 2.

alia, the Virgin Birth, Pontius Pilate," [1] etc.   He speaks
of the birth from the Virgin as one of " the three mysteries of renown, wrought in the silence of God." [2]
" Stop your ears," he says to the Trallians, " when any
one speaks to you at variance with Jesus Christ, who
was descended from David, and was also of Mary "; [3]
and to the Ephesians: " For our God, Jesus Christ, was,
according to the appointment of God, conceived in the
womb of Mary, of the seed of David, but by the Holy
Ghost." [4]

In face of such a testimony, no one, I think, can mis-
construe the fact that the Virgin Birth does not happen
to be mentioned in the brief Epistle of Polycarp (contemporary of Ignatius), in Hermas,[5] or in Barnabas.
Ignatius may be fairly held to speak for the sub-Apostolic age.

After Ignatius we come to the Apologists; and here
we find the earliest of these, *Aristides,* about 125 A.D.,
a Syriac translation of whose Apology has recently been
recovered, giving this as part of the general Christian
faith that the Son of God " from a Hebrew Virgin took
and clad Himself with flesh." Dr. Rendel Harris, who
edits the Apology, says: " Everything that we know of

---

[1] *The Apostles' Creed,* p. 59 (E. T.).   (Distinct from *Das apostol.
Glaubensbekenntniss.*)

[2] *Ep. to Ephesians,* 19.

[3] *To Trallians,* 9.

[4] *To Ephesians,* 18.

[5] Some, however, find an allusion in Hermas.

the dogmatics of the early part of the second century agrees with the belief that, at that period, the virginity of Mary was a part of the formulated Christian belief."[1]

A more important witness is *Justin Martyr*, who wrote about the middle of the century, though his life extends through the whole earlier part of it.   In his *Apology* Justin comes back again and again to the Virgin Birth, defending it from the objections of pagans,[2] and in his long *Dialogue with Trypho*, it forms one of the leading topics of discussion with the Jew.[3]   The references in Justin show that he was well acquainted with Matthew and Luke, including the early chapters.[4] We are not surprised, therefore, to find these Gospels, with the narratives of the miraculous birth, included in the *Diatessaron*, or Harmony of the Gospels, drawn up by his disciple Tatian.[5]

The testimony of the Catholic Fathers has been already referred to, and will be further spoken of below.

3. I have more than once referred to the attacks of Jews and pagans on this article of faith.[6]   I may here allude to them again as themselves furnishing important evidence of the place which this belief had in the faith of the early Church.   In Justin's argument, the belief

---

[1] *Apology*, p. 25 (in *Texts and Studies*, 1891).

[2] *I Apol.*, 21, 31, 33, 46, 54, 63, 64, etc

[3] *Dial.*, 23, 43, 66, 84, etc.

[4] Cf. Westcott, *Canon*, pp. 92–3.

[5] See above, p. 42.

[6] Cf. above, pp. 5, 95.

is always assumed, on both sides, as an unquestioned
article of the faith of Christians. The *Dialogue with
Trypho,* however, has mainly to do with the fulfilment
of prophecy, and does not touch on those baser calumnies
which, as we know from Celsus, were already in circulation in the second century among the Jews, and were
probably far older—calumnies attributing to Jesus an
illegitimate origin, through the union of his mother
(thus in Celsus [1]) with a soldier named Panthera. The
matured form of these fables is seen in the late Jewish
work *Tol'doth Jeschu*—a work, probably, of the eleventh
century.[2] These wretched slanders, which, however,
Voltaire served up as veracious history, averring the
Tol'doth Jeschu to be a work of the first century,[3] and
which a writer like Haeckel in our own time is not
ashamed to reproduce,[4] but which are repudiated by
every reputable authority, are still, in their own perverted way, a witness to the belief of the Church in
all ages in Christ's supernatural birth. As Origen re-
torts [5]—the Jew of Celsus has nothing to tell against
Jesus which is not based on the narratives of the Gospels. The name Panthera itself—or in its later Jewish

---

[1] Origen, *Against Celsus,* i. 32.

[2] On this work, and the whole subject, see especially Loofs, *Anti-
Haeckel,* p. 44. Cf. also Baring-Gould, *Lost and Hostile Gospels.* chs.
iii, iv.

[3] *Examen de Bolingbroke,* ch. x. 11.

[4] *Riddle of Universe,* ch. xviii.

[5] *Against Celsus,* ii. 13.

shape, Pandira—is probably nothing more than a corruption of παρθένος, a Virgin.[1] The unanimity and firmness with which the belief was held fast in face of the argument and ridicule of Jewish and heathen opponents only shows again how deeply rooted that belief must have been.

It is not, however, in their disputes with Jews and pagans, so much as in their controversies with the Gnostics, that we see most convincingly how tenaciously the Fathers of the early Church held to the fact of the birth from the Virgin, and what high value, in a doctrinal respect, they placed upon it. We have already seen that it was the fewest number even of the Gnostics who ventured to reject this doctrine; but it is now to be observed that, even where, in deference to tradition, they did not reject it in words, they subverted it, as was inevitable, in fact, by making the birth from Mary a more or less unreal and phantasmal affair.[2] Against all such perversions the Fathers firmly set themselves—maintaining, on the one hand, that Jesus had truly come in the flesh, and was of the real substance of Mary,[3] but, on the other, that He was supernaturally born, and had a superhuman dignity and pre-eminence as a new beginning in humanity. He came, as Tertullian said,

[1] Cf. Swete, *Apostles' Creed*, p. 47.

[2] Iren. i. 7; iii. 22; Tert., *Flesh of Christ*, 15, etc.; *Against Val.*, 27; Hippol. vi. 30; x. 12, etc.

[3] Iren. iii. 19, 22; Tert., *Flesh of Christ*, 15, etc.

" to consecrate a new order of birth." [1]   The doctrine of the Virgin Birth was thus brought into practical use as guaranteeing, on the one side, the true humanity, but not less, on the other, the divine Sonship of Jesus.

This is the ground taken up by Irenæus, by Tertullian, by Clement of Alexandria, by Hippolytus, by Origen—by *all* who discuss the subject. Gnosticism, with its denial, or explaining away, of the Virgin Birth, Irenæus speaks of as a " system which neither the prophets announced, nor the Lord taught, nor the Apostles delivered." [2]   Two of the headings of his chapters are: " Jesus Christ was not a mere man begotten from Joseph in the ordinary course of nature, but was very God, begotten of the Father Most High, and very man, born of the Virgin "—" Christ assumed human flesh, conceived and born of the Virgin." [3]   Here is a characteristic passage from Tertullian. I do not ask you to accept the reasoning, but only to note the belief that is in the heart of it. " It was not fit," he says, " that the Son of God should be born of a human father's seed, lest, if He were wholly the Son of Man, He should fail to be also the Son of God. . . . In order, therefore, that He who was already the Son of God—of God the Father's seed, i. e., the Spirit—might also be the Son of Man, He only wanted to assume flesh, of the flesh of man, without the seed of a man; for the seed

Flesh of Christ, 9.   [2] Iren. i. 8.
[3] iii. 19, 22.

of a man was unnecessary for One who had the seed of God." [1]   I inflict upon you only one other sentence from Origen, interesting because of the appeal the Apologist makes to the world's knowledge of the Christian doctrine.   " Moreover," he says, " since he [Celsus] frequently calls the Christian doctrine a secret system, we must confute him on this point also, since almost the entire world is better acquainted with what Christians preach than with the favourite opinions of philosophers. For who is ignorant of the statement that Jesus was born of a Virgin, and that He was crucified, and that His resurrection is an article of faith ? " [2] etc.

In the light of all that has been advanced, there can be little doubt, I think, in any candid mind, as to the place held by this article of faith in the esteem of the early Church. There can, I should say, be nearly as little hesitation as to the inference to be drawn from so remarkable a consensus as to the solid Apostolic basis of the doctrine itself. Others judge differently. To a similar marshalling of evidence Lobstein thinks it sufficient to reply : " The common source of all this patristic testimony is the double tradition contained in the Gospels of Matthew and Luke : the *consensus* so urgently insisted upon is accounted for by the fact that all the writers quoted went back to two of our Gospels." [3]   I might answer (1) that I am not so sure that all these

[1] *Flesh of Christ*, 18.   [2] *Against Celsus*, i. 7.
[3] *The Virgin Birth*, Pref. to Eng. Trans.

writers went back *only* to the written Gospels, for the essence of the argument of the Fathers in their controversy with those who rejected or wrested the meaning of the Gospels was an appeal to a tradition of the Church, presumed to be independent of the Scriptures; or ask (2) how the " double tradition " is itself to be accounted for, since, if " double," it must go back to some yet earlier fact or belief; or point out (3) that it is surely no slight matter that, by admission, we *have* a " double tradition," and the witness of " two of our Gospels." But I would specially urge, as I did before, that the fundamental problem is ignored of how these Gospels, if the stories were untrue, came to obtain the universal and unquestioning acceptance they did from the Church of the time. I contend again that this problem is insoluble on the hypothesis that the narratives are baseless legends; that they had no known backing of truth behind them. We shall see this better when we come, as we do in the next lecture, to consider the rival legendary theories.

LECTURE VI

I HAVE said that it is not enough for the objector to
deny the historical character of the narratives of the
Virgin Birth. He must find some method of explaining
how the narratives come to be there. It will be my task
in this lecture to consider the rival explanations of these
narratives offered by those who reject the historical fact.

It is plain that, if the Virgin Birth is not a reality,
the story of it can only be myth, legend, or invention—
a myth somehow hit upon independently by two of the
Evangelists. There are two ways open to us, accordingly, of establishing the Lord's birth from the Virgin
—first, by exhibiting the direct evidence for the fact,
which is what I have been trying to do; and, second, by
showing the untenableness of the rival explanations,
which is what I am about to attempt. My task is not
an easy one, if only from the number of the theories,
and the fact that they are, for the most part, irrecon-
cilably at variance with each other; though there is the
compensating advantage that one has seldom to travel
further for the confutation of any one of these theories

151

than simply the objections urged against it by the rest. This is a point in our favour. The Church, at least, it can fairly be pleaded, has always had one consistent story to tell on the Lord's birth. The theories that oppose the Virgin Birth are legion, and in entire disagreement with each other. As in the trial of Jesus before the Sanhedrim, " neither so did their witness agree together." [1]

There are certain considerations which may be urged against the class of mythical theories generally, as: (1) that the time is wanting for the myth to grow up—for we have never to forget that the Gospels we are dealing with had their origin at latest by 70 or 80 A.D. ; (2) that most of the theories can be shown to be inherently impossible, or impossible in the circumstances—as when, e. g., parallels are sought in Buddhism; and (3) not least, even assuming it possible for the myth to originate, there is the difficulty of showing how it could ever have got access to Jewish minds, and obtained general acceptance. I mention these things here only that you may keep their application before your minds in the subsequent discussion.

There are, as we have already seen, two main groups of theories on this subject—one which seeks the origin of the alleged myth on *Jewish* soil, and excludes Gentile influences; the other, now the more prevalent, which

[1] Mark xiv. 59.

seeks to explain the rise of the myth from *Gentile* sources, and either excludes Jewish influences altogether, or assigns to them a quite subordinate *rôle*. The conflict of these two classes of theories affords a preliminary illustration of what I have above said about radical disagreement. I may give one or two samples. Harnack, like Lobstein, insists quite positively that " the belief that Jesus was born of a Virgin sprang from Is. vii. 14." " It is in point of method," he says, " not permissible to stray so far [as in the Gentile theories], when we have near at hand such a complete explanation as Is. vii. 14." [1] Now hear the other side. " This at any rate," says Soltau, " is clear: the belief in the Virgin Birth of Jesus could not have originated in Palestine; anyhow, it could never have taken its rise in Jewish circles. . . . The idea that the Holy Spirit begat Jesus can have no other than a Hellenic origin. . . . The Virgin Birth, in particular, was certainly not first inferred from the words of the prophet Isaiah in vii. 14." [2] In the same strain writes Dr. Cheyne: " It has been too much overlooked that the mistranslation of *ha-'almah* in the LXX is so far from accounting for the belief in the Virgin Birth of Christ that it requires to be explained itself," [3] and he finds the explanation, as he does that of the Virgin Birth, in Babylonian influence.

---

[1] *Hist. of Dogma,* I, p. 100.

[2] *Geburtsgeschichte,* pp. 23–5 (E. T., pp. 47, 48, 51).

[3] *Bible Problems,* p. 193.

Schmiedel, Usener, and others, express themselves, as
we shall see later, with like decision. But now the advocates of the Gentile origin have the heavy guns of Harnack and his friends turned upon them. " The conjecture of Usener," says Harnack, " that the idea of
the birth from a Virgin is a heathen myth which was
received by the Christians, contradicts the entire earliest
development of Christian tradition, which is free from
heathen myths, so far as these had not already been
received by wide circles of Jews (above all certain
Babylonian and Persian myths), which in the case of
that idea is not demonstrable." [1] We shall hear more
of this also as we proceed. The two groups of views are
thus in direct opposition. One confutes the other. Under each head are numerous sub-theories—all equally
irreconcilable with each other.

I have already sought to show the difficulties which
attach to the theory of an origin of the idea of the
Virgin Birth on Jewish soil, or from Is. vii. 14. Lobstein thinks, indeed, that nothing was easier than to pass
from the case of children *promised* by God—e. g., Isaac
—to the idea of birth from a Virgin.[2] But it is precisely the taking of this remarkable step which is so
difficult to explain. The severely monotheistic Jewish
idea of God tended to separate Him from the world as
heathen conceptions of God did not; and it was the un-

[1] *Hist. of Dogma*, I, p. 100. Cf. Lobstein, pp. 76, 128.
[2] *Op. cit.*, p. 71.

likeliest thing to enter a Jewish mind that God's direct
agency would be employed in causing a Jewish maiden
to become a mother. Some, I know, have seen in the
story the influence of an ascetic motive, such as, e. g.,
had made itself felt among the Essenes.[1] Lobstein,
however, rightly rejects the idea that any ascetic motive
was active here, and points out that there is not the
slightest trace of such in the narrative, or in the life of
Jesus.[2] It is to be remembered that the one sect which
did reject the Virgin Birth was a Jewish one — the
Ebionites. It is not on soil of this description, therefore, that we can look for the development of a myth of
the Virgin Birth.

Without further dwelling on considerations which
have been sufficiently emphasised, I shall now endeavour
to illustrate the difficulties which arise in seeking to
carry through a theory of the Jewish origin of this supposed myth by looking at some of the special forms
which the theory assumes.

The general conception in these theories is something
like this. At the basis of the whole is the powerful impression made by Jesus on His disciples, which led them
to accept Him as Son of God and Messiah. This being
given, the need was soon felt of explaining the origin
and the secret of the spiritual power of One so remark-

[1] Thus Keim, *Jesus of Nazara*, II, p. 59.
[2] *Op. cit.*, p. 130.

able. Hence the rise of different modes of explanation.
1. The first and simplest was that suggested by the narrative of *the Baptism.* The descent of the Spirit on
Jesus at His baptism constituted Him the " Son of
God " in the theocratic sense. For our present purpose
this may be set aside. 2. A second and more realistic
explanation was the *naïve* one of an actual paternity of
God—a physical filiation—such as is alleged to be given
the narratives of the *supernatural birth* in Matthew and
Luke. This is supposed to have had its germ in a misunderstanding of Is. vii. 14. 3. The third and highest
form of explanation was that of a *metaphysical pre-
existence,* and descent into humanity, such as we find
in Paul and John. Lobstein gives the stages a little
differently: 1. The theocratic conception—Jesus the
Messiah; 2. The metaphysical; and 3. The miraculous
birth.[1]

So far everything seems plain, though, of course, the
vital element of proof is wanting that the narrative of
the Virgin Birth is myth at all. But, waiving meanwhile other objections, I would fix attention on one
crucial question: At what point in the development of
early Christianity is this myth of the Virgin Birth supposed to come in ?

1. Looking to the narratives themselves, the first and

---

[1] *Op. cit.,* pp. 59*ff.* Cf. Keim, and Godet's criticism in his *Com.
on Luke,* I, pp. 157*ff.* Bornemann gives yet another form: 1.
Supernatural birth; 2. Pre-existence theory (Paul); 3. Incarnation
of Logos (John), (*Unterricht,* p. 92).

most natural thing to say would be that the myth must come in *early*. The narratives, as we saw, are extremely primitive and *naïve* in idea and structure. They betray not the slightest trace of the influence of Paul or John. The language and style of Luke, who is taken to be the later of the two writers, carry us back into Jewish-Christian circles of the most primitive type. The myth, therefore, it would seem, represents the earliest stage in the formation of a Christology. It must be prior to Paul's Christological doctrine—so early at least as to be absolutely uninfluenced by the latter. This, I say, is the simplest and most natural form of the theory, but you must see at once the immense difficulty in which it lands us. The difficulty is the manifest impossibility of explaining the rise and acceptance of such a myth within so short an interval as, say, 25 or 30 years after the death of Christ. During the greater part of this time the Apostles, or most of them, were still at Jerusalem. In any case, if such a myth was in process of formation, and was taking root in the convictions of any important section of the Church, it is impossible that Paul and other early preachers of the Gospel should not have heard of it. But it is a leading point in the case of the opponents that Paul and the other Apostles and teachers of that period did *not* know of it. To the general difficulty of explaining how such a myth should arise on Jewish soil at all, there is added, in this form of the theory, an insuperable difficulty of time.

2. This first form of the theory, therefore, which puts
the origin of the myth of the Virgin Birth in the primitive period, *before* the preaching of Paul, has to be
abandoned. Lobstein does abandon it, and, driven
by the difficulty I have mentioned, takes the origin of
this myth to be, not even the second stage—the " theocratic " being the first—but the *third* stage in the development, after the " metaphysical." The idea of the
Virgin Birth comes in, in his view, between Paul and
John. " Between the primitive outlook of popular Messianic belief," he says, " and the point reached by specu-
lative thought in the Prologue to the Fourth Gospel, we
may place the tradition which has been preserved in the
double narrative of the Protevangel." [1] Lobstein, indeed, is not entirely consistent in this view, for in another place he says: " It is by no means proved that the
origin of the latter solution [the Virgin Birth] is subsequent to the elaboration of the theory of the pre-existence, for Matthew and Luke only received and set down
in writing far older traditions." [2] But then, if this is
so, we are back to a date of origin for this story in its
twofold form earlier than the Epistles of Paul, i. e.,
within less than 20 years from the Crucifixion—a form
of theory we have just seen to be inadmissible. If " far

---

[1] *Op. cit.*, p. 65.

[2] p. 78; cf. p. 26. This, of course, if accepted, would dispose of
Lobstein's other assertion (see above, p. 149), that the Church Fathers
of the 2d century must have drawn all their knowledge from our
Gospels.

older traditions " of the Virgin Birth existed, how explain their origin, or the alleged ignorance of the Apostles about them ?

But now take the other view, that the myth of the Virgin Birth originated not earlier than, but *concurrently with*, or possibly subsequent to, the Pauline " metaphysical " theory, as, in Lobstein's words, " a more concrete and realistic " solution of " the Christological problem," [1] are we free from difficulties ? I fear not. The difficulties only thicken.

(1) To begin with, the question has to be asked: Do myths arise as the solution of " Christological," or of any kind of problems ? If they do, I can only say I have never heard of them. Prof. Lobstein really cannot have it both ways. He cannot both have this myth growing up before Paul's teaching, and at the same time growing up along with it, or after it; and he cannot both have it as " a fruit of popular imagination," [2] " the fruit of religious feeling, the echo of Christian experience, the poetic and popular expression of an affirmation of faith," [3] a " pastoral epic of Christianity," [4] which are some of his ways of describing it, and, at the same time, a somewhat advanced " explanatory formula, an attempt to solve the Christological problem," [5] which is his other account of it. Poetry is one thing; explanatory formulas, reflective attempts at the solution

[1] pp. 66, 72.   [2] p. 72.   [3] p. 96.
[5] p. 77.   [5] p. 72.

of " problems," are another kind of thing altogether.
The theory is here incoherent. If this, which Lobstein
calls " the tradition consecrated by our Gospels, the myth
with which faith in the divine Sonship of Jesus is
poetically invested," [1] is something consciously framed
for " explanatory " purposes, then it is no poetic myth
at all : it is a fruit, not of imagination, but of invention.
If, on the other hand, Lobstein's meaning is that the
narratives in Matthew and Luke are simply given forth
as " poetry," expressions of ideas poetically conceived,
not as reality, they are still, in that case, neither
" myths " nor " explanatory formulas " : moreover,
such an explanation conflicts in the clearest way with
the nature of the narratives, for these, unquestionably,
are given forth, not as poetic fictions, but as facts to be
seriously believed.[2]

(2) Lobstein, however, has other difficulties to face,
if he adheres to his contention that his poetic-explana-
tory " myth " originated concurrently with Paul's
" metaphysical " theory, and ran its course independently of it. It is assumed by Lobstein, as it was by
Keim, that the idea of the supernatural birth, and Paul's
pre-existence doctrine, are conceptions which exclude
each other. This, of course, is not the case ; but whether
they are, or are not, compatible, how are we to explain

---

[1] p. 75. Cf. p. 77: "The dogma or myth inspired by religious
faith, created by popular imagination." "Dogma" or "myth"!

[2] Cf. the remarks on this point in Sweet's *Birth and Infancy of
Jesus Christ*, pp. 104–5.

their development side by side without mutual contact or influence ? It is too often forgotten that Paul's doctrine was not a private speculation of the Apostle's, but, as his Epistles show, the common doctrine of the Church. The Strassburg theologian Reuss may be quoted on this point. " We may here observe," he says, " that the writings of Paul, which carry us back, so to speak, into the very cradle of the Church, contain nothing to indicate that their Christological doctrine, so different from that of common Ebionitism, was regarded as an innovation, or gave rise to any disputations at the time of its first appearance." [1] This doctrine, then, could not but have been known to the originators of the myth of the supernatural birth. On the other hand, the growing myth must already by Paul's time have assumed a tolerably developed form. It rested, Lobstein has told us, on " far older tradition," and was accessible to Paul's companion Luke, who thought so much of it, and was so little conscious of contradiction to Paul's doctrine in it, that he put it in the forefront of his Gospel. It could not, therefore, be kept wholly from the knowledge of Paul. This paradox is so glaring that even Lobstein does not attempt to defend it. He allows that perhaps Paul *did* know of the story, but it had no interest for him : " he did not feel the need of seeking any subsidiary solution." [2] This, however, is a large, and, as

[1] *Hist. of Christ. Theol.*, I, p. 397 (E. T.).
[2] *Op. cit.*, p. 65.

we shall see, untenable assumption; and really gives up
the assertion, on which so much is based, that Paul was
wholly ignorant of the Virgin Birth.

(3) But even yet Lobstein is not at the end of his
troubles. The time difficulty comes back, and the critics
are not slow to point out that, even with the extension
of the period for the formation of the myth to Paul's
time, we are still barely 30 years from the origin of the
Church, and that a myth so fully formed and complex
could not grow up and find acceptance in that brief
space—least of all in a Church in which Apostles and
disciples of the first generation, including relatives of
Christ Himself (e. g., James the Lord's brother) were
yet present. Is it conceivable that myths so baseless,
and, *if* myths, so compromising to Mary's honour,
should find admission into such communities? There is
but one escape from the difficulty. We must push down
the formation of the myth later still—must put it, as
Keim did, earlier,[1] as Pfleiderer, Soltau, Usener, and
many others do now, *after* Paul, and even after John,
with his Logos doctrine. I only remark here that the
rock on which this form of hypothesis infallibly splits
is the date of the Gospels. It can only be defended by
the help of theories of the late origin and wholesale interpolation of the records which no sound criticism can
justify.

The theory of a purely Jewish origin of the myth

[1] *Jesus of Nazara*, II, p. 45.

must, therefore, with consent of the newer scholars, be
definitely surrendered. If this is given up, it is unnecessary to delay on theories of a more mixed kind—theories,
e. g., like Mr. F. C. Conybeare's, that the germ of the
idea of the Virgin Birth is to be found in the allegor-
isings of Philo.[1] He will be a skilful person who can
discern any trace of Philonic influence in the narratives
of either Matthew or Luke.

I turn, then, as a next step, to theories of a purely
Gentile origin for the alleged myth of the Virgin Birth.
Let me, at the risk of repetition, give you one or two
further examples of the grounds on which this new
method is adopted, that we may have the whole case
clearly before us. " Here," says Usener, in his article
" Nativity " in the *Encyclopædia Biblica*, " we unquestionably enter the circle of pagan ideas." " However
freely the Old Testament may speak of sons of God in
the figurative sense," says Schmiedel, in his article
" Mary " in the same work, " the loftiness of the Old
Testament conception of God precludes the supposition
of physical Sonship. . . . Nor would Is. vii. 14 have
been sufficient to account for the origin of such a doctrine unless the doctrine had commended itself on its
own merits. The passage was adduced only as an afterthought, in confirmation. . . . Thus the origin of the

[1] See Machen. *Princeton Theol. Rev.*, Jan., 1906, p. 72. Cf. Gore,
Dissertations, p. 61.

idea of a Virgin Birth is to be sought for in Gentile
Christian circles." "It has long been seen," says
Gunkel, "that the representation [in Luke] is quite
foreign to pure Judaism : the Judaism which comes from
the Old Testament, it is rightly said, knows of a miraculous creation (*Erschaffung*) of the child, but not of a
miraculous begetting through a divine factor." [1]   He
instances Gen. vi. as showing the horror at the idea of
a mingling of the sons of God with men.   You observe
how decisively, in all these writers, the idea of a Jewish
origin is set aside.

It is to be owned that, in this new type of theory, we
seem, at first sight, to be on more hopeful ground.   On
heathen soil the line between gods and men is ever a
wavering one : there is a freer mingling of the two orders.
In heathenism, accordingly, there is a tendency, which
the Jews, with their loftier monotheism, did not so
strongly share, to seek a godlike origin for godlike or
distinguished men.   The greatness of a hero is explained
by the presence of a divine element in him ; then a cause
is sought for this in some theory of origin, or incarnation, or indwelling of a divine genius.   As forms of this
tendency, you have such things in heathenism as the
raising of kings and heroes to divine rank—*apotheosis*
—as in the deification of the Roman emperors, which,
however, has nothing to do with origin ; or you have
incarnations of the gods in beasts, as in the Apis-bulls

[1] *Op. cit.,* p. 66.

of Egypt—a form of the animal worship of that country —but sometimes also incarnations in men, as in some of the Avatars of Vishnu, or the incarnations of Buddha; or, lastly, you have the coarser idea of the gods *begetting* men, as in the ordinary pagan mythology. It would be easy to show, and I shall have occasion to refer to it again, how far the so-called " incarnations " of heathenism differ in idea, in spirit, in their total meaning, from the Christian conception.[1] But I confine myself at present to the alleged analogies to the idea of the Virgin Birth on the soil of paganism. And here the question I propose to ask is the very pertinent one: Do we as a matter of fact find, or where do we find, the idea of a divine origin of heroes or great men *taking the form of a virgin birth,* analogous to what we have in the Gospels? I shall seek to answer this question by showing, first, that *nowhere* in heathenism do we find this idea; and next, that, even supposing the idea to be there (as I affirm it is not), no channels can be pointed out by which it could find entrance into the minds of the writers of the Gospels, or into the circles in which they moved, with any hope of acceptance. Impure fables we shall find in abundance, but no clear instance of a pure birth from a Virgin.

On this general question of pagan mythology, let me only premise two things:—

1. I would remark that *we need not wholly reject the*

[1] See below, pp. 216–17.

idea underlying even these heathen myths. Vile as many of them are, they have a value as showing the natural workings of men's minds—the universality of the instinct which connects superhuman greatness with a divine origin [1]—and may be construed in our favour as leading us to expect that, if there is a real incarnation, it will be accompanied by a miraculous origin. Thus far the argument of some of the Church Fathers was justified, when they pleaded that the heathen were the last who should object to the Virgin Birth, since their own mythology was full of stories of births from gods and goddesses.[2] The argument was a double-edged one, and its other edge is seen in the attempts now made to show that the Christian story is a product of the same myth-forming tendency which gave rise to the heathen fables; but it was a very natural one for the Fathers in their situation to use, and they never failed, at the same time, to denounce these pagan myths as vile tales and wholly fabulous.[3]

2. The other point I would remark upon is *the utter absence of the historical element* in these heathen myths, in which the contrast between them and the Gospel narratives is so obvious. The Gospels refer to events which happened in the immediate past—within a generation

[1] Cf. Gore, *Dissertations*, pp. 57, 59–60.

[2] Justin, *I Apol.*, 21, 22, 54, 64; *Dial.*, 70; Origen, *Against Celsus*, i. 37.

[3] Justin, *I Apol.*, 21, 64; Tert., *Apol.*, 12, 15, 21; Origen, i. 37, etc. See below, p. 169.

or two of the time when the accounts of them were published. They relate to an historical Person, and are given, as we saw, in an historical setting, with circumstantial details of name, place, date, etc. The myths with which they are brought into comparison—Greek, Roman, Babylonian, Persian—show nothing of this kind. They are on the face of them quite unhistorical —vague, formless, timeless; their origin lies far back in the dawn of time, mostly in the poetical personification of natural phenomena.[1] It is surely plain the comparison of things so different can only mislead. Parallels and analogies sought between them can only breed confusion.

With respect now to my main contention, it must strike you, I know, as strange to hear that the heathen world has no proper doctrine of a Virgin Birth—so continually are you told that pagan mythology is *full* of parallels of this kind; that " parthenogenesis was ' in the air ' "; [2] that, as Mr. Conybeare declares, " there was in that age a general belief that superhuman personages and great religious teachers were born of virgin mothers through divine agency." [3] I am confident, however, that

[1] Speaking of Mithraism, Prof. Dill says: "One great weakness of Mithraism lay precisely here — that, in place of the narrative of a divine life, instinct with human sympathy, it had only to offer the cold symbolism of a cosmic legend" (*Nero to Mar. Aurelius*, p. 622).

[2] Cf. Machen, *Princeton Theol. Review*, Jan., 1906, p. 72.

[3] *Ibid.*

I can make good my case, and only ask you not unthinkingly to accept these assertions, but to inquire with me where the proof is to be found of them.

Let us look in order at the main heads of the supposed analogy.

1. The nearest source which suggests itself for the idea of the Virgin Birth is *the popular mythological conceptions of the Greeks and Romans.* It is these chiefly—the fables of Hermes, of Dionysus, of Æsculapius, of Hercules, and the like — which the Church fathers had in view, and it is to these that writers of the standing of Holtzmann,[1] Schmiedel, and Usener bid us look. But surely to urge these coarse fables as analogies to the story of the Gospels is to show a strange blindness to the facts of the case. It is the fact that not one of these tales has to do with a Virgin Birth in the sense in which alone we are here concerned with it. The gods of whom these impure scandals are narrated are conceived of as beings like in form, parts, and passions, to mortal men. If they beget children, it is after a carnal manner. A god, inflamed by lust—Zeus is a chief sinner—surprises a maiden, and has a child by her, but it is by natural generation. There is nothing here analogous to the Virgin Birth of the Gospels. The stories

[1] Machen quotes Holtzmann: "These heathen representations of the coming of the great from above needed only to strip off their coarsely sensuous forms in order to be transferred to the world-conquering Son of God in the East" (as above).

themselves are incredibly vile.[1]   The better-minded in
Greece and Rome were ashamed of them.   Plato would
have them banished from his Republic.   They were, as
Tertullian tells us, the subjects of public ridicule.[2]   It
is a strange imagination that can suppose that these foul
tales could be taken over by the Church, and, in the
short space before the composition of our Gospels, become the inspiration of the beautiful and chaste narratives of Matthew and Luke!

Let me only give you two short quotations to show
how the early Church writers, who had to do with this
sort of argument, dealt with it, and how sensible they
were of the contrast.   " God's own Son," says Tertullian,
" was born,—but not so born as to make Him ashamed
of the name of Son or of His paternal origin.   It was
not His lot to have as His father, by incest with a sister,
or by violation of a daughter, or another's wife, a god
in the shape of a serpent, or ox, or bird, or lover, for
his vile ends transforming himself into the gold of
Danaus.   These are your divinities upon whom these
base deeds of Jupiter were done." [3]   Origen says:
" Since Celsus has introduced the Jew disputing with
Jesus, and tearing in pieces, as he imagines, the fiction
of His birth from a Virgin, comparing the Greek fables
about Danae, and Melanippe, and Auge, and Antiope,

---

[1] The stories cannot be reproduced here, but may be seen in any
good classical dictionary.

[2] *Apol.*, 15.   [3] *Ibid.*, 21.

our answer is that such language becomes a buffoon and not one who is writing in a serious tone." [1]

2. Take, next, *the fables set afloat about a philosopher like Plato, or rulers like Alexander or Augustus,* to which we are sometimes referred. In point of fact, the fathers and mothers of these personages were perfectly well known, and the flattery which ascribed to them a divine parentage deceived nobody. But even so, there is no real analogy with the Virgin Birth of the Gospels. A quite worthless fable made Plato a son of Apollo. But this was not connected with the idea of his mother being a Virgin. As Dr. Gore remarks: " None of the pagan writers cited refers to Plato as born of a Virgin." [2] Alexander, Soltau tells us, was given out by the priests to be a son of Zeus, and he himself spread abroad the anecdote " that he was not the bodily son of Philip, but "—think of it—" was begotten by a serpent cohabiting with his mother." [3] But even in this ridiculous story there is no suggestion that his mother was a Virgin. Similarly, the same authority informs us, Augustus " was careful that the fable should be widely diffused to the effect that his mother was once, while asleep in the temple of Apollo, visited by the god in the form of a serpent, and that in the tenth month afterwards he himself was born." The emperor, we are further told, " did everything in his power to promote the

---

[1] *Against Celsus*, i. 37.   [2] *Dissertations*, p. 291.
[3] *Op. cit.*, p. 23 (E. T., p. 46).

belief that Apollo was his father." [1] Here, again, there is no question of a Virgin Birth. Observe the contrast between these fables, unblushingly spread abroad by the persons immediately concerned, and by interested flatterers, and the stories in the Gospels. Where are the priests here to invent the story? Who will accuse Jesus or His disciples of acting as Alexander and Augustus are reported to have done?

3. A direct borrowing of this idea from contemporary heathenism is now accordingly largely given up, even by extreme writers like Dr. Cheyne and Gunkel, though its rejection disposes of at least three-fourths of the popular analogies. Shall we, then, look further afield—say to *the legend of Buddha*? Now, if anything in this region is certain at all, it is that Buddhism was not known, and its influence was not felt, in Christian circles, in the first century of our era. If it were necessary, I might show that the birth stories of Buddha are not found in the oldest books of the Buddhists themselves, are at least two or three centuries later than Buddha's own time, and in written form are much later still.[2] But supposing the stories to be older, and much more reliable than they are, I come back to my point that they are still not stories of birth from a Virgin. What real analogy, one may well ask, is there between the self-re-

[1] *Ibid.* (E. T., pp. 47, 77).
[2] Cf. the discussions in Kellogg's *The Light of Asia and the Light of the World*, pp. 37 ff.

strained narratives of the Gospels and the *extravaganza*
—for such it is—which relates how, when Buddha's
mother (a married woman) was asleep, she dreamed
that a white, six-tusked elephant entered her side, and
how, ten months later, a child was born? [1] It is certain,
as I have said, that the Gospel writers never heard of
Buddha, nor were the stories about him afloat in their
circles; but, if they had been, can you conceive of our
Evangelists appropriating and using them?

4. Foiled in these directions, shall we look *to Egypt*?
The Pharaohs were spoken of as Sons of Ra—without,
however, any necessary implication of peculiarity in
their birth. In one instance, however—that of Ameno-
phis III, of the 18th dynasty—it is alleged that there
is a parallel. The story seems really to have been an
expedient for legitimising the birth of the Pharaoh,
whose mother was an Asiatic, but unfortunately, like
the rest, it breaks down at the crucial point. The form
which the fable—we cannot call it a myth—took was
that the god Amon-Ra " incarnated himself in the royal
person of the husband [Thothmes IV] " of this queen,
and visited her on her couch, in order, as it is said, " that
he might be a father through her." [2] This evidently—
to say no more about it—is in no way a story of a Virgin

---

[1] Cf. Gore, *Dissertations*, pp. 58-9; Kellogg, *op. cit.*, p. 69. Buddhism, it is to be remembered knows nothing of a God or of a Holy
Spirit.

[2] Cf. Sayce, *Religions of Ancient Egypt and Babylonia*, p. 249;
Sweet, *op. cit.*, pp. 170-3.

Birth. But again, even if it were, what probability is there of the tale ever reaching or influencing Matthew or Luke?

There remains still ancient Babylonia as a possible source of origin for this supposed myth. Before, however, looking at the newer speculations on this subject, let me glance at a class of theories which, assigning *a very late date* to the rise of the idea of the Virgin Birth, are compelled, in the teeth, as we saw, of all textual authority, to assume extensive interpolation of the Gospel narratives, and *a gradual building up* of the Gospel story by successive additions. This is the general character of the theories of Schmiedel, Usener, Soltau, Völker, and others; but it will be sufficient to take that of Soltau as a type of the whole. It is a theory put forth with much assurance, yet will probably be regarded by sober judges as a species of *reductio ad absurdum* of this entire method of theorising.

According to Soltau, the idea of the conception of Jesus by the Holy Spirit did not arise till towards the end of the first century,[1] that is, till fully a quarter of a century after the Gospels containing the birth-narratives were, according to our best knowledge, already circulating in the Church![2] The conception by the Holy Ghost, however, is not the commencement, but in reality the *end* of a long development, the beginning of which,

---

[1] *Op. cit.* (E. T., p. 48).   [2] See above, pp. 58*ff.*

in the transference of the place of birth of Jesus from
Nazareth to Bethlehem, is curiously enough likewise
dated by this author at the close of the first century.[1]
It was pointed out before that Usener sees in John vii.
42 a hint of " the hidden path " by which the idea of
the birth at Bethlehem entered.[2] On this foundation,
once laid, the rest of the story was gradually built up—
the census, as a means of bringing Joseph and Mary to
Bethlehem, the visit of the shepherds, the adoration of
the Magi, etc. As yet, it is to be noted, there is nothing
of a Virgin Birth in the story. Where did these other
incidents come from? Here we arrive at Soltau's original contribution to the theory. Inscriptions, it appears,
relating to the birthday of Augustus, have been found
in Asia Minor, in which Augustus is hailed as a " god,"
and " saviour," his birthday is said to be a beginning
of " glad tidings," his reign brings " peace " and " harmony." [3] What can be clearer than that here we have
the real sources of the message and song of the angels
in Luke's story of the birth of Jesus? As if there
was the least probability that Luke ever heard of these
inscriptions, or as if he needed to go to them for
such terms as " Saviour," or " glad tidings," or such
ideas as " peace on earth," as the result of Messiah's
reign! Terms and ideas which stared him in the

[1] *Op. cit.* (E. T., p. 25). Sweet remarks that he brings the beginning and the end of the development together (p. 90).

[2] See above, p. 113.

[3] The inscriptions are given in the appendix to his book.

face in the pages of his Greek Bible! On the same
principle nearly all the writers in the New Testament
might be shown to have been diligent students of the
inscriptions of Halicarnassus, for the same ideas and
words occur in them! So the story of the Magi is
decomposed into three elements: (1) The star is suggested by what Suetonius relates of wonderful signs at
the birth of Augustus. (2) The Magi are introduced to
interpret the star. (3) The journey and the adoration
of the Magi are borrowed from the visit of the Parthian
king, Tiridates, and his Magians to the court of Nero
in 66 A.D. This journey, we are gravely informed,
" could only be explained if their act of adoration might
be transferred from the Antichrist Nero to the Messiah "! [1]   Finally, as the copestone of the structure,
there is introduced the idea of the Virgin Birth from
pagan mythology, as formerly described, with perhaps
suggestions from the births of sons of promise in the
Old Testament.[2] If, really, any one supposes that narratives so beautiful, poetic, and closely connected, could
originate in this fragmentary, haphazard fashion, he is
wellnigh past reasoning with. But the whole theory
falls like a house of cards once it is realised that the
completed Gospels were already there decades before
Soltau allows the process of development to begin!

I have already said that one thing fatal to the whole

[1] *Op. cit.*, p. 40; cf. pp. 49, 50.   [2] *Op. cit.*, pp. 41*ff.*, 49, etc.

group of theories we have been considering is the intense repugnance known to have been felt by the early Christians to everything connected with heathen idolatry. Harnack, as against Usener, reminds us " that the oldest Christianity strictly refrained from everything polytheistic and heathen," and on that account declares that " the unreasonable method of collecting from the mythology of all peoples parallels for original Church traditions, whether historical reports or legends, is valueless." " The Greek or Oriental mythology," he says, " I should leave entirely out of account; for there is no occasion to suppose that the Gentile congregations in the time up to the middle of the second century adopted, despite of their fixed principle, popular mythical representations." [1]

This difficulty is so obvious that writers like Gunkel and Cheyne now give up altogether the idea of a late borrowing of the myths from heathenism, and strike out a new line of theory, which, as it is the latest in order of appearance, is the last I shall trouble you with. The view advocated by Gunkel, Cheyne, Farnell, and others is, that the idea of the Virgin Birth was not a late borrowing from contemporary paganism, but came down by a long process of *transmission from Babylonian, Arabian, and Persian*—ultimately from Babylonian— *sources,* and had, by the time of Christ, assumed a definite shape among the Jews in a sketch of the person and

---

[1] Quoted by Machen, *Princeton Theol. Rev.,* Jan., 1906, p. 74.

attributes of the Messiah, which the early Christians had no difficulty in taking over in its entirety upon Jesus. As Gunkel says of the story of the Virgin Birth in Luke: "We see here, therefore, that a characteristically heathenish representation is taken over upon Jesus in Jewish Christianity." [1] This may be said almost to be the theory of Strauss revived, only that, instead of Old Testament prophecy furnishing the sketch of the Messiah which is applied to Jesus, it is heathen, specially Babylonian mythology, that is called upon to yield it.

An extract or two from Dr. Cheyne's book, *Bible Problems*, will show how the theory is worked out. On the basis of Arabian, Babylonian, Egyptian, and Persian parallels, Dr. Cheyne seeks to make plain how beliefs like those of the Virgin Birth of Jesus, His descent into Hades, His resurrection and ascension, arose. He remarks: "On the ground of facts supplied by archæology, it is plausible to hold that all these arose out of a pre-Christian sketch of the life, death, and exaltation of the expected Messiah, itself ultimately derived from a widely current mythic tradition respecting a solar deity." [2] Paul's statement "that Christ died and that He rose again 'according to the Scriptures,' in reality points," he thinks, "to a pre-Christian sketch of the life of Christ—partly, as we have seen—derived from widely spread, non-Jewish myths, and embodied in Jew-

[1] *Op. cit.*, p. 68.
[2] *Bible Problems*, p. 128.

ish writings." [1] A recent believing scholar, Jeremias, adopts substantially the same view, but sees in the heathen myths a case of real heathen prophecy (providentially ordained), to which the actual facts of Christ's life and death corresponded.[2]

You have now before you the very newest of these theories of the mythical origin of the idea of the Virgin Birth—a theory which, like its predecessors, lacks but one thing—*bottom*. You will perceive at once about this theory:—

1. It gives the death-stroke to all the theories that have gone before it—to the theory of a purely Jewish origin of the myth; to the theory of a late origin of the myth; to the theory of a borrowing of the myth from contemporary heathenism; to the theory of a wholesale interpolation of the documents containing it.

2. It cuts the ground from all the arguments derived from the supposed silence of Mark, Paul, John, and other New Testament writers. For this " pre-Christian sketch," including as one of its features the Virgin Birth, is supposed to be familiar to them all; Paul, in particular, is alleged to use it, if not actually to quote it as Scripture!

3. But lastly—that the new theory itself is absolutely baseless. Who ever saw, or heard of, or came on any trace of, this purely imaginary " pre-Christian sketch,"

---

[1] *Ibid.*, p. 113.
[2] In his book, *Das Babylonisches im N. T.*

based on Babylonian or other myths, which is first thought of as " plausible," then is converted into a certainty, and reasoned from as a fact! Jewish or Christian literature furnishes not a scrap of evidence for its existence. It is, what these writers would have the Virgin Birth to be, purely a fiction—a creation of the brain. The upshot, therefore, is, that this new theory, having destroyed all the others, itself shares in their downfall, and leaves the field clear for the only remaining hypothesis, which is the simplest and most satisfactory of any—*that the thing actually happened.*

This theory professes to derive the myth of the Virgin Birth from the ancient East, but I have now further to remark on it, as I did on the others, that no real case of a Virgin Birth is found in the instances brought forward. Dr. Cheyne himself will be our witness here. The term " virgin " in these old myths meant anything but what we now mean by it—meant, in fact, as he tells us, that the goddess-mother was " independent of the marriage tie," and could live a life of what we call " free love." [1] Out of this abyss of licentiousness he asks us to believe that such a representation as that of the Virgin-mother of the Gospels originated!

One proof, indeed, is brought forward by Gunkel, Cheyne, and others of these writers in support of the existence of this " pre-Christian sketch," and of their general theory of Babylonian influence. It is the repre-

[1] *Bible Problems,* p. 75.

sentation in the Apocalypse of the woman clothed with
the sun, who, with the man-child to which she gives
birth, is persecuted by the dragon (ch. xii.). Ingenious
parallels are worked out between this vision and the
narratives of the Infancy. The woman clothed with the
sun corresponds with Mary in the story of the Gospels;
the dragon, who seeks to destroy the seed of the woman,
corresponds with Herod, etc. Gunkel himself makes
the significant admission that he cannot find exactly
such a myth in any Babylonian records yet brought to
light.[1] Bousset, who combats the Babylonian theory,
thinks that the conception has an Egyptian origin.
Without, however, troubling ourselves about either
Babylonian or Egyptian elements in the imagery, we
may safely take the ground that, if a relation of dependence is to be assumed at all, it is immensely more
probable that the dependence is on the side of the Apocalypse, and not on the side of the Gospels. One can
understand how the Virgin and her divine Son could
suggest the imagery of the Apocalypse — the woman
symbolising really the Jewish Church—but not how the
grandeur of the symbolic picture could suggest the lowly
Mary. Herod's attempt on the life of Jesus might suggest the dragon, but hardly the dragon, Herod. Taken
in this light, the Apocalyptic passage is another witness
to the fact in the Gospels.

The theories of mythical origin have thus, one after

[1] *Op. cit.*, p. 196.

the other, been tried and found wanting. The Jewish theories confute the Gentile; the Gentile theories confute the Jewish; the new Babylonian theory destroys both, and itself perishes with them. The one thing that does not crumble beneath us is the historical fact.

LECTURE VII

IT is customary to seek to loosen the foundations of belief in the article of the Virgin Birth by affirming that no doctrinal interest is involved in its acceptance or non-acceptance. Faith in Jesus as the divine Redeemer—faith even in His sinlessness—is, we are told, in no way dependent on, or conditioned by, belief in His supernatural birth. The article, it is argued, may therefore safely be dropped from our creeds. It is this proposition I am to examine in the present and in the concluding lectures.

I do not deny that if it could really be shown that, as alleged, no important doctrinal interest is involved in the birth from the Virgin, it would do much to lessen our concern about the fact. Even then, as I said at the commencement, it would behove us to be cautious. We have still the record to be dealt with as an unassailable part of Scripture; we are poor judges of what may or may not be involved in so transcendent a fact as the Incarnation; and if, according to the evidence we have,

182

this was actually the way in which God brought His
Son into the world, it would be wiser for us to assume
that there *is* a doctrinal connection, whether we can see
it or not, than hastily to conclude that the Virgin Birth
is of indifference to faith. On the other hand, there
can be no doubt that it is a great help and support to
faith if we are able to see—as I think we may come to
see—that a connection between fact and doctrine *does*
exist, and that, on any showing, a miraculous origin
must be held to be involved in the constitution of such
a Person as Christ is. I freely grant that faith in the
Virgin Birth cannot be separated from the other elements of our faith in Christ. As Dr. Gore has said,
if Christ's subsequent life was miraculous, and His mode
of exit from it, " beyond all doubt this fact conditions
the evidence as to His Nativity." [1]

I have sought to show, as my argument has proceeded,
that certain things create a strong *presumption* that
there really *does* exist such a connection between fact
and doctrine as I speak of. I indicated that the very
zeal of the opponents points in this direction ; for people
do not usually waste their energies in efforts to overthrow a fact which they deem of no importance. I
dwelt also on the circumstance that, with few exceptions,
it is those who accept the Incarnation, in the full sense
of that word, who defend the Virgin Birth, while the

[1] *Dissertations*, p. 57.

attacks upon it, as a rule, come from those who reject the supernatural or miraculous aspects of Christ's life as a whole. The constancy with which these two things go together is only explicable on the assumption that there is a hidden bond between them. As the late Prof. A. B. Bruce—a man of sufficiently liberal mind—put it: " The connection is so close that few who earnestly believe in the absolute worth of Christ's Person will be disposed to deny the truth of the Evangelical narratives relating to the manner of His entrance into, and exit from, the world." [1]

There are, however, other considerations—exegetical, historical, elements in the theories of the opponents themselves—which go far to strengthen this belief that there is, and must be, a close connection between the fact of the Virgin Birth and the miracle of Christ's Personality. I may touch on these as preliminary to the direct argument.

1. *Exegetically,* it is very difficult, I think, to read the narratives in Matthew and Luke, and not see that the writers of these chapters, at least, believed that a close connection existed between the miraculous birth they recorded, and the kind of Personality Jesus was to be, the kind of life He was to lead, the work He was to do. In both of these narratives it will be observed that the conception by the Holy Ghost does not stand by itself as a simple marvel. It *grounds* something;

---

[1] *Miraculous Elements in the Gospels,* pp. 352–3.

and that something is the whole spiritual and ethical significance of the Personality of Christ. In Matthew, the angel declares to Joseph that that which is conceived by Mary is of the Holy Ghost, then goes on to direct how this wonderful child is to be named. " Thou shalt call His name Jesus; for it is He that shall save His people from their sins." [1] The miraculously born child is to be the Saviour. The language of Luke is even more significant. " The Holy Ghost shall come upon thee, and the power of the Most High shall overshadow thee; *wherefore* "—mark the illative particle—" that which is to be born shall be called holy, the Son of God." [2] Can it be doubted that, in the mind of the Evangelist, both the unique character of Jesus as " holy," and His divine Sonship in our humanity, are grounded in the fact of His miraculous conception? There is, indeed, nothing here about pre-existence: that is left for after revelation; [3] but all that is involved in His unique Sonship—for we see at once from the context that it is no mere physical filiation, but a unique relation of a higher kind that is intended—just as all that is involved in His character as " holy," and in His function as Saviour (cf. ch. ii. 11)—is regarded as conditioned by His being conceived by the Holy Ghost.

2. A like presumption of connection arises when we consider the use made of this fact of the Virgin Birth *historically*. We saw, in dealing with the witness of

---

[1] Matt. i. 21.   [2] Luke i. 35.   [3] See below, p. 209.

the early Church, how tenaciously the Fathers of that
age held by this fact in their controversies with pagans
and Gnostics—held fast by it, not simply as a piece of
tradition, not simply as a marvel, not simply as ful-
filling prophecy, but as a fact of vital *doctrinal* moment: the guarantee at once of the real humanity of
Christ, as against all docetic denial, and, not less decisively, of His superhuman dignity, as against all
Ebionitic lowering of His Person.

3. Finally, I would ask you to reflect what, *on the
theories of the opponents themselves,* is the significance
of this alleged myth of the birth of Jesus, and the principle of its origin. What gave rise to it? Mere poetic
fancy? No, we are told, but the desire to account for a
superhuman element discerned in Jesus; more specifically, to find an explanation of the divine Sonship
already ascribed to Him. Recall some of the expressions used. " The Gospel narrative of the supernatural
birth of Jesus," Lobstein says, " is an explanatory formula, an attempt to solve the Christological problem." [1]
" Viewed as the Logos in human form," says F. C.
Conybeare, " how should his birth be represented except
as from a Virgin? " [2] Soltau goes still further: " When
the Pauline and Johannine Christology, having been
translated into popular language [we should hear no
more after this of the incompatibility of the Virgin

[1] *Op. cit.,* p. 72.
[2] Quoted by Machen, as above, Jan., 1906, p. 72.

Birth with the Christologies of Paul and John], pene-
trated to the lower classes of the people, it was almost
bound to lead to the view . . . that Christ, in calling
God His Father, did not merely call Him so in the sense
in which all are children of God, but that He was even
bodily of higher derivation, of divine origin." [1] What,
I ask, does all this mean, if not that, in the view even
of these writers, the narratives of the Virgin Birth are
saturated with a doctrinal significance? The story of
the miraculous conception is doctrine translated into history. The doctrinal motive is of the very essence of it.
Its connection with the view taken of Christ's Person is
absolute. That character, surely, it does not lose, if,
refusing to regard it as myth, we accept it as history.

Still the allegation is persistently made that faith in
Jesus as Redeemer, even on the highest view we can take
of His Person and work, is *in no way dependent on belief in His supernatural birth.* The grounds on which
this is urged have already been partially before us, but
must here be more formally indicated.

1. It is argued that there is no *a priori* reason why
the *Incarnation*—assuming this to be a fact, which most
of these writers do not believe it to be—should not have
taken place in the way of ordinary parentage, but should
involve birth from a Virgin. There is no stain, it is
pointed out, in honourable marriage; and the divine Son

[1] *Op. cit.,* p. 44.

could as truly (perhaps more truly) have taken our
nature by the agency of two parents, as by means of one.
God, it is urged, does not work superfluous miracles—
these writers usually hold that He does not work any—
and there seems here no call for a departure from the
ordinary course of nature. I have already replied that
we are altogether incompetent judges of what may be
involved in so stupendous a fact as the Incarnation: that
it is, in fact, the objector, not we, who is laying down
a *priori* what God must do in the Incarnation of His
Son. But I shall try immediately to show that we can
go a great deal further than this.

2. As the Virgin Birth is thought to be not necessary
for the Incarnation, so, in the next place, it is argued
that it is not necessary for Christ's *sinlessness*. The inheritance of a sinful nature, it is said, is not precluded
by birth from a woman alone. If the mother herself
is sinful, the taint of corruption can be conveyed as
effectually through one as through two parents. Nothing, therefore, is really gained, in the interest of the
holiness of Jesus, by the exclusion of the father. The
element of truth in this objection must be acknowledged.
There was nothing, I grant, in the mere fact that Jesus
was born of a Virgin—in that fact, I mean, considered
by itself—to secure that Christ should be perfectly pure,
or free from stain of sin. In conjunction, however,
with the other factor in the miraculous birth—the conception by the Holy Ghost—we shall see afterwards that

there was involved everything to secure it. Meanwhile, let me put the question a little differently. It is objected that birth from a Virgin does not of itself secure sinlessness. But turn the matter round, and ask: Does not perfect sinlessness, on the other hand, imply a miracle in the birth? I think it will be found difficult, on reflection, to avoid an affirmative answer.

3. We are reminded, as before, that *the Apostles did not include the Virgin Birth in their teaching*—probably did not know of it—certainly did not make it the foundation of their faith, or insist on belief of it by others. All which, as we saw before, may be admitted, and still our main point stand untouched. No one alleges that the Virgin Birth was the ground of the Apostolic belief in the Incarnation; though, if the Apostles knew of it—as I think it probable they did—it no doubt contributed its share to that belief. If they did not know it at the beginning, of course they could not teach it; but it does not follow that, once it was made known to them, they would not value it, or see in it profound significance, or that they would speak slightingly of it, as our modern objectors do. A fact, as we have seen, may not be the original ground of our faith, yet may prove to be an essential implication of our faith; may not be the foundation of our faith, yet may be part of the foundation of the thing believed—of the reality itself. I refer you to what I said on this in the first lecture.[1]

[1] See above, pp. 25–26.

It is time now that I should approach this subject on its *positive* side; and here I hope to be able to convince you that the mode of our Lord's birth does stand in inseparable relation with the constitution of His Person—with His sinlessness, with His divine Sonship, with the reality of His Incarnation. It is, I know, a great demand on faith which is here made; but then it is a great subject we have to deal with. I shall develop my argument in the line of advancing from *the general fact of miracle* in the constitution of a Person such as Christ's is, to *the particular mode of miracle* implied in the Virgin Birth; and shall ask you to consider the subject successively from the three points of view: 1. Of the sinlessness (rather, the holiness) of Christ; 2. Of His uniqueness as a new creative beginning in humanity; and 3. Of His Incarnation as Son of God—the highest point of view of all.

1. I begin, then, with that side of Christ's Person that lies nearest to us, and ask: Is the Virgin Birth in any degree an implication of *Christ's sinlessness*?

Jesus was sinless—this, I think, I am warranted in assuming. It is a flawless character which the Gospels present to us. Jesus Himself, while so pure and unerring in His judgments on sin in others—laying His finger on the first uprisings of sin in the sinful thought or desire—is yet without trace of consciousness of sin. He confesses no sin, seeks no forgiveness, knows no repentance. He puts Himself as Saviour over against all others as sinners needing salvation. His Apostles and disciples—those who knew Him best—declare Him to be free from sin. " He did no sin," [1] says Peter. " In Him was no sin," [2] says John. " He knew no sin," [3] says Paul, repeating their testimony. With this correspond the declarations at His birth. " He shall save His people from their sins," [4] Matthew reports, in this explicitly distinguishing Him from the people He came to save. " Wherefore also that which is to be born shall be called holy," [5] Luke says, therein bringing His holiness into direct connection with the miraculous conception.

Here, then, arises a problem: this presence of an absolutely Holy One in our sinful humanity: How did it come about? Can nature explain it? Is not a miracle involved in the very statement of the fact? Undeniably, I think, it is. The late Prof. A. B. Bruce, already quoted, justly says: " A sinless man is as much a miracle in the moral world as a Virgin Birth is a miracle in the physical world." [6] It is very interesting to my mind to notice how our modern advocates of a humanitarian Christ, naturally born from Joseph and Mary, deal with this fact of the sinlessness of Jesus. My experience is that there is hardly one of them but hedges when he is brought face to face with it. Prof. Foster, in his

---

[1] I Pet. ii. 22. [2] I John iii. 5.
[3] II Cor. v. 21. [5] Matt. i. 21.
[5] Luke i. 35. [6] *Apologetics*, p. 410.

book on *The Finality of the Christian Religion,* will go
no further than to say that He is " the best we know." [1]
Prof. N. Schmidt, in his *The Prophet of Nazareth,*
says: " He seems to have had no morbid consciousness
of sin. His consciousness of imperfection was swal-
lowed up in the sense of divine love." [2] I asked an able
Ritschlian friend if he would grant me the perfect sinlessness of Christ. His reply was: " That is a the-
oretical question." I do not mean that there are not
those who accept the moral miracle, but deny the physical
(e. g., Schleiermacher, Keim, Beyschlag). I shall come
to their case immediately; [3] but it must be owned that
commonly in practice belief in the miraculous birth and
belief in the sinlessness of Jesus stand or fall together.
Prof. Bruce has remarked on this also. " It has to be
remembered," he says, " that faith is ever in a state of
unstable equilibrium while the supernatural is dealt with
eclectically; admitted in the moral and spiritual sphere,
denied in the physical. With belief in the Virgin Birth
is apt to go belief in the Virgin life, as not less than the
other a part of that veil that must be taken away that
the true Jesus may be seen as He was—a morally defective man, better than most, but not perfectly good." [4]

In order, however, that we may gauge the full extent
of this marvel of the appearance of the sinless One in
humanity, and realise the imperative need of miracle

[1] p. 482.   [2] p. 25.
[3] See below, pp. 197–8, 205.   [4] As above.

to explain it, we must go a good deal deeper, and look at the *radically sinful condition of the humanity* into which Christ came. This brings us back to the theology of the Apostles, which we have already in part considered. We are discussing doctrine, and it is in the light of doctrine that I ask you to look at this startling fact of the sinlessness of Jesus.

1. Take, first, *the teaching of the Apostle John.* We saw before that, to John, the cardinal fact about human nature is, that it needs regeneration. Natural birth does not fit a man for the kingdom of God. He must be born anew of the Spirit. Sin so cleaves even to the believer that, if any man says he has no sin, he is a liar, and the truth is not in him.[1] The holiness the believer has comes from a different principle—one supernaturally implanted. Now it is this human nature which, according to the Apostle, the Word assumed when He " became flesh." What was His relation to it? If Jesus shared in this human nature of ours, how did He escape its evil? Was there ever a point of time of which it could be said of *Him* that He needed regeneration, or was otherwise than perfectly holy in thought, and will, and deed? The suggestion, I think you will admit, to John's mind would have been blasphemous. Jesus was the Regenerator—the Giver of the Spirit—not one of the regenerated subjects of the kingdom. Whence, then, this complete separation between Him and the rest

[1] I John i. 7–10.

of mankind? What higher law operated in His case
to raise Him above the need of regeneration common
to all others? It is futile and superficial to say, as some
do, that, content with his Logos doctrine, John never
reflected on this question. How could he help reflecting? John knew as well as we do that Jesus, as a man,
was born—somehow. He knew that His mother was
Mary. Is it conceivable that he could think of His
birth, and not associate with it the idea of *miracle*?—a
miracle that must have operated in the very inception
of His being, to constitute Him the Holy One, separate
from sinners, that He was. Or can *we*, if we adopt
John's view of the radical need of regeneration in humanity, construe the earthly origin of this Holy One to
our thoughts in any other way?

2. Or, next, take *Paul's characteristic doctrine* of
the universal sin and condemnation of the race, and of
the carnal condition of man by nature. According to
Paul, every child of Adam has inherited a nature which
lacks in spiritual power, and is under a law of sin and
death,—the evil of which manifests itself in dispositions
and desires at war among themselves, and in revolt
against God and His holy law,—which, in its carnal
state, is "enmity against God."[1] The νοῦς, or better
part in man, is not extinguished; but its feeble protests
are ineffectual against the masterful forces of sin.[2] It
is not that, in Paul's view, the flesh is evil in itself.

---

[1] Rom. viii. 7.   [2] Rom. vii. 22, 23.

This misunderstanding of his doctrine is contradicted by the fact that human nature in all its parts and members is regarded by him as the subject of redemption.[1] But sin has taken possession of this nature, governs and controls it, so that to be " in the flesh " is the synonym with Paul of being subject to sin, and specially to its inferior impulses. Every man is thus bound by the law of a sinful nature to corruption and death, and cannot by any power of his own deliver himself from his wretched estate.[2]

What then, the question comes back, of Jesus, who is born into this humanity expressly for its redemption? Is it humanity in its integrity, or humanity in its fallen and sin-corrupted state, that Christ assumes? Does Jesus, like others, stand in solidarity with Adam, and share the sinful nature, the loss of spiritual power, the perverted and godless desires, inherited from that first forefather by natural generation? Surely Paul would have replied, had such a question been put to him, " Perish the thought! " Jesus was to him One who stood absolutely free from, and above, this law of sin and death. But does not this, again, by the clearest necessity, imply miracle in the constitution of His Person? Assume, if you will, that Paul had not heard of the Virgin Birth, though I think this unlikely. He knew at least that Jesus had a *human* birth, and, in the very nature of the case, he must have conceived of that

---

[1] Rom. vi. 13, 19.   [2] Rom. vii. 23.

birth as involving miracle, for only by a miracle could such a sinless Person flower out in our sinful humanity. I pointed out before, accordingly, that in every one of Paul's references to the earthly origin of Christ there is some significant peculiarity of expression.[1] And again I say, if we accept Paul's premises as to the radically sinful condition of human nature, I fail to see how we, any more than he, can escape the conclusion that Christ's entrance into our humanity must have been exceptional and miraculous.

This, I confess, is one of the things I can never understand in certain of our modern interpreters of John and Paul. They think, apparently, they have explained everything in the Christology of these Apostles, when they have used such terms as " Logos " or " Heavenly Man," or spoken of a " metaphysical," in distinction from a " physical " conception of Christ's origin. They seem altogether to forget that for Paul and John also Jesus was a man who was actually born, and that problems were presented by His birth, not the less hard, but all the more difficult and pressing, just because of their high doctrine of pre-existence, and their belief in Christ's sinlessness. Jesus had an earthly origin, and in that origin, as these Apostles well knew, He was differentiated from every other by the fact that, from the first moment of His existence, He was absolutely pure, —that He was possessed of a Spirit of holiness which

[1] See above, p. 117 *ff*.

overbore all temptation, even to the slightest evil, and made Him continuously and perfectly a doer of the will of His Father. They must have explained this to themselves *somehow*. Can it be doubted that they explained it to their own thoughts in a way which involved miracle?

Here, then, I draw my first strong line—*there is a miracle involved in the production of the sinless humanity of Christ*. But just here, I know, I will be pulled up. " Miracle "—I can think I hear some one say—" Yes, *spiritual* miracle—moral miracle—miracle, if you like, in the region of the soul; but not a *physical* miracle—not a miracle in the bodily sphere—a miracle which suspends the ordinary course of natural causation —which is incompatible with a double parentage, or requires us to assume birth from a Virgin." Some who uphold the sinlessness of Christ have taken exactly this ground. Schleiermacher, Keim, Beyschlag took this ground: Ritschlians like Kaftan, Loofs, Häring, etc., take it now. Even Lobstein, in his own way, admits the moral miracle, while denying the physical.[1] This, in fact, is the contention of these writers. Here, they say in effect, is the real kernel of truth in the Infancy stories; the element which makes them truly valuable; preserve this, and you have all that is essential to faith in these representations.

The reply I have to make to this form of theory, which

[1] *The Virgin Birth*, p. 101.

fain would separate the spiritual from the physical miracle, is simply this—and here I draw my next broad line
—*the thing cannot be done.* My ground for this assertion is that, in the nature of things, spiritual and physical are so intimately related, that you cannot have a
change so vitally affecting humanity on the spiritual
side, which does not involve a corresponding change on
the physical side, or in the sphere of organism. We are
dealing here, I ask you to remember, not with a simple miracle of sanctification—Jesus being viewed, after
the analogy of ordinary Christian experience, as a perfectly sanctified man. Sanctification, we instinctively
feel, is not the category which suits One like Him, for
sanctification implies that there is sin to be cleansed
away, and He had no sin, needed no cleansing. He is
the Sanctifier, not one of the sanctified. We could not
apply to Him the language of John—" He is faithful
and righteous to forgive us our sins, and to cleanse us
from all unrighteousness." [1]   He was never aught but
pure. The miracle, therefore, which made Him what
He was,—which faith is compelled to postulate for the
explanation of His Person,—is one that goes down to the
primal origin of His earthly being. It cannot stop at
any intermediate point, but must be traced back to the
first germinal beginnings of His existence, or even behind them. But this plainly involves the physical as
well as the spiritual side of His humanity.

[1] I John i. 9.

The subject is difficult to explain, but let me try to illustrate for a moment, as I have tried to do elsewhere,[1] from the scientific doctrine of evolution. It is well known that certain distinguished evolutionists, while handing over man's body to be accounted for by the ordinary processes of evolution, yet hold that man's mind cannot be wholly accounted for in a similar manner. The rational mind of man, they urge—I agree with the view, but am not called upon here to discuss it—has qualities and powers which separate it, not only in degree, but in kind, from the animal mind, and put an unbridgeable gulf, on the spiritual side, between man and the highest of the creatures below him. In other words, there is, in man's case, a rise on the spiritual side—the constitution of a new order or kingdom of existence—which requires for its explanation a distinct supernatural cause. Now the weakness of this theory, I have always felt, lies in its assumption that, while man's mind needs a supernatural cause to account for it, his body may be left to the ordinary processes of development. The difficulty of such a view is obvious. I have stated the point in this way. " It is a corollary from the known laws of the connection of mind and body that every mind needs an organism fitted to it. If the mind of man is the product of a new cause, the brain, which is the instrument of that mind, must share

[1] In my volume on *Ritschlianism*, Essay on "The Miraculous Conception."

in its peculiar origin. You cannot put a human mind
into a simian brain." [1] In other words, if there is a
sudden rise on the spiritual side, there must be a rise on
the physical—the organic—side to correspond.

Now apply this, with all reverence, to the origin of
such a new and sinless Personality as we have in Jesus
Christ. How is this to be accounted for on the supposition of a miracle in the spiritual sphere only? A
miracle is allowed to be necessary on the spiritual side.
It is, further, not a miracle of ordinary sanctification.
It is a miracle that operates in the first moment of His
conception. But, in a new creation like this, can we
separate the two sides of Christ's Personality? Surely
we must say that a perfect soul such as Jesus had needed
as its counterpart a perfect and harmonious organism.
It is as much part of our faith that Jesus had a pure
and perfect physical nature as that He had a pure and
perfect soul; indeed the one is not conceivable without
the other. We may distinguish as we please between
the spiritual and the natural, but the fact is that man,
as we know him, is a unity. The disturbance of sin is
felt as strongly in the disordered passions of his body
as in the unregulated affections of his spirit.

I thus come back to the point from which I started,
that, viewing Jesus as a Sinless Personality, there is
involved a supernatural act in the production of His
bodily nature. One lesson I would draw from this be-

[1] *Ritschlianism*, p. 230.

fore going further. I was speaking in last lecture of alleged heathen analogies to the Virgin Birth. But I would ask you now to observe how completely we are outside of the range of all heathen myths in this idea of supernatural birth as grounding a Sinless Personality. No such idea as that is found anywhere in heathenism. In Christianity it is of the essence of the conception. This simple fact sets the miraculous birth of Jesus wholly by itself, and sweeps away the entire baseless fabric of analogies sought in other religions to this unique act of God in our redemption.

2. Thus far I have been considering how far miracle is implied in the perfect *sinlessness* of Christ. This, however, is only the first round in the ladder of ascent to the full apprehension of the dignity of Jesus. We have not said everything about Jesus when we have said sinlessness. We mount a stage higher when we regard Him, as He is set forth to us in Scripture, as the *Second Adam* of our race, and *new creative beginning in humanity*. This, in truth, is already implied in what has gone before, for it is evidently no ordinary Person—no single individual of the race — who had the creative origin in body and soul just described. We connect here with what Paul says of Christ as standing to the second creation in a like relation to that in which Adam stood to the first;[1] but still more directly we connect

[1] Rom. v. 14.

with Christ's own consciousness, and with the facts about Him in the Gospels.

We look first here to the birth-narratives, and find that these, while not anticipating the pre-existence doctrine of later revelation, ascribe to the child to be born of the Virgin *a unique and incommunicable dignity.* " God shall give unto Him the throne of His father David." [1] He is the goal of prophecy—the Immanuel, " God with us," of Isaiah's oracle. He is Lord, King, Saviour. He is prepared for by a forerunner, heralded by angels, worshipped by shepherds and Magi, greeted by prophetic voices in the Temple. We might be tempted to set this down to poetry, but, when we advance to the history in the Gospels, we find that everything there corresponds. No one can read the Gospels without perceiving that the Evangelists throughout ascribe an absolute worth to Christ's Person. What is more, Jesus Himself does the same. His consciousness of a unique dignity is seen in almost every statement He makes, every act He performs. His universal relation to humanity is already implied in His favourite designation for Himself—" Son of Man." He is of the race, yet in a manner stands apart from it. He belongs to humanity, yet stands as Saviour over against the world He came to save. He reveals God to man, and man to himself, yet is not merely a prophet, but above all prophets—the Son. He does not simply, like the prophets, bring words

[1] Luke i. 32.

of God to men, but is Himself " *the* Truth "—the embodied revelation of God. Throughout He is identified with His message: He speaks with absolute authority: " But *I* say unto you "; by relation to Him the destinies of men are determined. Nor are these mere empty claims on Christ's part; they can be verified. The ages have accepted Christ at His own valuation. In Him, the conscience of the world being judge, there *is* presented the realised ideal of humanity. In Him we *have* a revelation of God which the world can never grow beyond. In Him we *do* see presented the type of the absolute religious relation of Sonship to God. His thoughts and ideals *do* to-day dominate the highest thought and sentiment of the world. In Him the spiritual forces *are* concentrated on which we depend for the world's moral and spiritual salvation.

Here, then, we have a Person unlike every other in history; who stands on a plane infinitely higher than every other; whose birth-hour, as we proclaim by our very manner of dating our letters, divides time for us into two great sections—*before* and *after* Christ;—One who, sinless in character, is yet more—perfect, archetypal man, realisation of a type of humanity utterly beyond the powers of nature to produce. How do we account for Him? This New Redeeming Head of the race that Schleiermacher tells us of, in whom the God-consciousness had absolute supremacy; this miracle of ideal perfection—" ideal man "—whom Keim and Beyschlag

acknowledge; this " Revelation-Person," in such solidarity with God in mind and purpose—in His appropria-
tion of the divine world-end as His own—that Ritschl
will have us ascribe to Him " Godhead "—How came
He to be there? Will natural explanation suffice? Can
you explain it without miracle?

The answer which our Gospels give to this question,
and in which most of us, I think, will now be disposed
to agree, is, that *a natural explanation does not suffice.*
It did not suffice for the explanation of the Sinless Personality; it will not suffice for the new Creative Head
of humanity. Paul is quoted against us on the Virgin
Birth. But assuredly Paul did not believe that One
whom He expressly puts in contrast with the first Adam
as the new Spiritual Head by whose obedience the bale-
ful consequences of the first Adam's transgression were
annulled, and righteousness and life brought to the
world, was Himself a natural descendant of that first
Adam, involved in the liabilities and doom attached to
his sin. This is simply to say that, however Paul conceived of the wonder, he did not believe that Christ had
a non-miraculous origin.

This is the Scriptural answer; but what of the answer
of the moderns? The thorough-going humanitarians
who are to-day the chief opponents of the Virgin Birth
will hear of no miracle in Christ's origin at all. I have
already availed myself of the admission of others—
mostly now of older date—Schleiermacher, Keim, Bey-

schlag, and the like, who grant that there must have been a miracle in the constitution of Christ's Person, though the miracle was not physical. These writers do not concede the full truth of the Incarnation; to them Christ is still only "ideal man," "archetypal man," "Revealer"; but even so they grant that ordinary generation does not suffice to explain Him—that there must have been in His origin a direct creative act. Here, for instance, is Schleiermacher, who anticipated a century ago the objections with which we are familiar to the Virgin Birth, and this is what He says: "Every one who accepts in the Redeemer a sinlessness of nature and a new creation through union of the divine with the human, postulates in this sense a supernatural generation" (*Erzeugung*).[1] Or here is Keim. After pages of argument *against* the birth from the Virgin, what does he come to? This: "As little are we able . . . to refrain from the acknowledgment that in the Person of Jesus a higher human organisation [note these words] than heretofore was called into being by that creative will of God that runs in parallel though viewless course side by side with the processes of creaturely procreation."[2] I value these admissions, so far as they go. They break the back of a pure naturalism, and seem to me, in principle, to be the surrender of the case.

To this, of course, the reply, as before, will be given —"Yes, but the miracle was spiritual, inward, the

---

[1] *Der christ. Glaube*, Sect. 97.   [2] *Jesus of Nazara*, II, p. 64.

bestowal of spiritual endowment—not *physical.*" But this brings me back to the old point: *Can* we, in the establishing of such a new creative beginning,—in the origination of One who, while holding of humanity, is yet outside the chain of its heredities and liabilities,— think of a spiritual miracle which has not also its physical side? I contend that we cannot. We have heard even Keim speak of "a higher human organisation," which, if the words mean anything, surely points to something physical. The best proof of all of *the inadequacy of this half-way position* is that, historically, it has never been able to maintain itself. It did not do so in the school of Schleiermacher, the great bulk of whose disciples—Neander, Ullmann, Tholuck, and the rest—went on to the full acknowledgment of the Virgin Birth. It did not do so in the school represented by Keim, which mostly sank down to the level of pure humanitarianism. Current indications show that the same fate (or return to a more positive position) is certain to attend the half-way position of a section of the school of Ritschl. Ritschl himself, while laying the whole weight of Christianity on what he called the "revelation-value" of the Person of Christ, persistently declined to discuss how the revelation came to be there: how Christ came to be the unique Being He was.[1] But in this seeming humility, there is really an abdication of thought on questions one *must* ask. I feel sure of this, that any one

[1] Cf. *Recht. und Versöhnung,* III, p. 426.

who applies his mind earnestly to the conditions of the problem, even as Ritschl states it, will find little difficulty in going at least so far as to say that miracle there was, and must have been, in the origin of One, sinless and divinely unique, as Jesus was.

Further discussion I leave to my last lecture, and close here by again emphasising the complete distinction of this Christian circle of conceptions from everything found in heathen mythology. A supernatural birth which has for its end the founding of a new humanity, and the introduction by a Redeemer of the divine forces needed for a world's salvation, is wide as the poles apart from those fables of the lust of the gods with which the birth of the mythical heroes of paganism is associated.

LECTURE VIII

DOCTRINAL BEARINGS OF THE VIRGIN BIRTH: THE INCARNATION—SUMMARY AND CONCLUSION

I HAVE sought in the preceding lecture to show that a creative miracle is implied in the absolute sinlessness of Jesus, and in His uniqueness as the Head of a new humanity. The full height of our argument, however, is not reached till we go a step higher, and, with the universal Church, see in the appearance of Christ in our world the entrance of a true divine Being into humanity—the Incarnation of the Son. I come now, accordingly, as the last stage in this long journey, to show that, if miracle is implied in the sinlessness of Christ, and in the uniqueness of His Person, much more is such a miracle as the Gospels record an integral part of the mystery of the Incarnation.

I have always felt it astonishing that any one should hold the Virgin Birth to be inconsistent with, or excluded by, *the doctrine of the pre-existence of the Son of God*, as taught by Paul and John. The idea, I suppose, is that the narratives of the birth of Christ say nothing about His pre-existence, but speak as if He

first began to be at His birth at Bethlehem. And it may
at once be granted that the narratives in the Gospels say
nothing of pre-existence. There is no reason to suppose
that the full mystery of our Lord's Person was unlocked
to Mary, or to any in that early circle. The Saviour
had to be manifested in His life, work, claims, death,
resurrection, and exaltation to the right hand of power,
before it could be fully seen Who or What He was, and
how far the compass of His Being reached. This, of
itself, as before urged, is an evidence of the early date
and primitive character of these narratives of the Virgin
Birth, that they are so entirely uninfluenced by the
views of the pre-existence and essential divine dignity
of the Son which are developed in the Apostolic writings.

It is all there already, perhaps, in germ—this higher
truth of the Lord's Person. It was not credible, to any
mind reflecting deeply on it, that One who had so supernatural, so directly divine, an origin,—of whom the
angel could say, " He shall be great, and shall be called
the Son of the Most High "—" the Lord God shall give
unto Him the throne of His father David "—" He shall
reign over the house of Jacob for ever; and of His Kingdom there shall be no end "—" that which is to be born
shall be called holy, the Son of God," [1]—should not be
more than human. Such expressions stretch out at least
to meet the later pre-existence doctrine. They need, to
sustain their significance, a frame as ample as that

[1] Luke i. 32–5.

which the Apostolic doctrine yields. The Evangelist
Matthew made no mistake when he read unto them the
whole meaning of the great Isaianic prophecy of Immanuel.

It was all there, perhaps, in germ; but it was not yet
unfolded. On the other hand, the Apostolic doctrine of
the pre-existence of the Son does not exclude, but, if you
assume that this pre-existent Being was actually born
as a man, positively requires us to postulate a miraculous
birth. That seems to me as self-evident a proposition
as the mind of man can frame. It is sometimes said
by those who argue for the opposite view (e. g., Sabatier
and Lobstein), that Paul and John did not *need* this
explanation; they had a better one.[1]   But this does not
touch the point at all. That Jesus had a pre-existent
life—was Son of God in a transcendent or " metaphysical " sense, which is what these writers mean by a
" better " explanation—does not touch this other question which has yet to be faced: How did this pre-existent
Son become man? It cannot be doubted that it is the doctrine of these Apostles that He did become man. " The
Word became flesh." [2]   It is not the Logos or Word in
His abstract being, but the Logos *incarnate*, that interests John. The burden of his teaching is that Jesus
Christ has " come in the flesh." [3]   So, if, as Lobstein
says, " it cannot be doubted that in the mind of [Paul]

---

[1] Lobstein, *Virgin Birth*, p. 57.   [2] John i. 14.
[3] I John iv. 2.

the Lord's personality has a heavenly origin," [1] it can as little be doubted that in Paul's mind this heavenly Person entered by birth into the conditions of a true human existence. " Being in the form of God . . . He emptied Himself, taking the form of a servant, being made [becoming] in the likeness of men." [2] He " was born [became] of the seed of David according to the flesh " [3] was " born [became] of a woman." [4] How, then, was this entrance into humanity accomplished? Was it *docetically*—in mere seeming? Assuredly not, in the view of these Apostles. It was a *true* humanity which Christ assumed. He came truly in the flesh. There was a true entrance into human life by a birth. But *such* a birth, in the nature of the case, was a miracle. What was the nature of the miracle? Do not the narratives of the Virgin Birth supply the answer?

The reply has already been dealt with that there is no trace of such a miraculous birth in the writings of Paul and John. Even if it were so—even were it admitted that Paul and John had no knowledge of the Virgin Birth, or did not reflect on the subject—I would point out that the fact of Christ's being born stands there just the same, and the problem still awaits solution of *how* the miracle of the Incarnation came about. But is it in the least likely that Paul did not reflect on it?— Paul, whose mind was so logical, who carried out his

---

[1] *Op. cit.*, p. 63.　　　　[2] Phil. ii. 6, 7.
[3] Rom. i. 3.　　　　[4] Gal. iv. 4.

principles so consistently, who in his later Epistles (Ephesians, Colossians) traces the implications of his Christology and of Christ's Mediatorship in their cosmological aspects in so vast and bold a way—is it likely that he would be so utterly oblivious of the problem raised on the human side by his own doctrine of the Incarnation, or would remain unconcerned about it? Or would John?

I have tried to show in previous lectures that Paul *did* reflect on this problem.[1] Not to go back on what was then said, take only that great liturgical passage in I Tim. iii. 16. Paul shows there with sufficient clearness his sense of the profundity of the problem: " Without controversy, great is the mystery of godliness "; and in the next clause he tells us where, in his view, the essence of the mystery lies: " Who was manifest in the flesh." Whether, therefore, Paul had the full answer to the problem or not—and I have given reasons for thinking that he was not ignorant of it—he knew at least that the problem was there, and that the constitution of Christ's humanity was in some sense miraculous. The case is even clearer in regard to John. There is no doubt, really, that John knew of the Gospel histories of Christ's supernatural birth, and there is just as little doubt in my own mind that he cordially accepted them as a solution of his own problem of *how* the Word became flesh.

[1] See above, pp. 116 ff.

Objection, however, may now be taken on the ground
—no doubt in some cases will be taken—that, even
granting all that we affirm, this idea of an Incarnation
of a pre-existent divine Being, going so far beyond the
simpler conceptions of the birth-narratives, is, after all,
only a metaphysical speculation of Paul's and John's
own, borrowed from Philonism—a quasi-philosophical
form in which these Apostles sought to embody their
impressions of Christ's greatness—and, therefore, cannot be legitimately used as a basis for arguing back, in
our day, to the Virgin Birth. I said at the commencement that it was no part of my business to discuss the
reality of the Incarnation, but, by way of clearing the
ground, a word or two may be said on the point now
raised.

The best way of removing any feeling of the kind
now expressed is to keep clearly in mind how the conception of Christ's pre-existence and divine Sonship was
actually reached. It did not arise, as the objection assumes, from metaphysical speculation. It arose from
facts which were the common possession of the Church;
and it was not a conception peculiar to these Apostles,
but, as we see from their writings, was widely shared
by the Church of their day.[1]

1. First, as the basis of this conception, came *the life
of Christ Himself*—His words, works, claims, the prerogatives He ascribed to Himself, the profound personal

[1] See above, p. 161.

impression He made on His disciples, which won them
to the confession that He was the Son of God and the
Messiah—a Person superhuman in character, attributes,
and functions. " Thou art the Christ, the Son of the
living God," [1] confessed Peter. We see this fact-basis
of the Apostolic conviction most clearly of all in John—
the most transcendental of the Apostles in His estimate
of Christ. John did not reason *down* from some metaphysical conception of the Logos to the divine dignity
of Christ; he *rose* to the belief that Jesus was the Incarnate Word from what he had seen and heard of Him in
His earthly manifestation. His feet were on the earth
all the time. " That which we have heard," he says,
" that which we have seen with our eyes, that which
we beheld, and our hands handled, concerning the Word
of life . . . that which we have seen and heard declare
we unto you." [2] " The Word became flesh and dwelt
among us, and we beheld His glory, glory as of the only
begotten of the father, full of grace and truth." [3]

2. Next, after the shock and temporary eclipse of the
Cross and Tomb, came *the resurrection in power*, followed by the brief, memorable period of intercourse of
the disciples with their Risen Lord, the exaltation to
heaven, and, finally, *the outpouring of the Spirit* at
Pentecost; and in the light of it all, coupled with the
hope of His Return, they saw their Master to be in the
fullest sense divine. The resurrection and exaltation

[1] Matt. xvi. 16.   [2] I John i. 1, 3.   [3] John i. 14.

threw back an illuminating, magnifying light on the
teaching, works, and claims of His earthly life—" declared [or " defined "] to be the Son of God with power
by the resurrection from the dead," [1] says Paul—and it
became clearly manifest to their minds how that here
divine greatness and love had been humbling itself to
suffering and shame for man's redemption.

3. But now—and here is a point I think important—
to recognise Christ in the light of His heavenly glory as
a divine Person was *already to affirm His pre-existence*;
for reflection must at once show us that divinity is not a
thing you can make or unmake. If Christ is divine
now, He has in nature *ever* been divine; the temporal in
His earthly manifestation is discovered to be but the
veil of the eternal; His presence on earth was the revelation of an eternal life He had with the Father. With
this agree His own words which John has preserved
about a heaven from which He had descended, and a
glory He had with the Father before the world was.[2]

Such, then, is the conception of Christ's Person which
lies at the basis of the Apostolic doctrine; and, accepting that doctrine, we see at once how stupendous a
miracle is implied in it. Christ's birth, we are to remember, is not the origin of His Personality, but only
its entrance into the conditions of a human life. But
that entrance was a real one. The Son of God *became
man.* Now this is miracle: the very constitution of

[1] Rom. i. 3.   [2] John vi. 33, 38; viii. 58; xvii. 5, etc.

such a divine and human Person is miracle: the most
astounding miracle, as said before, the universe has ever
seen. " Ask it in the depth, or in the height above,"
said Isaiah to Ahaz, and, on the refusal of the king, the
prophet declared that the Lord Himself would give him
a sign—that of the virgin (or maiden) who should conceive and bear the child Immanuel.[1] God has fulfilled
His word, and in the Incarnation has given us a sign
greater than anything in the depth beneath or in the
height above. And when we think of the wonder of this
divine One who has appeared in our midst, and of the
glory to which He has now been raised—" angels, and
authorities, and powers," as Peter says, " being made
subject to Him " [2]—do we not feel that faith postulates
a beginning which shall correspond with the end—a beginning as unique as the event itself is without parallel ?

Here also we reach the final point of view for seeing
the absolute distinction between the Scriptural doctrine
of Christ's origin, and anything found in *heathen mythology*. As analogies have been sought in heathenism for
the Virgin Birth, so analogies have been put forward
also for the Christian doctrine of the Incarnation.
Heathenism has, indeed, its incarnations of gods in
beasts and men. But the differences between these and
the Christian conception of the Son of God becoming
man are practically infinite. The heathen incarnations
are many: Christianity knows of but one. In the

---

[1] Is. vii. 11*ff.*   [2] I Pet. iii. 16.

heathen incarnations there is no idea of a true and per-
manent union of a divine being with a humanity which
becomes his for ever; in Christianity the union is perfect and abiding. The heathen incarnations are repeated
over and over in different forms. Vishnu, e. g., has
many Avatars — in fish, in tortoise, in boar, in lion.
Only when we come to the eighth have we the incarnation in the hero Krishna. The Son, in Christianity, is
incarnate once and for ever. The heathen incarnations
are monstrous, immoral, degrading; always purely
mythological. In Christianity we have the assumption
of a holy humanity for holy ends; and the act is historical, with its result in an actual human life, death,
and resurrection, which can be historically verified. The
idea of incarnation itself is different. In Christianity a
Divine Being voluntarily unites Himself with the race
for holy and redeeming ends. Heathenism has no such
conception.

We are now well within sight of the conclusion of our
inquiry; but there is yet one step remaining to be taken,
which to some may seem the most crucial of all, though
it is not really so. I have sought in these lectures to
impress you with the conviction that a *miracle* is involved in the constitution of the Saviour's Person—
even in His sinlessness and archetypal manhood—supremely in His Incarnation. I have further sought to
show that this miracle is not simply an *inward* or *spir-*

itual miracle, but has a *physical* side as well. But now it will be asked: " Yes, but does this show that the miracle must take the form of *birth from a Virgin*?" Let it be granted that there is a miracle; let the miracle be as stupendous as you please; grant that it involved the physical as well as the spiritual side of Christ's humanity; this will prove at most, it may be said, a supernatural factor in Christ's birth, but not necessarily the Virgin Birth of the Gospels. Can that be shown to be a form which this miracle of Incarnation must necessarily assume?

My reply to this, in the first place, must be that, in the nature of the case, the particular form which the miracle of the Incarnation shall assume is not a matter which *can* be laid down *a priori*. It is God Himself who must say in what way He shall accomplish this wonder. What we do see is, that there must be a miracle in the constitution of such a Person as Christ is, and we turn to *history*—not to *a priori* speculation—to see what form the miracle actually did take. It may be impossible to show *a priori* that the supernatural origin necessarily implies a Virgin Birth; but, on the other hand, if the existence of a supernatural factor in the bodily origin of Jesus is admitted, assuredly all *a priori* objection to the Virgin Birth vanishes, and few, in fact, who accept the one will be found stumbling at the other. This is the connection between the propositions I have been advancing and the narratives in the Gospels. The record in the Gospels simply supplies, in the form of history, what faith, on its own grounds, postulates. The history, therefore, becomes credible, and worthy of all acceptation. For that at which naturalism stumbles in the Synoptic narratives is not simply the *form* of the miracle, but the idea of a miraculous conception in *any* form. If once it is granted that a new act of the Creative Cause enters into the production of Christ's humanity, what is there longer incredible in the supposition that it should enter in the manner which the Gospels represent? Along this line of consideration, even if there were nothing else, the doctrinal significance of the Virgin Birth is put on a secure footing. For if this was, *de facto*, the form which the miracle of the Incarnation assumed, beyond question the Virgin Birth encloses in it, whether we can see it or not, the whole " mystery of godliness."

But is it the case that we can see no reason for the miracle assuming this form? No reason, at least, in congruity, if not in actual necessity? Let me, as the concluding part of my argument, ask you to look reverently at this question.

I assume here the result of my previous reasoning, that, if miracle is concerned in the birth of Christ at all, it is impossible to stop short of the conclusion that the miracle must be, in part, a *physical* one. The *Te Deum* sings: " When thou tookest upon thee to deliver man, thou didst not abhor the Virgin's womb." Every birth

is in a sense a miracle—a mystery of God. Ps. cxxxix.
says: " My frame was not hidden from thee, when I
was made in secret, and curiously wrought in the lowest
parts of the earth. Thine eyes did see my imperfect
substance, and in thy book were all my members written, which day by day were fashioned, when as yet there
was none of them." [1] Similarly, the miracle of the Incarnation, whatever the nature of it, was one wrought
in the secrecy of the mother's being. This is the fact
overlooked by mediating writers like Prof. Fricke, of
Leipzig, who cannot understand why any one should
take offence at the article, " Conceived by the Holy
Ghost," yet objects to any one dragging down this expression into the region of what he calls " the physiological." [2] In one respect the protest of this writer is
justified. Nothing is more objectionable than the attempt sometimes made to give a sensuous interpretation
to the words of Luke about the miraculous conception.
Talk about " physical filiation " such as one meets with
even in Lobstein,[3] suggests pagan analogies, and is
wholly out of place in connection with the creative
energy of a purely Spiritual Agent, such as the Holy

[1] Ps. cxxxix. 15, 16.
[2] *Christliche Welt*, 27 Oct., 1892; cf. my *Ritschlianism*, p. 234.
Prof. Fricke, like others of this mediating tendency, stops short of a
complete Incarnation. Jesus is to him One who has the Spirit
without measure—the Incomparable One. Naturally, therefore,
there is weakness in his view of the Virgin Birth.
[3] *Op. cit.*, pp. 67, 126.

Spirit is conceived to be. On the other hand, the Holy Spirit is undoubtedly regarded as, in Lobstein's words, " the author of the corporeal and material life of Jesus," and this physical *result* of His action is not to be lost sight of.

I recognise, then, to the full a miracle in the origin of Jesus which involved His bodily nature. I desire neither to minimise nor to explain away the miracle. To me the stupendous miracle is always the Incarnation itself, and any lesser miracle which is involved in that loses its power to offend. This is why, in these discussions, I have laid no stress on the interesting facts of " Parthenogenesis," or virgin births in nature, sometimes brought forward as throwing light on the birth of Christ. I do not say that these facts have no bearing on the subject; in some respects they have a very close bearing. It has been plausibly argued by Mr. Griffith-Jones, e. g., in his book, *Ascent Through Christ*, on the ground of these facts of parthenogenesis, that, if the Virgin Birth is *above* nature, it is not *contrary* to nature;[1] and this, by consent of scientific men themselves, must be admitted. It was Prof. Huxley who wrote, as quoted by Dr. Gore: " The mysteries of the Church are child's play compared with the mysteries of Nature. The doctrine of the Trinity is not more puzzling than the necessary antinomies of physical speculation; virgin procreation and resuscitation from apparent death are

[1] *Ascent Through Christ*, p. 262.

ordinary phenomena for the naturalist." [1]   Prof. G. J.
Romanes, too, in his *Darwin and After Darwin*, makes
the remarkable statement: " Even if a virgin has ever
conceived and borne a son, and even if such a fact in
the human species has been unique, it would not betoken
any breach of physiological continuity." [2]   This accords
with what one frequently observes in the miracles of
Scripture.   Miracle may transcend nature altogether,
as in the raising of the dead; but more commonly miracle is a heightening or utilising of powers already in-
herent in nature.   The supernatural is grafted on the
natural.   Parthenogenesis, up to a certain point, is a
fact in nature, and has this value, that it shows that
Virgin Birth is inherently a possibility, and repels the
objection sometimes made that such a birth would not
give a complete humanity.[3]

Still the question will be pressed, *Why* parthenogenesis?   Why not simply a heightening of the ordinary
powers of nature, for which we have at least *Old Testament precedents*?   Why this superfluous miracle?   But
is there not a very obvious answer to this question?   In
the Old Testament examples—Isaac, Samson, Samuel
—you have a supernatural heightening of the powers of
nature, indeed—but to what end?   Not to the overstep-
ping of nature in any degree in the result, but only to

---

[1] Gore, *Bampton Lects.*, p. 247.   [2] I., p. 119.
[3] Cf. R. J. Campbell, quoted above, p. 3.

the production by way of nature of beings who are entirely natural—men and nothing more. Isaac, though the seed of promise, had no peculiar distinction even as a man. Samson, though endowed by the Spirit with superhuman strength, was assuredly no model for imitation. Ethically he was a piece of the commonest of human clay. Samuel was a distinguished prophet, but still simply a man. John the Baptist, Christ's own forerunner—another child of promise—though Jesus said of him that among those born of women there had not arisen a greater, was yet profoundly conscious of his inferiority to Him whose way he came to prepare, and Jesus Himself declared that one but little in His Kingdom was greater than he.[1] All these were sinful men. In no case in the world's history has natural generation issued in a being who is sinless, not to say superhuman. But here in Jesus is One who, as we have seen, is not only sinless and archetypal, but has in Him all the potencies of Godhead. Is it not reasonable to expect that His manner of entering the world will be also different from that of others ?

Assuming this to be so, as a general presumption, I think we can see at least some reasons why the miracle involved in the Incarnation should take this form of a Virgin Birth.

1. When the question is put: Why, granting a creative miracle in Christ's origin, the conditions might not

[1] Matt. xi. 11.

be met by ordinary generation, may not the reply be given—*Cui bono*? " Conceived by the Holy Ghost "—does not this explain all? If a creative origin is in any case postulated, why the complication with a second and external factor, namely, the paternal? The objector asks: Why a superfluous miracle? But may it not be legitimately retorted that, seeing the miracle is already there, the superfluity consists in his own insistence on the element of human paternity? The creative miracle we assume, remember, is one that goes down to the foundations of life in the mother. Does not such a miracle of itself supersede human fatherhood?

2. Again, the Incarnation is an event *sui generis*, and we have seen reason to expect that there will be something in the manner of it also *sui generis*. It is reasonable, that is, to think that there will be something in the *mode* of the Incarnation that will unambiguously proclaim its extraordinary character; that will draw attention to it as an event wholly unique, exceptional, unexampled, in the history of mankind. Plainly, under the conditions of ordinary paternity, this exceptional character of Christ's origin would have been veiled, if not nullified. By His birth from a Virgin it is thrown into strongest relief. This is the right use, it seems to me, to make of the Old Testament analogies, which, so far as they go, favour my contention. They show that, when God has a new beginning to make, or a great work to do, even if it be by ordinary men, He takes pains to

mark the fact by some signal interposition. How much more in this new creative beginning, which transcends all previous analogies! Luke, probably, has this thought in his mind in the genealogy of Jesus which he connects with his narrative. In that genealogy, you observe, he carries back the descent of Jesus not, like Matthew, to David and Abraham simply, but to Adam, whom he significantly names " the Son of God."[1] Jesus also, at the commencement, is " Son of God." There is unmistakably a meaning in this. In Luke, as in Paul, Jesus is brought into direct comparison with Adam, the head of the first creation, and " figure of Him that was to come."[2] And the point of comparison can only be that Adam was not, like the others in list, a son of man by ordinary generation, but took his origin directly at the hands of God. Evolution, as I have tried to show elsewhere,[3] does not contradict this view, but, as I think, confirms it. Whatever light evolution may throw on secondary factors, there seems little doubt that direct creative action is also involved in man's origin, both in body and in soul. Luke would seem to imply that was so also in Christ's case. The Gospels show us the manner.

3. There is a third consideration in this connection which Dorner specially emphasises.[4] We do not lean to a Roman Catholic doctrine of immaculate conception

[1] Luke iii. 38; cf. Matt. i. 1.   [2] Rom. v. 14.
[3] Cf. my book, *God's Image in Man.*   [4] Cf. my *Ritschlianism*, p. 237.

when we say that in Mary *a fitting instrument* was prepared in mind and body for this supreme function of
being the mother of the Redeemer. But natural generation involves the introduction of another influence—of
a strain of a different quality and kind. Was there
then a second and male parent prepared, as there was a
female? Or would not the mingling of different and
inferior influences have been a positive drawback for
the end contemplated—a disturbance calling for a new
miracle to counteract and correct it? Natural generation, on this view, does not afford relief from miracle,
but rather *doubles* the miracle.

Gathering up the threads of my reasoning, I think
I may claim to have proved that it is a very superficial
view which affirms that there is no doctrinal connection
between the Virgin Birth and the fact of the Incarnation. I grant at once, as I have done earlier, that for a
naturalistic Christ you do not need a supernatural
origin. More—if you do not hold a supernatural Christ,
you will not long retain belief in a supernatural origin.
On the other hand, when you have the certainty of the
Incarnation, the whole force of that certainty will be
thrown into the scale of the Gospel narratives. In the
Virgin Birth you will feel that you have what you might
most naturally expect in such a new creative beginning.
It is the form of miracle which most clearly corresponds
with the nature of the fact. Our faith in the event does
not, of course, rest on the power of our minds to deduce

it from the Incarnation, but on the history; but, with faith in the Incarnation to start with, and the admission of the necessity of a miracle of some kind, as involved in that, we may readily perceive the fitness and credibility of the miracle as recorded.

Here, then, I conclude my argument, and, in doing so, it may be convenient that I should briefly recapitulate the chief positions I have endeavoured to establish. I may sum them up thus:

1. The only two narratives we have of the birth of Jesus tell us that He was born of a Virgin.

2. The Gospels containing these narratives are genuine documents of the Apostolic Age.

3. The texts of these narratives have come down to us in their integrity.

4. The two narratives of the Virgin Birth are independent.

5. The narratives, nevertheless, are not contradictory, but are complementary and corroborative of each other.

6. There are strongest reasons for believing that Matthew's narrative comes from the circle of Joseph, and Luke's from the circle of Mary.

7. The Gospel of Mark, which embraces only the public ministry of Jesus, does not contradict the other narratives.

8. The Gospel of John does not contradict the other narratives, but presupposes them.

9. John unquestionably knew the earlier Gospels, and is traditionally identified with opposition to the earliest known impugner of the Virgin Birth, Cerinthus.

10. Paul does not contradict the Virgin Birth. On the contrary, Luke, a chief witness of the Virgin Birth, was the companion of Paul, and Paul's language seems to presuppose some knowledge of the fact.

11. The doctrine of Paul and John—as of the New Testament generally—implies a miracle in the origin of Christ.

12. The Gospels containing the narratives of Christ's birth were, so far as known, received without question by the Church from their first appearance.

13. With the exceptions of the Ebionites—the narrowest section of the Jewish Christians—and some of the Gnostic sects, the Church from Apostolic times universally accepted the fact of the Virgin Birth. The Nazarenes, or main body of the Jewish Christians, accepted it.

14. The early Church set high value on the Virgin Birth doctrinally, as attesting (1) the true humanity of Christ, and (2) His superhuman dignity.

15. The prophecy of Isaiah vii. 14 is rightly applied by Matthew to the birth of Jesus.

16. Yet, as most critics now admit, this prophecy was applied by no one in those days to the Messiah, and therefore could not have suggested the invention of this story.

17. It is granted by a majority of recent critics that the myth—as they call it—of the Virgin Birth could not have originated on Jewish soil.

18. It is as conclusively shown by Harnack and others that it could not have originated on Gentile soil.

19. Pagan myths do not afford any proper analogies to the Virgin Birth of Christ, or the doctrine of the Incarnation.

20. The perfect sinlessness of Christ, and the archetypal character of His humanity, imply a miracle in His origin.

21. The doctrine of the Incarnation of the pre-existent Son implies a miracle in Christ's origin.

22. The miracle in Christ's origin had of necessity a physical as well as a spiritual side.

23. The Virgin Birth answers historically to the conditions which faith postulates for the origin of Christ.

In light of these propositions, I cannot acquiesce in the opinion that the article of the Virgin Birth is one doctrinally indifferent, or that can be legitimately dropped from the public creed of the Church. The rejection of this article would, in my judgment, be a mutilation of Scripture, a contradiction of the continuous testimony of the Church from Apostolic times, a weakening of the doctrine of the Incarnation, and a practical surrender of the Christian position into the hands of the advocates of a non-miraculous, purely humanitarian Christ—all on insufficient grounds.

APPENDIX

OPINIONS OF LIVING SCHOLARS

INTRODUCTORY NOTE BY PROF. ORR

THE papers dealt with in this Appendix were procured by Dr. W. W. White, of the Bible Teachers' Training School, New York, from the scholars named, in further illustration of the subject of the Virgin Birth. Some of the papers are exceptionally valuable, and the hope may be expressed that means will be taken to have them published *in extenso*. It is unfortunately not possible to do more in this Appendix than indicate leading points by summaries and extracts.

It is right again to say that my own lectures were written, and a full synopsis of them was published, before these papers were seen by me. The papers came to hand in New York while the lectures were being delivered (some later), and no use has been made of them in any way, beyond the reading of certain extracts, on days appointed for the purpose. I thought it better to take the full responsibility for my own work, and to keep the contributions of other writers distinct. Each author is therefore responsible only for his own production, and not in the least for any views I have expressed. Naturally also there are views in some of the papers with which I disagree. But I am deeply grateful for the large amount of common ground, and for the corroboration of my positions on the most essential points, which the discussion by so many minds reveals.

I have not, except in one case (that of Dr. Jacobs) ventured on any criticism or counter-argument, even where my views do not fully accord with those of the writer. The only point on which I should like to enter my personal dissent is in respect of the opinion expressed by certain of the contributors that the Virgin Birth, even if true, is not essential to Christianity. I have given my reasons in the lectures for thinking that this is not a tenable position. It is a fair question to raise, whether or not the evidence justifies belief in the Virgin Birth. But it seems to me self-evident that, *if the Virgin Birth is believed to be true*, it must be held to be an essential element in the Incarnation, as it actually happened. It was the way in which God chose to bring about the Incarnation, and it cannot but be vitally connected with the fact of which it was the instrumental cause. The historical testimony also must not be lost sight of. May I add that it appears to me that the writers in question, in showing how deeply the idea of the Virgin Birth is an implication of just views of Christ's Person, holiness, and work, do much to modify their own contention as to its non-essential character.

In the list of authors and subjects that follows, the order is that in which the papers are noticed in the succeeding pages. I ought, perhaps, to mention that, while responsible for the summarising of the papers given to me, I am not responsible for their transcription, into which occasional errors may have crept.

AUTHORS AND SUBJECTS

The Rev. Prof. WILLIAM SANDAY, D.D., LL.D.,
Oxford University, Oxford.

" The Origin and Character of the First Two Chapters of
St. Luke."

Sir WILLIAM RAMSAY, D.C.L., D.D.,
University of Aberdeen, Aberdeen, Scotland.

" Luke's Narrative of the Birth of Christ."

The Rev. GEORGE H. BOX, M.A.,
Vicar of Linton, Ross, Herefordshire, England.

" The Jewish-Christian Origin of the Gospel Narratives of
the Nativity."

The Rev. Prof. W. E. ADDIS, M.A.,
Manchester College, Oxford.

" Why Do I Believe in the Virgin Birth? "

The Rev. Canon RICHARD J. KNOWLING, D.D.,
The College, Durham, England.

" Why I Believe the Doctrine of the Virgin Birth to be
True."

The Rev. Principal ALFRED E. GARVIE, M.A.,
New College, London.

" The Doctrine of the Virgin Birth of Jesus Christ Our
Lord: A Psychological, Ethical, and Theological Investigation."

The Rev. H. WHEELER ROBINSON, M.A.,
Rawdon College, near Leeds, England.

" The Old Testament in Relation to the Virgin Birth."

The Rev. Prof. THEOD. ZAHN, D.D.,
Erlangen University, Erlangen, Germany.

" Why I Believe the Doctrine of the Virgin Birth to be
True."

The Rev. Prof. REINHOLD SEEBERG, D.D.,
Berlin University, Berlin, Germany.

" Born of the Virgin Mary."

The Rev. Prof. H. BAVINCK, D.D.,
The Free University, Amsterdam, Holland.

" The Virgin Birth of our Lord."

The Rev. Prof. E. DOUMERGUE, D.D.,
Montauban, France.

" The Miracle of the Supernatural Birth of the Christ."

The Rev. H. C. G. MOULE, D.D.,
Bishop of Durham, England.

" Why Do I Believe in the Virgin Birth of our Lord?"

The Rev. W. R. GRIFFITH-THOMAS, D.D.,
Principal of Wycliffe Hall, Oxford.

"The Virgin Birth—Reasons for Belief."

The Rev. Prof. HENRY COWAN, D.D.,
University of Aberdeen, Aberdeen, Scotland.

"Testimony of the Sub-Apostolic Church and Age to the
Virgin Birth of our Lord."

JOSEPH JACOBS, Litt.D.,
Yonkers, N. Y.

"The Virgin Birth from the Standpoint of Jewish Science
and of Folklore."

Prof. ISMAR J. PERITZ, D.D.,
Syracuse University, Syracuse, N. Y.

"The Hebrew-Christian Attitude Toward the Virgin Birth."

PASTEUR HIRSCH,
Paris, France.

"The Evolution that has Led from the Miraculous Birth of
Jesus Christ to the Dogma of the Immaculate Conception."

The Rev. Prof. GABRIEL OUSSANI, D.D.,
St. Joseph's Seminary, Dunwoodie, N. Y.

"The Christian Doctrine of Christ's Virgin Birth."

SUMMARIES OF PAPERS

I

THE REV. PROF. WILLIAM SANDAY, D.D., LL.D., OXFORD

Dr. Sanday's valuable paper discusses the origin and ₁haracter of the first two chapters of Luke. He observes:

In regard to the first two chapters of St. Luke, the one conclusion that impresses itself upon me most strongly is that, whatever the date at which the chapters were first set down in writing—and the question of date is secondary rather than primary—in any case the contents of the chapters are the most archaic things in the whole New Testament. I am quite prepared to assume Harnack's date for the composition of St. Luke's two historical writings, viz., that they were begun and finished somewhere in the fifteen years between 78 and 93 A.D.—I should myself be inclined to say, more probably in the earlier part of that period than the later, but that is a trifle. I shall also venture to assume what has been consistently maintained by all the leading English scholars who have dealt with the subject and has now received the powerful and, as I believe, decisive support of Professor Harnack, that it was really St. Luke, the companion of St. Paul, who edited and gave to the world the Third Gospel and the Acts as they now stand.

He examines the view of Harnack that " the substance of the chapters reached St. Luke in the form of oral tradition, and was first committed to writing by him," and indicates his preference for the alternative, " that he received them already in writing and reproduced this document as he reproduced others with a certain amount of freedom."

On the latter point he says:

Whatever may be true as to the linguistic clothing of the narrative, I am prepared to maintain, as against Harnack, that in any case the chapters are not a free composition of St. Luke's, but that there is some definite authority to which he closely adhered behind them. . . . The whole mental attitude of the narrator is different from St. Luke's and much more primitive. . . . I think we may say that the real author of these first two chapters was a Jew, a Jew by birth, and a Jew by all his antecedents and interests.

Illustration and argument follow.

The deeply interesting conclusions reached are thus stated:

I submit that these varied observations taken together go far to justify the proposition with which I started, that the substance of these two chapters not only differs materially from all that we know of the character and standpoint of St. Luke, but that it is really an example of a type of thought and feeling fundamentally older than anything else in the New Testament. Nowhere else is the novel element in Christianity so little disengaged from the conditions out of which it arose. We should say, I think, looking at the broad phenomena of these chapters, that they were the product of a

circle like that which the author introduces to us, the circle
of Zacharias and Elisabeth, of Joseph and Mary, of Simeon
and Anna. They are pious folk, brought up in the spirit
of the older dispensation, but looking out beyond it—looking out so far as to catch sight of the coming " redemption
of Israel," but hardly as yet the salvation of the world, at
least in the sense in which it was empirically realised. The
ancient prophets indeed looked forward to a time when the
knowledge of the Lord should cover the earth as the waters
cover the sea, but it was all to be through the medium of
Israel. In that the author of these chapters agreed with
them. But neither they nor he seem to have anticipated
such a throwing open of the gates to the Gentiles as actually
took place, while the children of the kingdom were cast out.

Johannes Weiss has expressed the opinion that the narratives of these chapters may have begun to circulate among
the Jewish-Christian communities of Judæa " in the sixties "
(*Schriften d. N. T.*, p. 383). He is careful to add that, in
doing this, he does not attribute to them a higher historical
value than other critics. That is a point that we reserve for
the present. But in the meantime we may ask whether even
so early a date as the beginning of the sixties satisfies the
conditions. Perhaps it may. Perhaps it is possible that by
this time people had begun to slip back into the old mode
of speech according to which " Herod, king of Judæa " was
understood to mean Herod the Great. But it would be even
more in keeping with the contents of the chapters if they
had been written down as much as twenty years earlier. It
is always possible, especially in a secluded district or a
secluded household, to be behind the times. But I very much
doubt whether there is anything in the chapters that would
not be even more vividly natural if they had taken their
first shape before the great missionary successes of St. Paul.

That hypothesis I must leave as a matter of speculation.
, . . But the ground on which I would take my stand is that

the substance of the chapters is, in all essential characteristics, older than anything else in the whole New Testament.

The paper closes with the paragraphs:

There is just one more inference that I think we may draw. In his book Harnack has called attention to "the womanly element" in the Third Gospel, of which he proceeds to enumerate fourteen examples. (*Lukas der Arzt*, p. 109*ff*. In this he believes himself to be putting forward something new; but it is rather curious that in this country the observation goes back at least more than twenty years (Farrar, *The Messages of the Books*, 1884, p. 81, "the Gospel of womanhood"); and in recent years it has become almost a commonplace.

But, if this is true of the Gospel as a whole, it is true pre-eminently of the first two chapters. Here we may speak more strongly, and say that the whole story is told from a woman's point of view. Observe especially the notes of time in i. 24, 26, 36, 56, 57; also the description vv. 40–44, and the stress that is laid on the thoughts of the Virgin Mary, ii. 9, 48, 50, 51. It is not too much to say that the whole story is told from the point of view of a woman, and more particularly of Mary. Impressions of this kind cannot perhaps be insisted upon; but for myself I believe that the last link in the chain by which the substance of the chapters reached St. Luke—and I should not be surprised if the first link too—was a woman.

II

SIR WILLIAM M. RAMSAY, D.C.L., D.D., ABERDEEN, SCOTLAND

Sir Wm. Ramsay, like Dr. Sanday, discusses Luke's narrative.

His paper opens with a striking declaration:

That in the man Jesus Christ the Divine nature was incarnate, is an essential and fundamental part of the Christian religion: "the Word was made flesh and dwelt among us." This fundamental principle is common to all the four Gospels and to the New Testament as a whole. If you try to eliminate it, there remains practically nothing: that is the result clearly demonstrated in many attempts which have been made to cut out the superhuman and Divine from the life of Jesus as set forth in the Gospels. Some scholars who have made the attempt leave a slight trifling remainder; others frankly confess that there is nothing worth notice left; others again substitute a fanciful romance elaborated out of their own inner consciousness and unsupported by ancient authority for the narrative of the Gospels. That Jesus was not merely human, but truly superhuman and Divine is the Christian teaching and faith and belief, and to deny that is to separate one's self from Christianity.

Prof. Ramsay thinks " it is different when we approach the question how the Divine nature came to be in the man, and how the superhuman was brought into relation with the human," and contends that the answer to this question is not " of the essence of Christianity."

" All the four Gospels and Paul agree in regarding the exact circumstances and manner of the birth of Christ as a matter only of historic and moral interest, not an essential and necessary part of the faith." [1]

He nevertheless holds that Luke's narrative is true, resting ultimately on the authority of Mary.

They [the facts] came ultimately to Luke's knowledge in some way which he does not explain precisely; but he suggests in his own fashion that Mary was his ultimate authority. He knew what was kept hid in her heart. He tells us that no one knew the facts but herself, and explains that Elisabeth told Mary her inmost heart, but not that Mary told even Elisabeth; yet he claims that he was able to impart information with certainty. This is as much as to declare that in this matter the knowledge came to him from her either directly or through a trustworthy intermediary.

" Two general questions," he says, " must suggest themselves: viz., as to the authority and credibility of the story, and as to whether Luke used a written or an oral authority."

In opposition to Harnack, he lays stress on Luke's high rank as an historian:

The facts mark out Luke in my estimation as a great and judicious historian, and his narrative as entitled to high rank in respect of authoritativeness. Reasons for this opinion cannot be stated here, for they depend on a survey of his history as a whole.[2] But, except for those who invoke

[1] I have indicated my dissent from this view, p. 234.

[2] The question is discussed in *St. Paul the Traveler*, *Was Christ Born in Bethlehem*, and *Pauline and other Studies*.

superhuman agency, his credibility must rest on his sources of information and his critical sense in distinguishing between good and inferior sources. In Luke i. 3–4, he claims to have excellent sources and to set forth what is certain. Those who hold, like Prof. Harnack, that he was the companion and coadjutor of Paul, must admit that he had access to first-rate authorities, if he chose to use them. . . . What reason is there to think either on the one hand that Luke's narrative was here affected by popular report (which inevitably carries legend with it), or on the other hand that he used mainly or exclusively a good authority? The only good ultimate authority was Mary herself, and, as we have seen, the expression is skilfully calculated to suggest that the writer relied on her. . . . The story has not the character of legend. It is precise, clear, definite, whereas legend is vague, fluid, intangible. While the words are Luke's,[1] the facts breathe a different personality, and that not a man's, but a woman's and mother's. Only the child's mother noted and remembered his growth at every stage—ii. 40, 52. Contrast the warm love that breathes through these sayings with the kindly affection that records the growth of John—i. 80.

The maternal feeling is too strong to have been created by Luke in a popular report, as any person possessed of literary capacity will recognise if he reads the story with this object and from this point of view. The song of Mary is not Luke's composition (as Prof. Harnack argues); it is the Biblical rapture of a mind fed on the Old Testament from infancy, and expressing its emotion in its only language of exalted emotion (but Luke was a Hellene and a convert from paganism, to whom Biblical language could never and did never become the inevitable organ of expression during

---

[1] This has been brought out clearly by Prof. Harnack in his *Lukas der Arzt*, with much of whose reasoning everyone must agree though it is too verbal to carry complete conviction. I have argued to the same effect on grounds of fact, *Christ Born at Bethlehem*, ch. iv.

rapture). Luke translated and perhaps gave a more marked lyrical form, but he did not and could not invent the hymns of this story. They are the expression of the Jewish mind; he was a Greek, as incapable of inventing them as he was of inventing the character of Jesus. . . . We must, I think, conclude that Luke's account rested ultimately on the witness of the best authority, viz., Mary herself.

This raises the question of the intermediary:

The character of the narrative, the womanly and motherly feeling that breathes through it, gives the assurance that it reached Luke not after passing through several intermediaries, but through the report of some person who had been intimate with Mary in her later years, "who knew her heart and could give him what was almost as good as her own immediate account." Further, "one may venture to state the impression that the intermediary is more likely to have been a woman than a man. There is a womanly spirit in the whole narrative, which seems inconsistent with the transmission from man to man," and which (one may add) could not have been preserved in the narrative of Luke even after hearing it from a woman unless he had had a strong natural sympathy with women; and that he had this is proved clearly by the marked prominence which he gives them (alone of all writers of the New Testament) in history.

So much stands written in my book, *Christ Born at Bethlehem*, ch. iv.

Prof. Ramsay adopts as probable Prof. Sanday's suggestion that the intermediary was Joanna, the wife of Chuza, Herod's steward (Luke viii. 3); but differs from Dr. Sanday in holding that Luke did not use a written source.

As respects credibility, he thinks that in one or two points—as in the reference to the angel—there may have been misapprehension on the part of Luke, or of his informant, but is strong in his affirmation of the substantial truth of the narrative:

That the narrative, though perhaps containing certain misapprehensions, is substantially a true account resting on Mary's authority, seems to me beyond question; and I should take the hymns of Mary and Zachariah to be the truest, because the most perfectly Biblical parts. There is one consideration which must lead us to regard the misapprehensions as unimportant. The compelling power of everything connected with the life of the Saviour was the greatest force in history. It was this force that produced the Gospels, driving the facts into the minds of men so that they could not but speak the things which they had seen and heard, and impressing the image of Jesus on their imagination so deeply that it shines with almost undiminished brilliance through the Gospels, although they were written so many years after his death and are not unaffected by the time and circumstances in which they were composed. This compelling power is the reality that underlies the unfortunate and misleading name, " verbal inspiration," and the revolt from that term should not blind us to the great truth of which it is a misconception. This compelling power operated both on the intermediary and on Luke in this narrative.

Prof. Ramsay differs from most in declaring: " I am quite unable to accept the view that Matthew states Joseph's view as Luke states Mary's. There seems no real, only a fancied analogy." [1]

[1] I venture to dissent, see pp. 83–4.

III

THE REV. GEORGE BOX, M.A., VICAR OF LINTON, HEREFORDSHIRE, ENGLAND

It is impossible to do justice to this long and able paper by extracts, but certain points may be noted. The paper seeks to establish, as against the new school of comparative mythology, the Jewish-Christian origin of the narratives of both Matthew and Luke.

On Matt. i. 11 the author says:

The first impression produced by the perusal of Matthew's narrative is, undoubtedly, that we have here a genuine product of the Jewish spirit. In spirit as well as in letter and substance it reflects the characteristic features of Jewish habits of thought and expression. How strong this impression is—and how well founded—may be gathered from the remarks of so unprejudiced an observer as Prof. S. Schechter. "The impression," he says, "conveyed to the Rabbinic student by the perusal of the New Testament is in many parts like that gained by reading an old Rabbinic homily. On the very threshold of the New Testament he is confronted by a genealogical table, a feature not uncommon in the later Rabbinical versions of the Old Testament, which are rather fond of providing Biblical heroes with long pedigrees.

Illustrations follow.

I conclude, then, that the whole narrative embodied in the first two chapters of the First Gospel is thoroughly Jewish in form and general conception, and that while Hellenistic colouring is unmistakably present in the story, it shows decisive indications of the influence of Palestine, and is, in fact, addressed to a circle of Hellenistic Jews who were under Palestinian influence.

The integrity of the narrative is upheld against those who would separate the genealogy from ch. i. 18–ii. 23. Mr. Box finds " Midrashic " elements in Matthew's narration:

What, then, is the character and historical significance of Matthew's narration (Matthew i. and ii.)? To the present writer it seems to exhibit in a degree that can hardly be paralleled elsewhere in the New Testament the characteristic features of Jewish Midrash or Haggada. . . . It sets forth certain facts and beliefs in a fanciful and imaginative setting specially calculated to appeal to Jews. The justification for this procedure lies in the peculiar character and idiosyncrasy of the readers to whom it is addressed. . . . The task that confronts the critical student is to disentangle the facts and beliefs—the fundamental ground factors on which the narration is built—from their decorative embroidery. What then are these fundamental *data*?

. . . . . .

The fundamental fact which underlies the genealogy of the First Gospel, and to which it bears witness, is the Davidic descent of the family of Joseph to which Jesus belonged. Its artificial form merely serves to disguise a genuine family tradition, which may have been embodied in a real birth-register. May it not be a sort of Midrashic commentary, in genealogical terms, on the real genealogy which is more correctly preserved in the Third Gospel?

On the Virgin Birth and the citation from Isaiah:

In the narrative that follows (i. 18–25) we are confronted by similar phenomena—the underlying fact accompanied by

explanation. The fact assumed and explicitly stated is the
Virgin Birth, which is supported (in the compiler's characteristic manner) by a citation from Scripture, viz., the LXX.
version of Isaiah vii. 14.

Now it is generally agreed that the narrative cannot have
been suggested by the citation. It is certainly remarkable
that Is. vii. 14, is the only passage in the LXX. (with one
exception, viz., Gen. xxiv. 43) where the Hebrew word
'almah, which means a young woman of marriageable age, is
rendered παρθένος. In the overwhelming majority of instances παρθένος (= Virgin) corresponds to its proper Hebrew equivalent běthûlā. Moreover, of any Messianic application among the Jews of these words concerning the Virgin's Son there is not elsewhere, we are assured on the high
authority of Prof. Dalman, even a " trace " (*The Words of
Jesus*, E. T., p. 270. . . . Badham's attempt (*Academy*,
June 8, 1895) to show that the belief that the Messiah was
to be born of a Virgin was current among Palestinian and
Alexandrian Jews rests upon highly precarious and uncertain evidence—mostly quotations from Martini and others
from Midrashic texts which cannot be verified. In some
cases they look like Christian interpolations. Consequently
we are justified in the conclusion that the narrative was not
suggested by the citation, but the citation by the assumed
fact of the narrative.

In the second part of the paper the Jewish-Christian
origin and the integrity of Luke i., ii., are considered
and defended. Considerations which seem to the author
" decisive " are adduced against the theory of interpolation of vers. 34, 35 of ch. i.

On the origin of the narrative, the view of Lagarde,
Resch, and Dalman is approved that (in Dalman's

words) these chapters " have throughout a colouring distinctly Hebrew, not Aramaic, and not Greek." The author agrees with Dr. Briggs that the language of the (mainly poetic) sources of Luke's narrative was probably " not Aramaic, but Hebrew."

On the important point of the relation of the two narratives we have the following:

That the Nativity-narratives in the First and Third Gospels are essentially independent has already been indicated. The fundamental facts on which they agree and on which they revolve may very well have been derived from a common source, viz., the early Jewish-Christian community of Palestine. The meagre historical content of Matthew's narrative is explained by the apologetic and polemical purpose that dominates it. He selects and uses only such material as is immediately useful for the practical purpose he has in view, and in view of this it is surely unsafe to argue from his silence that he was unacquainted with other traditional incidents which were treasured in the Palestinian circle. And in fact there is, I believe, one direct point of contact between the two narratives which suggests that Matthew was not unacquainted with the Hebrew hymns and poetical pieces which are so striking a feature of the Lucan account. I refer to the annunciation by an angel to Joseph set forth in Matt. i. 20, 21 [passage cited]. . . . Matthew is here using and translating from a poetical piece in Hebrew, derived doubtless like the hymns in Luke from the Palestinian community; and this conclusion is confirmed by the explanation of the name Jesus, which, as already mentioned, can only be elucidated by a play upon words in Hebrew.

The theories of pagan origin (Soltau, Schmiedel,

Usener, Gunkel) are acutely discussed, and the final result is reached:

The conclusion is forced upon us, therefore, that if the story of the Virgin Birth is a legend it must have grown up within the Jewish-Christian community of Palestine, and must represent a primitive Christological dogma expressing the idea of the perfect moral and spiritual purity of Jesus as Son of God. The Christian consciousness it might be urged, working on such a passage as " Thou art my Son, this day have I begotten thee " (Ps. ii. 7), together with the Scriptural promise of the fulness of the Spirit that should rest upon the Messiah (Is. xi. 2) may have been led to transfer these ideas to the physical beginnings of Jesus' life. But in the absence of any analogous developments in the Christian consciousness elsewhere this is hard to believe. Why did the Christological process assume just this form, and in this (a priori most unlikely) quarter? The impulse must have been given from without. But unless the idea came from heathen sources—which to the present writer seems inconceivable in so strictly Jewish a circle—then it must have grown out of a conviction, cherished within a limited Palestinian circle of believers, that the traditional belief among them was based upon facts of which some members of this community had been the original depositories and witnesses.

When subjected to the *criteria* properly applicable to it, and when the evidence is weighed in the light of the considerations advanced above, such a tradition, it seems to the present writer, has high claims to historical credibility. The alternative explanations only serve to raise more difficulties than they profess to solve.

In any case the hypothesis of pagan mythological influence is to be ruled out.

IV

THE REV. PROF. W. E. ADDIS, M.A., OXFORD

Well known as a radical critic of the Old Testament, Prof. Addis is nevertheless, like Dr. Briggs, a convinced defender of the Virgin Birth. In his paper, " Why do I believe in the Virgin Birth ? " he first clears the ground by setting aside reasons which fail to convince him. Among these is the prophecy in Is. vii., which, on the usual grounds that the sign was for Isaiah's contemporaries, that the Hebrew word '*almah* does not mean " virgin " in the strict sense, etc., he thinks is not applicable to the Virgin Birth. He is careful to distinguish between " belief in the Incarnation, and belief that the Incarnation was effected in a human body and soul of a pure Virgin," and says: " It is certain that some who do not accept the story of the Virgin Birth do accept the Catholic doctrine of the Incarnation." [1] He believes that the evidence for the Virgin Birth is " strong enough for rational acceptance," but admits that it could conceivably be much stronger than it is. He rejects any aid from " parthenogenesis."

On the positive side his argument is lucid and convincing. The main portions are here reproduced.

[1] I have stated in the lectures that I have had difficulty in discovering them; they are certainly few.

Granting that " a previous judgment already disposing us to believe " is necessary, he says:

Now, I think this prejudgment reasonable, and I should be inclined to state the case thus. The word of His supposed parents, however high their repute, would never convince me that an ordinary child had been born without having any man for his father. My point is that Christ was not an ordinary man. I confess that He is in a sense absolutely unique and incommunicable the Son of God, free from the least taint of sin, the head of a redeemed and renewed humanity. That being so, the Virgin Birth is no longer a difficulty to me; on the contrary, it is what I should expect, and any other hypothesis would present to my mind far more serious obstacles. I freely admit that such a birth involves a miracle; only the whole being and work of Christ is to me a miracle. I cannot look upon Him as a mere man; I do not set out with the assumption that He, through whom all things were made, was subject either in His birth or resurrection to the laws of the material universe. Of course *a priori* reasoning of this kind is not enough. It does not follow that a thing actually happened, because it appears to us likely and becoming that it should happen. Still the grounds just mentioned create a rational presumption. This presumption is clinched by the evidence of the Gospels and of the early Church, and is thus elevated into positive faith.

. . . . .

The careful study of the Synoptic Gospels creates several definite impressions in the mind. We feel that no man could have invented the story of Christ's life and character. On the one hand the picture drawn is natural, consistent, unique in its originality and attractive power; on the other hand, Christ towers high above the heads of His reporters, and is assuredly no creation of theirs. Nor are we left in any doubt that Christ was in the fullest sense man. He was hungry and weary; He was moved like other men by personal love and grief and even by anger. He drained the chalice of suffering, and it was said of Him that while He saved others, He could not save Himself. Still in one respect He stands by Himself. Never once does He make the faintest approach to confession of sin or moral imperfection. He who was so lowly of heart reveals no consciousness of sin, and though He poured forth His thanks to God, the Father of all, He expresses no gratitude for personal sin pardoned or even averted. He did indeed submit to a baptism, principally designed for the remission of sins. Nevertheless the revelation imparted to Him there was a declaration, not that any sin of His had been washed away, but rather He was the beloved Son in whom the Father was well pleased. True, He acknowledged that God alone is good. The distinction, however, between the progressive goodness of a Son who "learned obedience" and the divine goodness, absolute and infinite from all eternity, does not imply the least taint of personal fault or shortcoming in the Son of Man. We ask, therefore, how it was that our Lord in His human nature was free from the tendencies to evil which are the sad inheritance of the human race. To this, belief in the Virgin Birth offers the easiest and simplest answer: the Son of God became Man. He did not "shrink from the Virgin womb," yet He did not enter the human life by the common road. Being man "of the substance of His mother" He purified the flesh which He took by the very act of uniting it to His Divine Person. I do not question the fact that God was able in other ways to ensure the spotless sanctity of Christ's human nature. I contend, however, that the Virgin Birth provides, so far as I can see, the most natural and simple way of doing so; any other means which we can imagine would, I think, be more, not less, miraculous. From miracle of some kind we cannot escape, so long as we hold fast to the faith explicitly stated by St. Paul and implied in the New Testament throughout that our blessed Lord "knew no sin." Hence Dr. Martineau, rejecting the miraculous element altogether, is driven, reverent and religious as he is, to the conclusion that Christ was morally defective, a supremely good man, but still not perfectly good. (*Seat of Authority*, p. 651, where Dr. Martineau says that the words "without sin" must not be pressed beyond their relative significance.)

We may follow the same idea along another line of thought. St. Paul speaks of our Lord as the "Second Adam." We may put this in more modern language by considering Christ as the beginning of a redeemed humanity, as one who makes "all things new." Explain it as we will, the fact is surely patent enough that we are "very far gone from original righteousness." Even the most sceptical historian will scarcely refuse to admit that Christ introduced a new era, compared with which all other changes grow pale and insignificant, in the history of the human race. It was then in every way most fitting that He should enter the world in a new manner, breaking the long chain of birth which had transmitted sinful inclination from age to age, and inaugurating a new order. A first start had to be made, and He who was untouched by carnal passion was to raise us from "the death of sin to the life of righteousness." . . . And just as Christ's sinlessness is a miracle, so but in a much higher degree is His Incarnation. We may, if we please, dismiss miracles and believe that God is incarnate in collective humanity and reveals Himself in the progress of the race. But we are playing with words if we try to hold fast the faith that God was incarnate in the man Christ Jesus and made the perfect revelation of His character and will in Him, unless we are prepared to accept this as a stupendous miracle. Apart from miracle, we cannot worship Christ as the "very image of God's substance." A man more perfect than He may come in the slow progress of evolution. We have still to "look for another." This, of course, is tantamount to the absolute abandonment of Christianity.

Such are the reasons *a priori* which prepare the way, and may well incline us to believe that our Lord was born of a pure Virgin. This being so, what positive evidence have we for the traditional belief? We have the narrative by St. Luke at the beginning of his Gospel. Recent criticism has enabled me to appreciate more clearly the worth of the evidence given in the Third Gospel. Harnack, following in the line of Sir John Hawkins and Mr. Hobart, has produced an accumulation of evidence which makes it difficult to doubt that our Third Gospel really was written by Luke, the beloved physician and companion of St. Paul. Now Luke spent two years with St. Paul at Cæsarea, and had ample means of intercourse with Christians of Jewish race who had listened to our Lord and known His mother and His brethren. We turn next to the First Gospel; certainly the story told there is hard to reconcile even in important details with the history as given by St. Luke. One thing, however, is plain as noonday: the accounts in the Third and First Gospels are independent of each other, so that to the witness of St. Luke written down at latest about 80 A.D., we may confidently add the testimony of the first Evangelist derived from another source.

Reference follows to the witness of the early Church:

"Moreover there is really nothing to be said on the other side. For proof of this I must refer the reader to Mr. Allen's masterly review of the whole question in the *Interpreter* for 1905. . . . And how did the idea of Christ's Virgin Birth arise? It is far too ancient to be explained by the influence of Greek ideas, and besides the stories of birth from a divine and human parent are not stories of Virgin

Birth at all, but something quite different. The early chapters of Luke, as well as Matthew, are intensely Hebraic in thought and style. But of Virgin Birth, as of any notion that virginity was more honourable than marriage, the Old Testament says nothing. Its leaning is all the other way. We do not forget the words in the text, "Behold a virgin shall conceive," etc. But to these words St. Luke does not refer at all. St. Matthew adduces them as a prediction of a fact accepted on other grounds.

V

The Rev. Canon R. J. Knowling, D.D., Durham, England

Canon Knowling's paper, "Why I Believe the Doctrine of the Virgin Birth to be True," puts clearly the chief points with which readers of his excellent books and articles will already be familiar. The following paragraphs will be of interest:

The testimony of St. Irenæus has just received a remarkable strengthening by the recent discovery of a writing of the same great saint, which is accepted by Dr. Harnack as coming beyond all doubt from him, a writing in which St. Irenæus comes before us in the character of a catechist, seeking to build up his friend, Marcian, in the knowledge of the facts and of the doctrine of the Faith. In this newly recovered document we find frequent references to the fact of our Lord's Virgin Birth, and inferences and lessons are displayed against those who refuse to credit it, and it is stated, as Irenæus so forcibly remarks elsewhere, that the tradition thus affirmed is the common tradition, not of any drawn from the acceptance of this fact; keen opposition is one church only but of the whole Christian world. . . . Outside Christianity there were only two sources for the derivation of the story of the Virgin Birth—Jewish or pagan. But it is not too much to say that the whole tendency of Jewish thought was wholly different, and that such a fable as the birth of the Messiah from a Virgin could have arisen anywhere more easily than among the Jews. On the other hand, where was the Christian Church to be found which would have made itself responsible for this remarkable birth? We have only to turn to the language of the early Christian Apologist, Aristides, and its horror of the impurities of gods and goddesses, to be assured that such a story would not have commended itself for a moment to the early Christian consciousness, unless it could be justified by the statements of the Evangelists. . . .

The present writer has elsewhere laid stress upon the fact that St. Luke in his intercourse with James, the Lord's brother, in Jerusalem, an intercourse attested by one of the "We" sections of the Acts (xxi. 17) would have had means of learning the details of the Saviour's birth. And he is glad to see that the same view is not only emphasised by the Bishop of Ely [*Cambridge Theological Essays*, p. 406], but is rendered possible and probable by Dr. Harnack's own admission, that St. Luke had intercourse not only with John Mark, Silas, Philip, but also with James, the Lord's brother. (*Lukas der Arzt*, p. 3.) . . .

In this connection it is very difficult to believe that what was known to St. Luke was unknown to St. Paul, a point which the Bishop of Ely has recently emphasised. The present writer would express his strong conviction that far too much has been made of the silence of St. Paul in his Epis-

tles. Without going into the subject (upon which he has
expressed himself elsewhere) he will simply quote the words
of the famous Berlin professor, Dr. Weiss, that a new creative act of God, a cancelling of the natural continuity is
" an almost indispensable consequence of St. Paul's theology" [*Bibl. Theologie des N. T.*, pp. 289, 290], in face of
the fact that the second Adam is the pure and sinless head
of humanity in contrast to the first Adam, by whose transgression and sinful taint has been inherited by every member of his race.

VI

THE REV. PRINCIPAL A. E. GARVIE, D.D., NEW COLLEGE, LONDON

Principal Garvie entitles his paper: " The Doctrine
of the Virgin Birth of Jesus Christ our Lord: a Psychological, Ethical, and Theological Investigation." He
proposes to concentrate attention on " the relation of
the fact of the Virgin Birth to the doctrine of the Person
of Christ, His religious consciousness, and moral character."

He thus defines his personal attitude:

While himself prepared to answer affirmatively the question, *Why I believe the doctrine of the Virgin Birth to be
true?* as regards the *evidence* for the fact he holds that it
offers a high degree of probability, but not of absolute certainty; as regards the *significance* of belief in the fact, he
holds that it cannot be regarded as essential to Christian

faith in the divinity of Jesus, and yet that it is accordant with and confirmatory of that faith. There are too many exact scholars and genuine Christians on the other side to warrant a confidence, which would be both immodest and uncharitable. In bearing his own personal testimony he will endeavour to show that, in view of the universal sinfulness of mankind, the unique perfection of Jesus is explained most reasonably and credibly by the fact that His birth was due, not to natural generation, but to a supernatural act of divine grace, conditioned by human faith.

Dr. Garvie emphasises first " the Universal Sinfulness of Mankind." He remarks:

About this starting-point it might seem unnecessary to say anything, were it not that there is an opinion gaining currency in circles that are not thoroughly informed on these matters that somehow modern science has compelled Christian theology to rid itself altogether of the doctrines of original sin and total depravity. That the fresh light thrown on the beginnings of human history demands some modification in the statement of the doctrines may be freely conceded, but what must be firmly denied is that the words of the prophet, " All we like sheep have gone astray " (Is. liii. 6), or of the Apostle, " All have sinned, and fall short of the glory of God " (Romans iii. 23), have become obsolete, and been superseded.

He shows how Mr. F. R. Tennant, " while denying any hereditary taint in the congenital instincts or appetites of the child, recognises that the desires, which may afterwards come into conflict with conscience in the child's development have a long start of conscience, and that accordingly the moral life is a race in which every child starts handicapped: ' When will and conscience enter, it is into a land already occupied by a powerful foe,' " and he

welcomes this statement as a proof that from a thoroughly modern stand-point the fact of the universal sinfulness of mankind is not denied, only the explanation of it hitherto given is modified. The modification appears to go further than the data allow. The moral resemblance of parents and children seems to require some explanation such as the influence of the early environment does not sufficiently give. Even if we admit that sin, as involving personal choice, cannot be transmitted; yet the possibilities—instincts and appetites—which through personal choice become actualities of sin we seem to be justified in believing are in some measure determined by heredity. To put the conclusion in the most guarded terms there does appear to be universal in the race, and continued from generation to generation, a tendency which is the potency of sin.

With this is now contrasted " the Unique Perfection of Jesus ":

The universal sinfulness of mankind includes religious defect as well as moral depravity; for moral evil is properly described as sin only in man's relation to God, as distrust of and disobedience to God. The unique perfection of Jesus, which stands out in solitary splendour on that dark background, is in His religious consciousness as in His moral character. As regards the absolute transcendence of the moral character of Jesus there is general agreement. [Lecky, J. S. Mill, and Schaff are quoted.] . . . There is one thing altogether lacking in the moral experience of Jesus which is found in all the saints—there is no repentance of sin, and no prayers for pardon. Only if He was, as in the Gospels He is represented as being, an absolute exception to the race in having no sin to repent of or seek pardon for, can this be regarded as consistent with the absolute moral perfection. Even the memory of sin once committed would be sufficient to forbid such an attitude. If his moral life had been a race in which he had started handicapped, or if His will and conscience had entered "into a land already occupied by a powerful foe," to repeat Mr. Tennant's figures of speech, would such a moral conscience have been possible? Even if we were to suppose that, when His moral life began, will had such energy, and conscience such illumination, that this most powerful foe had at once been reduced to subjection, we should only be shifting the miracle from the beginning to a later stage of His moral development. In either case the moral experience of Jesus presents to us a problem for which some solution must be found.

But His religious consciousness of Divine Sonship, His filial dependence on, communion with, submission to God as His Father is no less absolutely unique in its perfection. Never before, or since, has God been so known, trusted. loved, obeyed, served. [Harnack is quoted.] . . . The vision, the confidence, and the obedience of faith were seen in Jesus as in no other.

In this absolute perfection of Jesus, both as regards *moral character* and *religious consciousness*, there is so great a contrast between Him and humanity in its universal sinfulness, that He cannot be included in the normal process of evolution. . . . For those who deny this absolute perfection, or who doubt that it necessarily involves as absolute a transcendence of the ordinary conditions and limitations under which human personality has its start, course, and goal, there may be here no problem clamouring for a solution; but for those who accept the Christian confession of Christ as Divine Saviour and Lord there is a question urgently demanding an answer.

This leads to the consideration of the **Virgin Birth of Jesus**:

The writer is persuaded that the fact of the Virgin Birth is one of the data to be recognised in any adequate answer. It is sometimes maintained that the Gospels offer us three alternative, and not complementary, answers to the question. The Johannine doctrine of the Incarnation of the Logos, and the Synoptic testimony to the descent of the Spirit on Jesus at His baptism are held to be rivals to and substitutes for the explanation of the higher nature of Jesus offered in the statement in Matthew and Luke regarding the Virgin Birth. It is to be noted, however, that the first and third Evangelists seem to have had no consciousness that they were offering two contrary explanations; and without laying any undue stress on the suggestion, the writer cannot rid himself of the impression that the very emphatic repetitions in John i. 13, regarding believers as the children of God, " which were born, not of blood ($a\mathit{i}\mu a\tau\omega\nu$, bloods), nor of the will of the flesh ($\sigma a\rho\kappa\acute{o}s$), nor of the will of man ($\mathit{a}\nu\delta\rho\acute{o}s$) but of God," contain a covert reference to the mode of the birth of the Logos, which is in the next verse described " the Word became flesh." Without pressing these arguments, we may discover on closer scrutiny that the three explanations harmonise. As has been already urged, Jesus must have been an exception to the universal sinfulness of the race from the very beginning of His moral development, and how could the descent of the Spirit in His thirtieth year explain the sinless childhood, boyhood, youth? Is it not probable that the $\sigma\acute{a}\rho\xi$ which the $\lambda\acute{o}\gamma os$ became was prepared for His habitation? The humanity had to be so constituted that the personal unity with the divinity would find in it no hindrance. As will afterwards be shown, human faith was the condition of the divine grace in the supernatural act by which the humanity was constituted, and this seems to me a more reasonable and credible explanation than the assumption, which must otherwise be made, that from the moment of union the humanity was so overborne by the divinity as to be reduced to passivity, so that none of the congenital instincts or appetites could assert themselves before the emergence of will and conscience. In the faith of the mother and of Joseph mankind offered its welcome, rendered its service to the Incarnation of the Word.

The additions of Roman Catholicism (immaculate conception of the Virgin herself, etc.) to this doctrine are dismissed as without warrant.

The author proceeds:

In endeavouring to show that the Virgin Birth does offer us some explanation of the unique, absolute perfection of Jesus, we must beware of too confident a statement. We are not in a position to affirm that it was only in this way and no other that it was possible for the personal development of Jesus in goodness and godliness to get such a beginning, without any handicap (to repeat the figure already used). We may, if we please, conjecture that even if Jesus had been born naturally, the divine grace might have so guarded the infant mind, heart, will, that no factor was allowed to enter into His personal development which could have hindered this unique, absolute perfection. But, while in the evangelical narratives we have no evidence for such an assumption, the record of the Virgin Birth lies before us, and this we are compelled to explain as a fable (an enterprise which in the writer's judgment has been so far unsuccessful), or to accept as a fact to which either we can assign no significance or value, and which, therefore, becomes a burdensome mystery, or which, as the writer prefers, we must endeavour so to interpret that it becomes intelligible.

Stress is laid on the ethical conditioning of the Incarnation:

The features of this supernatural conception which are to be emphasised are on the one hand the divine grace which is spontaneously *initiative*, and on the other hand the human faith which is responsively *receptive*. . . . In the Incarnation of the Son of God faith from the beginning was the accompaniment of grace. Our Protestant dread of the superstition of *Mariolatry* should not be allowed to prevent our frank and full recognition of the blessedness and honour of the mother of Jesus in the trust and the task committed to her. She was not " disobedient to the heavenly vision," nor distrustful of the heavenly race. " Behold the handmaid of the Lord; be it unto me according to thy Word " (Luke i. 38). We may venture to believe that this *human faith* was the necessary condition of the Divine grace in the supernatural act of the conception. . . .

The faith of Joseph, also blessed and honoured of God as the chosen guardian of the mother and the child, must not be overlooked. He, too, had his trust and task from God. He humbly and obediently accepted the divine communication in regard to his betrothed. In their companionship during the trying days until the birth of the child doubtless his faith confirmed and sustained hers. If the paternal function physically was not his, it was his morally and religiously. He might be regarded as one of the parents of Jesus, not according to the flesh, but according to the Spirit.

The reasonableness of the Virgin Birth is thus shown:

Granted the necessity that His personal life should not be a race in which He started handicapped, and that His conscience and will should not enter a land already occupied by a powerful foe, the postulate is fulfilled it may be maintained confidently, in the Virgin Birth in such a way as least disturbs the laws and order of human development. A heredity and an environment are provided, adequate to, and appropriate for, the absolutely unique result, in which the supernatural does not suppress violently, or expel entirely the natural, but completely pervades and transforms it. The divine initiative in the supernatural conception starts a process which runs a normal course, and yet attains the abnormal result. There is not a prodigality, but an economy of the miraculous.

The essay closes by showing that the value of Christ's life as a pattern is not affected by His supernatural birth.

VII

The Rev. H. Wheeler Robinson, M.A., Rawdon, by Leeds, England

The aim of Mr. Robinson's very full paper is " to approach the Nativity narratives from the standpoint of men and women whose thought was dominated by the Old Testament Scriptures." In the difficulty of summarising a paper which involves so much detail, it may be simplest to give the author's conclusions in his own words. He says:

The points which have been ascertained may now be collected:

1. The mystery of the physiological process of conception

and birth, regarded as a point of entrance for divine activity. The continuity of life, under divine control, from the moment of conception onwards.

2. The idea of Spirit as acting on and through persons to personal ends. The close interrelation of " soul " and " body " in the Hebrew idea of personality. The absence of any idea that Virgin Birth was necessary to eliminate the taint of sin from the personality of Jesus.

3. The absence of any O. T. prophecy of Virgin Birth, yet the consonance of such birth with Hebrew ideas of virginity.

The author adds:

There is no need to appeal to direct Gentile influence on the formulation of the belief. Given these conditions of thought, and the unique personality of Jesus, we may proceed to explain away the narratives as a natural inference —if we want to explain them away. But this raises the whole attitude to miracle. . . . On historical grounds, we are driven to admit the truth of the Resurrection of Jesus in a unique way. Why may we not, then, accept a unique beginning as well as a unique ending to this unique life?

The paper concludes:

In accepting for himself the Virgin Birth in this sense, and on the lines here briefly outlined, the writer feels bound to state that it ought to be possible for Christians to find common ground, whatever their differences on the physiological question. If God is recognised to be in Christ, all theories of the manner of His presence are secondary to the fact itself. . . . It is possible that there never will be agreement amongst believers on such a subject; and there is no New Testament warrant for the exclusion of any who cannot accept the Nativity narratives in the sense intended by their writers, which it has been the chief aim of this paper to elucidate.

VIII

THE REV. PROF. THEOD. ZAHN, D.D., ERLANGEN, GERMANY

This distinguished scholar contributes a paper which is in part a confession of personal faith, and in part a discussion of points in the testimony of the Gospels—especially of the Gospel of John.

To the question, "Why do I believe the doctrine of the Virgin Birth to be true?" he replies:

My answer to this question can be given in very few words: I believe that that doctrine is true, or, in other words, I believe that the miraculous event which is set forth in that doctrine did actually happen, because I believe in Jesus Christ, who did redeem me and will redeem me from the guilt of sin and from the power of Death. These words *contain* everything that I can give in answer; but they do not *say* everything that is to be said to-day. The same disturbance of the Christian minds of all countries and of all denominations, which has been the occasion to ask a number of theologians, of English, French, and German speech, about their personal attitude towards that doctrine, renders some explanation necessary of my above-given confession of faith.

Later he says, after contrasting the primitive with the " modern " faith: " Therefore my faith in Jesus as my Redeemer stands and falls with the grateful recognition of the facts which form the contents of the Gospel."

Do these facts include the Virgin Birth? He grants, " No word of Jesus has come down to us which refers to it *distinctly*. Nowhere did Paul *unequivocally* declare his belief in it." Yet he contends: " The Virgin Birth of Christ was an article of faith of the Church as early as the first century, and we may assume that it will be so as long as there is a Church, for that article is a necessary element of the faith on which the Church lives."

Dealing with the testimony of the Fourth Gospel, Zahn takes up a number of points to show that John was not unacquainted with, or indifferent to, the earthly origin of Jesus. His characteristic positions are seen in the following:

We can no more imagine that John did not know the tradition of the Virgin Birth than that he did not form any opinion about that report. Not only the unanimous tradition of the ancient Church, but likewise the comparative study of the Gospels forces us to recognise that the Fourth Gospel was written later than the other three, and that the author expected his first readers to have a knowledge of the fundamental outlines of the Synoptical tradition. Since, further, the accounts in Matthew i. and Luke i. manifestly originated independently of each other, it follows that the essential features in which both accounts agree was a matter of general knowledge at the time when these Gospels were composed, and it results from Luke i. 2*ff*., that this occurred at the time and under the eyes of the " eye witnesses from the beginning." Besides, Matthew. ch. i., already takes into consideration the Jewish slurs cast upon the respectability of the birth of Jesus; the latter, of course, are nothing but a malicious caricature of the Christian tradition of the Virgin Birth. Therefore, even the Jews of Palestine knew that tradition as a common belief of the Christians among them. Considering all this, it is incredible, from a historical point of view, that that tradition did not arise until after the years 60 to 70, and it is as incredible that it was unknown to the Fourth Evangelist and his first readers. If Cerinthus denied it, John knew it, and we may suppose that he confessed his faith in it. This can even be proved.

According to the usual text of John i. 13, this passage treats of the men to whom Jesus has imparted the right and the capacity to become children of God. That applies to all who in the time of the Evangelist believed in the name of Jesus (i. 12). Of these, he says that they are begotten and born, not of double blood, that is, by the mixture of the blood of two people, not of a will of the flesh, not of the will of a man, but of God. Even if there did not follow the statement in i. 14, that the Logos became flesh, it could not be misunderstood that verse 13 says of the birth of the children of God exactly what is said by the tradition of the Virgin Birth of Jesus. The begetting and the birth of the Only Begotten Son of God is directly used as the model for representing the begetting and birth of children of God, who have become so through Him. For, why else should John nor have been satisfied to deny that the children of God are products of a will of the flesh like the children of man? Why does he assert beyond that negatively that they were not called into being by the mixture of the blood of a man and a woman and not by the will of a man? Just this triple denial seems unnatural, even if John wanted to compare the birth of the children of God with the Birth of the Only Son of God. Why is he not satisfied with the simple opposition of flesh and spirit as Jesus uses it according to John iii. 6, where he speaks expressly of the Second Birth in opposition to the natural birth. To that we must add some

grave stylistic objections to the traditional text of i. 13. Its
connection with i. 12 is very hard; for, not the definition
of the faith in the name of Christ, which forms the close of
verse 12, but the definition of the quality of being a child
of God is what is determined by verse 13. Just as unnatural seems the connection of the clause about the incarnation of the Logos in verse 14 with verse 13 by an " and."
Wherever in the Prologue John passes to a new sphere of
thought, he uses the asyndetic form (verses 3, 6, 9), and
by the word " and " he adds only such sentences as belong
to the same sphere as the preceding idea. Compare the
sentences in verses 1, 4, 10, 11–14. All these objections disappear, if we recognise as the original text the reading
which in any case is exceedingly ancient and which says,
" He was not born of double blood and not of a will of the
flesh, nor was He born of a man's will, but of God, and the
Logos became flesh and we saw His glory," etc. This is
not the place to show in detail that these clauses without
any connection in relative form with verse 12 could be read
in all Church copies of the Occident from Irenæus to the
last years of the fourth century, and that the reading even
left its traces in the far-off Orient. Tertullian was probably
right in accusing the Valentinians of being the first to
change the singular in verse 13 to the plural. That this
reading passed into Church copies of the Greek Orient is
readily understood. Since in verse 14 the subject is not
left indeterminate, as in verses 10 and 11, but is given by the
name of the Logos, it seemed as if the Logos and His entry
into human life was mentioned here first, and not in verse 13.
But just in verse 14 the use of the name of the Logos was
necessary, because John wanted to remind of verse 1 and
wanted to say that He who at the beginning was God with
God, had become, by the begetting and birth described in
verse 13, a man of flesh and blood and at the same time
the One Begotten Son of God. It is very easily understood

that some orthodox Greek connected verse 13 with verse 12 by an interpolated relative pronoun; that way, the interpretation of that clause as referring to a special class of select spiritual men, which was popular among the Gnostics, was rendered impossible, and its interpretation was insured as referring to all faithful Christians.

John has therefore not only indirectly shown his familiarity with the Virgin Birth of Jesus and omitted any opposition to it, but he has confessed it with full sounding testimony. If the Fourth Evangelist is the disciple who, in compliance with the last will of the dying Jesus, took Mary into his house (John viii. 26) we cannot imagine any stronger testimony than this; for, what men can know of the birth of Jesus, that was known to the mother who has borne our Lord.

IX

The Rev. Prof. R. Seeberg, D.D., Berlin, Germany

Prof. Seeberg's discussion of the article, " Born of the Virgin Mary," turns in part on his peculiar Christology, which he explains to mean that the Divine Spirit as the Personal Redeeming Will of God (dogmatically the " Logos ") united Himself with the man Jesus so as to become One with Him, penetrating Him by His energy, and forming Him to be His organ. His paper, however, is a very thorough handling of the cru-

cial points in the controversy, with the result of showing that the derivation of the Virgin Birth from pagan
myths or from O. T. prophecy is inadmissible, and that
nothing militates against the acceptance of the historical
fact. He sums up in the following propositions:

The result of the historical examination is therefore briefly
this:

1. The miraculous origin of Jesus, reported by Matthew
and Luke, has the meaning that God created Jesus as He
created Adam, in order that He might be His organ.

2. That miraculous origin of Jesus is to be recognised as
an historical fact, because well-informed authors report it
without any tendency or object in view, and because it is
testified to by the unprejudiced belief of the entire ancient
Church, as well as by the Jewish slanders of Mary.

3. On the other side, the denial of the Virgin Birth on the
part of the radical Jewish-Christians is caused by a tendency.

4. The efforts to show the story to have been a myth,
either by falling back on pagan myths or on Jewish conceptions or views, are historically untenable.

5. The silence of the old source of the Gospels, of the
primitive Christian Baptismal Confession, of John, of Paul,
and of the other authors of the New Testament, is unintelligible as long as we face it from the point of view of
the modern popular Dogmatics; but it is readily understood,
if we take the question up from the point of view of the
original Christology.

He asks in closing whether the article has a religious
significance which warrants us retaining it in our Creed,
and answers the question in the affirmative. " We have,"
he says, " to pay regard to the ' weak in faith,' but we

must not make them masters of the faith of the Church."
He shows that a profound doctrinal interest is involved
in the Article, when taken in connection with a just
view of Christ.

If we now look at the resistance we men make to God,
and see how our whole nature, burdened and weakened by
the long inheritance of sinful tendencies and habits, op-
poses the will and the truth of God, we can hardly understand how a man who has that tendency towards evil in him
from his birth could become the organ of God in the absolute way that Jesus did. The more closely we become acquainted with the man Jesus, with the absolute truth of
His words, with the perfect union of His will with the
divine will within Him, with the freshness and originality
of His powerful human individuality, the more loudly does
the question arise whether this man really could have originated like all other men, open from the first to evil, and
inclined towards it. . . . Here is the point where the history
of the miraculous birth of Jesus comes in. It solves for
us a riddle which is much greater than the riddle which it
itself presents to us.

X

THE REV. PROF. H. BAVINCK, D.D., AMSTERDAM,
HOLLAND

This eminent Dutch theologian devotes considerable
space to the right *method* of investigating the subject of
the Virgin Birth. He contrasts the *analytical* method,

common in scientific and historical investigation, which supposes that the inquirer does not know anything of the subject he inquires into, and proceeds by unbiassed consideration of the phenomena presented to it; and the *synthetic*, shown to be needful also in science, which starts from ideas already given.

In every science both these methods are employed, and it is only a question of degree as to how far one or the other method has predominance.

Prof. Bavinck shows that the one-sided application of the analytical method to the Gospels can only lead to destructive and negative results, and illustrates from modern criticism. " The Virgin Birth especially is from the standpoint of analytical investigation a stumbling-block." The analytic method in theology, as in every science, needs to be completed by the synthetic.

In psychology, the psychical phenomena lead up to the knowledge of the soul itself; but in the same way the knowledge of the soul helps us to understand and interpret the psychical phenomena. A man's character may be explained by his words and deeds, but the knowledge of the person himself gives us more insight into his feelings and acts. . . . Life, conscience, will, religious and moral feelings, etc., are only understood because we bring with us an idea about all these things, borrrowed from our own living personality. . . . The words and the acts of Christ certainly shed light upon His Person; but the Person of Christ on the other hand makes clear His speech and deeds. The miracles of Jesus are seen from a quite different point of view, if I acknowledge Him to be the holy Son of God, from that in which they would if I honour Him only as a religious genius. And so it is with the whole substance of Christian belief.

Accordingly, Prof. Bavinck holds,

in all these and other theological investigations, the principal and real question is: What think ye of Christ? Consciously or unconsciously, this question is always put in the foreground, and all investigations on either side are ruled by the answer to this question. . . . By this alone theology preserves its religious character. The answer does not depend on critical and historical investigation, but on the regeneration of the heart. No man speaking by the Spirit of God calleth Jesus accursed, and no man can say that Jesus is the Lord but by the Holy Ghost.

In dealing with Christ's image in the New Testament, Prof. Bavinck gives special attention to one point—the identity of the self-consciousness that we find in Christ everywhere.

It is always the same Person, the same I, that encounters us in the Christ of the New Testament. This self-consciousness is quite human, more human than in any one of us, but humanity is not the essence, but the form of its existence.

Later in the paper, Prof. Bavinck connects with this an argument with the Virgin Birth. Because Christ was an eternal divine Person,

He could not be quite passive in the moment of conception as we are: He was sent by His Father into the world, but he came also Himself with full consciousness and will. . . . He could not be conceived, as we are, quite passively, and could not come in this way into existence, but, because He previously existed, His conception was His own deed. He assumed consciously and freely our human nature.

Another point of view from which Prof. Bavinck argues the necessity of the Virgin Birth is the relation of Christ to the world as Saviour.

He did not become this by natural development of His earthly life in the way of evolution. He came as a Saviour, because He was such before according to the counsel and will of His Father. Then it behoved Him to be like unto His brethren in all things, but nevertheless to be a unique Person, not a common member of mankind, but the Head of a new Covenant, the root of a new generation.

He connects this with the terms of the old theology, that

He could not and might not be born under the Covenant of works, subordinate to Adam, and subjected to the guilt, sin, and death of the race. But, like Adam himself, He had to be formed directly by the hand of God, not of the dust of the ground, but of the human flesh and blood in Mary's holy womb.

Unlike some others, Prof. Bavinck holds that, viewed in the light of the divine personality and redeeming mission of Christ, the Virgin Birth is

not a strange fact in His life, not a superfluous addition without significance for His own Person and for our belief, but a natural and necessary event in the life of our Lord, as natural and necessary as His death and resurrection. It is in full harmony with the whole.

Rejection of this mystery is therefore not an innocent

thing. One cannot defend such a rejection by an appeal to the silence of the Apostles. Though we believe in the supernatural birth of Christ, we do not mention it every day in our preaching. The central facts of the Gospel are the death and resurrection of our Lord, not His supernatural birth and incarnation. The Cross of Christ has therefore been the *kerugma* of the Apostles, and ought to be ours also. But though we do not mention this mystery every day, it is quite another thing to deny and reject it. That the Christian Church has never done. From the first, when Mary told this mystery of her heart, the Church believed her. There has not been any opposition to this doctrine but from the side of the Ebionites and the Gnostics—not on critical and historical, but on dogmatic grounds. And just so in these days, the rejection of the Virgin Birth is generally combined with the rejection of the Apostolic testimony about the resurrection and ascension, the Messiahship and divine Sonship of our Lord.

XI

The Rev. Prof. E. Doumergue, D.D., Montauban, France

Prof. Doumergue describes his paper as " simply the reflections of an historian, who is accustomed to apply the historical methods."

He dismisses the *a priori* objection to miracle, and limits himself to pointing out that the miracle of the Supernatural Birth is really " less miraculous than, for instance, the Resurrection." "No doubt, we can find for the Resurrection certain analogies in nature; but the analogies for the miraculous Birth are of a different and more significant character." He instances the facts of *Parthenogenesis*.

With reference to "legends," he asks whether these do not rather speak to "a human need, a human instinct," to which the miraculous birth of Christ corresponds.

He then comes

to the great argument, the direct, positive argument in favour of the Supernatural Birth. It is the corollary of the entire Life of the Christ, and of the part (*rôle*) which the witnesses of that Life, the Evangelists and the Apostles, attributed to the Christ.

The present crisis, which is so troublesome, so harassing, is the result of the contest between two theologies: one leads quite naturally to the affirmation; the other leads, no less naturally, to the denial of the Supernatural Birth.

It is on that fact, and because of that fact, that the two schools separate; much more than because of any other fact, even the Resurrection.

And why? Because, very logically, the decisive question is always the question of origin and of nature. Whence does the Christ come? Whence does Christianity come? What is the nature of the Christ, and of Christianity? One Theology answers: the Christ is God who has become a man; the other Theology answers: he is a man who has become God. Heavenward! Earthward!

That is exactly, precisely, the special point—the point, however, on which everything depends, on which the present theological discussion in the entire world turns.

He illustrates the character of the new humanity-theology from Wernle, who contends that, though Jesus had a sort of moral divinity, " in spite of it all, he did not pass beyond the limits of pure humanity " (*des rein menschlichen*).

In dealing with the argument from silence, he has an interesting quotation from Biedermann:

One understands how as rationalistic a theologian as Biedermann, who does not admit for himself the miraculous birth, writes: " John does not explain how the Logos became flesh, but he knows, evidently, the Miraculous Birth."

He points out that " in order to originate, to form, to develop, a legend needs time," and the time in this case is wanting. The style of the reports of Matthew and Luke shows that " these reports belong to the most ancient documents which are contained in the New Testament." He adopts the view of Zahn that Matthew's narrative is a protest against the slander that Jesus was the son of Mary conceived in adultery.

But if Matthew protests against the slanders, to what epoch must those slanders go back, which were older than the epoch in which Matthew wrote? Again we are face to face with a primitive belief.

We can, therefore, at the least, conclude with Bovon, the dogmatist of Lausanne, who is so independent of traditional orthodoxy: " In the present state of the question, it would require a great deal of assurance to declare that Jesus was not born as the Biblical authors report."

XII

The Rev. H. C. G. Moule, D.D., Bishop of Durham

The Bishop of Durham furnishes a succinct and devout statement of the reasons for believing in the Virgin Birth of our Lord, which it is to be hoped will be published in another form. He builds his argument largely on the character of Jesus in the Gospels, regarding which he says: " More and yet more, as life advances, and as experience tests and discriminates opinions and arguments, the supreme and self-evidential value of the *Evangelic Portrait of our Lord* affirms itself to my deepest reason."

It is perhaps only necessary here to quote a striking passage on the contrast of the Canonical with the Apocryphal Gospels, and his closing summary.

I call attention here, as we may do everywhere in the Canonical Gospels, to the eloquent contrast between the restraint and sober dignity of their narratives, which yet are so full of wonders, and the narratives of the so-called Apocryphal Gospels and the kindred literature; such as the *Gospel of the Infancy*, the *Anaphora Pilati*, and the lately recovered fragments of the *Gospel of Peter*. These writings, broadly speaking, emanate from the same age of the world and from the same race and region as the Canonical Gospels. But compare the character of the two literatures, in their picture of the supernatural. The canonical writers never, for a moment, give us the grotesque, the gigantesque, in their accounts. The apocryphal writers revel in such things. The flight into Egypt appears in them as a succession of fantastic miracles. The dying thief addresses the Lord on the cross in a long oration; he is sent with a written order for admission to the guardians of Paradise; he appears in regal pomp after death in Galilee. The Lord's resurrection in the *Gospel of Peter*, is described as the exit from the sepulchre of a Being whose head is higher than the clouds in the sky, and the cross moving automatically, follows him as he steps forth. I know few methods at once so simple and so impressive for revising a consciousness of the majestic sanity and veracity of the Canonical Gospels as to peruse, in close succession, a few pages of the apocryphal stories and then, let us say, the last two chapters of St. John or the first two chapters of St. Luke.

Yes, the great yet tender narrative of Annunciation and Nativity bears in its very tissue all the deepest characters of truthfulness. Some of its finest and most beautiful lines suggest powerfully that its writer drew his knowledge from a quarter authentic above all others, from the Holy Mother herself. Nothing is more easy than to think that St. Luke had ample opportunity for consulting her. . . .

So I close my answer to the question at the head of my essay. To sum it up in an inverted order, beginning from the end: I believe the spotless Virgin Birth of our most Holy Lord because I have a strong confidence in the trustworthiness of the original assertion of it in the Gospels. I believe it because I take it to be supremely and profoundly *congruous* with the altogether unique Person and Character of Him of whom it is asserted. I believe it in harmony (a harmony which is a powerful aid to a reasonable faith) with a continuous belief, unbroken throughout the whole Christian era from the apostolic age to ours, and which has found a continual verification, from the spiritual view-point, in the adoring faith of the saints of God.

XIII

THE REV. W. H. GRIFFITH-THOMAS, D.D., OXFORD

Dr. Griffith-Thomas entitles his paper, " The Virgin Birth—Reasons for Belief," and aims at stating " in brief and popular language the general position." " Without concentrating on any particular arguments in favour of the doctrine it is proposed to give several reasons which singly and cumulatively support a belief in the Virgin Birth." It is another paper to which general currency should be given.

The author follows lines analogous to those in the foregoing lectures in discussing the genuineness and integrity of the Gospel records, the early witness of the Church, and the necessity of the miraculous birth to account for the uniqueness of the life of Jesus. " It may fairly be contended that such an unique life demands an unique origin and entrance into the world."

" The one rock," he argues, " on which all non-miraculous theories are shattered is the historic Person of the man Christ Jesus. He has to be accounted for. The effect demands an adequate cause, and we Christians claim that the Virgin Birth alone gives this adequate explanation of His mode of entrance upon His earthly life."

On the silence of the Apostles, Dr. Griffith-Thomas remarks:

The preaching of the fact of the Incarnation rather than the mode is the true method of presenting the Gospel; first what Christ is and only then how He came to be what He is. In these considerations of the true perspective of Christian teaching we may rightly explain the silence of St. Paul and St. John. There was no need of the Virgin Birth for evangelistic purposes, but only for the intellectual instruction of Christian people. Adequate reasons could be given for silence on this point in the earliest years of the Church, but to argue from this silence to a disbelief, or at any rate to an ignorance of the doctrine on the part of the early Christians, is not only precarious in the highest degree, but really contradicts the facts associated with the early date of Luke's Gospel.

He concludes:

We see no reason for rejecting the testimony of the Gospels and the witness of the whole Church to the Virgin Birth. If the narratives of the Gospels are not true they are a deliberate fiction, for there is no other alternative. And if the Church has been mistaken for centuries it is certainly the greatest and most widespread persistent delusion that has ever been known. Two almost insuperable difficulties appear in this connection. (1) How did the idea of the Virgin Birth arise so soon if it was not based on fact? (2) How were the narratives of the Gospels accepted so early and universally if they were not historical? . . .

The ultimate decision will only be arrived at by settling the question what Jesus came in the world to do. If the one thing that man needs is illumination, then ideas will suffice and no Divine Incarnation is necessary, but if there is such a thing as sin in the world we must produce a Divine

Sinless Redeemer to deal with it. For such a Redeemer the only adequate explanation, so far as His earthly origin is concerned, is the ancient belief of the Church Universal that He was "conceived of the Holy Ghost, born of the Virgin Mary."

XIV

THE REV. PROF. HENRY COWAN, D.D., ABERDEEN, SCOTLAND

Prof. Cowan writes on the "Testimony of the Sub-Apostolic Age to the Virgin Birth of our Lord," and his paper is a carefully marshalled statement of the evidence on that subject. The testimonies of Ignatius, Aristides, and Justin are presented. *The Pastor* of Hermas is one of the books sometimes alleged to be silent on the Virgin Birth, but Prof. Cowan points to a passage "in which the Virgin Birth appears to be allegorical'ᵥ declared." He shows how the Apocryphal *Protevangelium of James* and the pseudonymous *Gospe₁ of Peter* attest (the former directly, the latter by suggestion) the Virgin Birth. The fact is made use oᵢ that "several heretical sects which flourished in the Sub-Apostolic Age either accepted the Virgin Birth oᵢ adopted a Christology suggested by it, and thus recognised the authority of the tradition regarding it." Lateᵢ testimonies—Christian, heretical, Jewish—follow.

As respects results:

The general belief of the Church in the closing years of the Apostolic Age has a bearing on the genuineness and historicity of Matthew i., ii., and of Luke i., ii.; on their genuineness because such belief removes any *a priori* reason for supposing that the narratives of the Infancy had no place in the Gospels as originally composed; on their historicity because if the records of those four chapters were in any important particulars untrue, the errors must have been repudiated by many instead of being generally accepted by the Church.

He thus comments on the alleged silence of St. John:

Whatever weight, rightly or wrongly, may be attached to this silence is outweighed by that belief in the Virgin Birth which sub-apostolic testimony shows to have been general during the closing years of St. John's life. For surely if such belief was really unfounded, St. John must have known it to be so, owing to his special intimacy with Mary, who was consigned to his care and lived in his home. The propagation, moreover, of the alleged error took place before his very eyes; for he lived in his old age at Ephesus, the capital of that province of Asia where the Virgin Birth is specially known to have been acknowledged.

If John, then, knew that the belief which had become so widespread among the Christians around him was erroneous, can we conceive of him, as an honest man, sanctioning by silence the growth of what he knew to be a fable into a prominent part of the Christian Creed? Silence in such a case would have been unpardonable; while on the other hand, any protest which he made could not but have been memorable and effective. The absence of protest on his part is explicable only on the supposition that the Church's belief in her Lord's Virgin Birth was well founded.

XV

MR. JOSEPH JACOBS, LITT.D., YONKERS, N. Y.

Mr. Jacobs writes as a Jew on "The Virgin Birth from the Standpoint of Jewish Science and of Folklore."

His blunt position is: "There is no Jewish standpoint with regard to the Virgin Birth."

Throughout the wide extent of Jewish literature there is not a single passage which can bear the construction that the Messiah should be miraculously conceived. The passage (Is. vii. 14–16) is now universally recognised by Christian scholars to be entirely mistranslated by the Septuagint and by the Gospel of St. Matthew. The only basis for any such construction being put upon the passage is a mistranslation of the Septuagint of a word which in Hebrew has no reference to virginity. The word, *'almah* used in that passage is derived from a root meaning to be mature, and simply implies that the young woman in question is of a marriageable age. The fact that it is used in Proverbs xxx. 19, of "the way of a man with a maid," is sufficient to prove that there is no idea of virginity attached to the word. This is now recognised by all scholars, Christian as well as Jewish. The fathers of the Church took the opposite view for obvious reasons, and their theories prevailed to the end of the eighteenth century, when, to use the words of the Rev. Dr. Skinner in the Cambridge Bible for schools, "it began to be recognised that on the philological question the Jews were right." . . .

The Jewish interpretation of the Scriptures never saw in

this passage anything corresponding to a Virgin Birth. This is sufficiently indicated by the absence of any suggestion in the very wide apocryphal and apocalyptic literature of the Jews which can be dated before the birth of Christ. These visions and prophecies are filled with innumerable traits of a supernatural kind, but they never suggest that the Messiah shall be born otherwise than as a man. The traits of the Jewish Messiah in these works have been brought together in an excellent work by Prof. James Drummond, *The Jewish Messiah, a Critical History of the Messianic Idea among the Jews, from the Rise of the Maccabees to the Closing of the Talmud.* There is not a scintilla of evidence in all this literature of anything corresponding to the Virgin Birth. Indeed, in the celebrated dialogue between Justin Martyr and the Jew Trypho, who has been identified by some with the Rabbi Tarphon of the Talmud, the latter distinctly remarks of the Jews of his time: "We all expect that the Christ will come into being as a man for men" (*Dialogue*, XI, 9).

During the Middle Ages several renegade Jews tried to convince their former co-religionists of the truths of Christianity from the traditional Scriptures and holy books revered by the Jews. The whole of the two Talmuds of Jerusalem and Babylon and the Midrashic literature connected with them were ransacked to prove the Trinity, the Virgin Birth, etc., but not a single passage could be discovered which directly, or by implication, implied that it was the Jewish belief that the Messiah would be born in any supernatural manner. Mr. F. P. Badham, in *The Academy* of London (June 8, 1895, pp. 485–7) has brought together eight passages from the mediæval controversialists which might seem to have some bearing on the subject. The majority of them no longer exist in the MSS. of Rabbinic literature, and are quoted by apostates whose *bona fides* leaves one in doubt. Most of the passages come from Raymond Martini's

Pugio Fide, who had access to books no longer extant, but, even granting the authenticity of these passages, they are much too vague to bear the interpretation placed upon them by the Dominican monk.[1]

The latter part of the paper is taken up with examples borrowed from Hartland, Charency, etc., to show that virgin birth is a common feature in the folk-lore of nations. " In Greek mythology it was quite usual to consider the birth of many deities and demigods as occurring without the intervention of a father." He instances Semele, Cybele, Adonis, Hephæstus, etc. Miscellaneous legends are cited from Persia, Tartary, Korea, Japan, China, Peru, etc. He says, " Perhaps the most remarkable analogy of the virgin birth of Jesus is that of the virgin birth of Plato as reported by Diogenes Laertius in his life of Plato." " Thus," he says, " from all portions of the globe evidence accumulates—and I have given only a selection of the most striking cases—that it is the natural instinct of the folk to claim for their heroes and demigods a supernatural birth, in most cases through Parthenogenesis." One remark more: " To an outsider, indeed, it appears that all these attempts to prove the supernatural character of Jesus' birth and family are logical consequences of the attempts to give Him a divine character."

[Dr. Jacobs has been misled by his authorities. The cases he cites from Greek mythology (Perseus, Adonis,

---

[1] See above, pp. 168*ff.*

Cybele, etc.) were not, even in the legend, cases of virgin birth (cf. Smith's or other Classical Dictionary), and in no case did they relate to historical personages. It is not alleged in the worthless fable of Diogenes Laertius that Plato was born of a virgin (cf. Gore, *Dissert.* p. 291). The unsifted stories from other peoples are useless for comparison with an historical account, and in any case bear no analogy to the Virgin Birth of Jesus. Even if fables be found of a boy growing out of an egg (Korea), or of the Japanese god of fishes being born from the hand of the first woman, or of a woman conceiving from eating a red fruit which she found, and giving birth to the ancestors of the Chinese Emperor, what has this to do with the stories in the Gospels?]

XVI

Prof. Ismar J. Peritz, Ph.D., Syracuse, N. Y.

Dr. Peritz writes as a Jewish convert on "The Hebrew-Christian Attitude Towards the Virgin Birth." He divides Jewish converts to Christianity into three classes, according as their training and habit of thought have been: 1. Talmudic; 2. Historical; and 3. Critical. He finds in the Talmud, Targums, and later Jewish literature, certain ideas which prepare the way for

the teaching of the New Testament on the Virgin Birth
of Christ—especially the ideas of the pre-existence of the
Messiah, of the Memra-Logos, and of the Metraton (an
angelic representative of the Divinity). He indicates
certain parallels to the Virgin Birth in a Midrash of
Rabbi Moses Hadarshan, a French exegete of the eleventh century, who "had evidently imbibed Christian
conceptions." On the historical side, he dwells on the
services rendered by Hebrew-Christians in modern times
to the defence of the Virgin Birth, instancing specially
Neander and Edersheim. In the critical field, he gives
an account of the labours of Dr. G. Dalman, who, though
he "does not specifically discuss the Virgin Birth, deals
with it in part in connection with his treatment of the
title 'Son of God.'" He claims that the representative
Hebrew-Christian attitude is in harmony with that of
the New Testament, and is on the side of the unique
birth, life, character, and mission of Jesus the Messiah.

XVII

Pasteur Hirsch, Paris

This writer discusses historically "The Evolution
that has led from the Miraculous Birth of Jesus Christ
to the Dogma of the Immaculate Conception."

XVIII

The Rev. Prof. Gabriel Oussani, D.D.,
Dunwoodie, N. Y.

Prof. Oussani writes from the Roman Catholic point
of view, and likewise traces "The Various Developments of the Doctrine of Christ's Virgin Birth in the
Catholic Church." On the Virgin Birth itself he makes
a strong point of the patristic testimony, and of the
inseparable connection between this doctrine and the
dogma of the divinity of Christ. His argument is thus
put:

Granted that the Eternal Son of God did at a certain
moment of time take flesh by a real incarnation in the
womb of Mary; granted that He was born as man, without change of personality or addition of another personality, but simply by the assumption of new nature and
by an entrance into new conditions of life and experience;
granted in this sense the Incarnation of the Son of God
in the womb of Mary—can we conceive it to have taken
place by the ordinary process of generation? Do not we
inevitably associate with the ordinary process of generation
the production of a new personality? Must not the denial
of the Virgin Birth involve the position that Jesus was
simply a new human person in whatever specially intimate
relations with God? And this argument becomes almost
irresistible when the question is removed from the idea of
incarnation strictly considered, to the associated idea of
the sinless humanity, the humanity of a second Adam.

Christ was a new departure in human life, a marvellous phenomenon, which becomes still more marvellous, more impenetrable and altogether unintelligible were we to ascribe to Him the same process of generation as to other mortals.

With reference to the later developments he is careful to put them on a different basis from the doctrine of the Virgin Birth. Thus, the dogma of Mary's *perpetual* virginity has

a powerful support in early Christian tradition, theology, and worship. It must be admitted, however, that viewed as an historical fact it has no explicit support in Scripture. The dogma must therefore be considered as the result of a development, which development, strictly speaking, does not necessarily imply its theological or historical truth or falsehood.

As regards *Joseph's* perpetual virginity, it

has no ground whatever either in Scripture or in early Christian tradition and literature. The Gospel's statements, were they to be rationally interpreted, are explicitly against it, although, as a specimen of dogmatic or rather theological process of evolution, it falls quite naturally within the sphere of progressive development, so apparent and visible in both Catholic and Protestant theology alike.

And generally:

It is evident, however, that if a process of development can be shown to have taken place in the second and especially the third stage of the doctrine concerning the parentage and birth of Christ, no such process can be shown to have taken place in the first stage of the doctrine, as it is perfectly demonstrable that the doctrine, in its first stage, relating to the divine conception of Christ and His Virgin Birth, was the primitive belief of the apostles, evangelists and disciples of our Lord, and at a time when theological development could not yet have taken place in the Church. Hence, if the doctrine of the perpetual virginity of Mary and of Joseph can be attacked on Scriptural and critical grounds, that of the Virgin Birth of Jesus stands as solid as a rock.

The remaining part of the paper discusses the theories of the origin of the doctrine of the Virgin Birth from Jewish and pagan sources.

INDEX

OTHER FINE VOLUMES AVAILABLE

1980-81

TITLES CURRENTLY AVAILABLE

NOTES

NOTES

NOTES

NOTES

NOTES